THE
A to Z
OF
LONDON
MURDERS

Condemned cell at Newgate.
Author's collection

THE
A to Z
OF
LONDON
MURDERS

Geoffrey Howse

Wharncliffe Books

This book is dedicated to my Godchildren
**Darren, Adam, Ivan, Suki, Ricky
and Joanna**

First published in Great Britain in 2007 by
Wharncliffe Books
an imprint of
Pen & Sword Books Ltd
47 Church Street
Barnsley
South Yorkshire
S70 2AS

ISBN: 978 1 845630 33 1

A CIP catalogue record for this book is available from
the British Library.

Typeset in Plantin by
Mousemat Design Limited

Printed and bound in England by CPI

Pen & Sword Books Ltd incorporates the imprints of
Pen & Sword Aviation, Pen & Sword Maritime,
Pen & Sword Military, Wharncliffe Local History,
Pen and Sword Select, Pen and Sword Military Classics
and Leo Cooper.

For a complete list of Pen & Sword titles please contact
PEN & SWORD BOOKS LIMITED
47 Church Street, Barnsley, South Yorkshire,
S70 2AS, England
E-mail: enquiries@pen-and-sword.co.uk
Website: www.pen-and-sword.co.uk

Contents

CONTENTS

CONTENTS

Introduction

True crime, particularly murder in all its horrible forms, seems to hold a fascination for enormous numbers of people. For some inexplicable reason murders committed in England's capital city have more often made international headlines than similar crimes committed elsewhere. Of what are usually described as 'notable British murders', over fifty per cent have taken place in London itself. When one takes into account those murders not considered to *be* 'notable', one is faced with an unimaginably long list of horrible but sadly, *commonplace* crimes. As if any murder could be commonplace. For somebody, or in most instances for many individuals connected to a victim, every murder is a tragedy. I can't help but feel that in some way I am letting many hundreds of London murder victims down by not mentioning them by name in this book. The reality is that in the vast majority of cases, particularly in more recent years where unprovoked murder for petty gain seems to be prevalent, the victims become little more than a name on a list, a statistic. It is almost as if their passing is without consequence. I certainly do not hold that view but one has to be practical, unless there is something remarkable about the crime itself, the victim or indeed, the perpetrator, virtually a list of names on a sheet of paper is all one is left with and for all but a few personally connected to each victim, a 'memorial', does not make either very interesting or indeed riveting reading.

Sadly, murder has been all too common an occurrence over the centuries. It is only advances in scientific analysis and modern methods of detection that have enabled the more covertly executed murders to be discovered. The all too obvious signs of murder are more easily recognised as such, but stealthily planned crimes can still go undetected for years and sometimes may never be discovered; as demonstrated within these pages, accounts of hitherto unknown victims of murder but for a chain of events, such as serial killings, would probably never have come to light.

I have included a historical overview of murders in the capital from 1593 to 2006. I have generally not included the political murders that took place mostly during the seventeenth century, when such figures as Thomas Wentworth, Earl of Strafford (1593-1641) and William Laud, Archbishop of Canterbury (1573-1645) were beheaded on Tower Hill by Act of Attainder, Strafford, as one commentator put it, 'being murdered with the sword of justice'; but you may like to consult my own book, *Foul Deeds and Suspicious Deaths in London's East End* for a comprehensive account of both these cases, where you may also read about the murders of Simon of Sudbury, Archbishop of Canterbury and Sir Robert Hales, the King's Treasurer, dragged out of the Tower of London by rioters during the Peasants Revolt of 1381 and beheaded on Tower Hill. Because there are so many London murders and murderers to cover over a long timescale, I have only included a relatively small portion of them, in terms of the actual number of crimes committed. Due to the amount of space allotted to me, unless the case covered takes in other districts of Greater London, I have not included murders that fall outside the present day N, NW, S, SE, SW, EC, E, W and WC postcodes.

Britain as a whole in more recent years and London in particular over many centuries has welcomed an influx of foreign visitors and migrants. London's history has

A late Victorian engraving of New Scotland Yard, designed by Norman Shaw, to resemble a Scottish baronial castle, and built on the site of the uncompleted National Opera House. In 1829, the London Metropolitan Force was formed and moved into its Whitehall headquarters in the area known as Scotland Yard, the name by which the police headquarters became known. By the 1880s, it was clear that the force was rapidly outgrowing its headquarters and New Scotland Yard was built on the Thames Embankment. Author's collection

been largely enhanced by the diversity of its ever-increasing population. Such tolerance has not always been met with reciprocal acts of kindness by certain relatively new arrivals, as some cases included here show. I have not made any mention of the crimes or the names of the perpetrators of the deplorable bombings that took place in London on 7 July 2005. The victims were many and their loss as well as the appalling injuries sustained by some of the survivors, much to be mourned and regretted; but the misguided views that these murderers were purported to have held and the cause they claimed to represent, brought uncalled for shame and unwarranted troubles to their

own otherwise peaceful communities. I cannot and will not dignify or further their cause or glorify their names by including them here.

During the 1980s, when I was a theatrical producer, I had the pleasure of working with the actor Michael BOOTHE, who was a founder member of the Save London's Theatres Campaign and a keen and active supporter of the actors' union, Equity. He was a gentle soul, a talented actor and singer, with a gregarious personality. In his private life he was gay but outwardly there were no obvious signs that this handsome, well-dressed, matinee idol, was anything other than straight. Michael's tragically early death in 1990, in

what police believed was a homophobic attack, rocked not just the theatrical world but the entire nation, such was its ferocity. I found it extremely difficult to write about Michael's murder but as his killers have yet to be brought to justice, I just want to shake a stick at them to let them know that their deplorable act has not been forgotten.

A little over a year ago a white boy, just turned eighteen, not known to me personally but well known to some I hold dear, was brutally stabbed to death in London by his 'best friend' of ethnic origin, over a £20 debt and a petty argument over a scratched car. Rarely a month goes by these days when some such similar tragedy has not occurred on London's streets. The term black on black, with regard to one black person killing another, to distinguish it from someone from one race killing a person from another, has passed into modern parlance and become an all too common feature of our newspaper columns. To me, life seems to be cheapened by such phraseology. Pointless racist murders are being constantly perpetrated on London's streets and disenchanted youths join or form dangerous gangs in which clashes between rival factions have all too often resulted in tragedy. Indeed, life for some elements of our society seems to be *very* cheap. This wonderful gift from God should not be so regarded. I could not have spent the

A late Victorian postcard view of Holloway Prison. Author's collection

many thousands of hours poring over gruesome documents detailing the most unspeakable things we human beings have done to one another, to produce this book, without a belief in the afterlife and a conviction that the crimes that have gone unpunished in this life, will not go unpunished in the next. What has become increasingly and worryingly apparent, is that an escalating amount of petty, often drug-fuelled crimes are turning quickly and almost effortlessly to the commission of the ultimate criminal act: murder.

The religious and racial tolerance that most law-abiding citizens have exercised in London and elsewhere in Britain is now being exploited by some less tolerant individuals from outside our own shores. Murder in London by foreign nationals is no longer an unusual occurrence. An increasing degree of general lawlessness and a disregard for the values that have made this nation great over many centuries should never be diluted or compromised to allow infiltration at any level by outside forces that wish only to pick the cherries off this wonderful cake, or in some avaricious instances to strip Britain of its identity and impose extreme fundamentalist views alien to the indigenous population of these islands.

It is perfectly clear to me with regard to murder, that more prudent use of capital punishment might be the only way of satisfying certain contingents of the British public. This thirst for revenge and retribution is a natural reaction to those closely affected by violent crime. Unfortunately, it has, through bitter experience become transparently clear, that to execute an individual on evidence that puts them in the frame beyond what was termed 'reasonable doubt', was not infallible. Unless there is incontrovertible proof and there can be absolutely no doubt whatever that murder was committed by an individual, there is no excuse whatsoever in law or otherwise for taking that person's life. Although I am in principle against capital punishment I would be more inclined to support its re-instatement if certain safeguards were put in place; and certainly in the case of proven serial killers, where there is absolutely no doubt of their guilt, their swift dispatching would save the Exchequer considerable sums.

Albert PIERREPOINT, Britain's most prolific hangman in the twentieth century, had a reputation for being the most efficient and swiftest executioner ever. Recent hangings in Iraq have demonstrated an unspeakably uncivilised approach to the execution of even the highest profile criminals imaginable. In the United States of America the retention of capital punishment for murder and certain other crimes is not without controversy. Hangings are rare. The electric chair has resulted in some distressingly inhuman executions. The preferred use of lethal injection in some states is in my view even worse, as for decades in Britain, that has been the method of putting down unwanted or terminally ill dogs and cats. I fail to be convinced that in any instance lethal injection could be regarded as either a humane or justified form of execution for any member of the human race, as some recent executions have demonstrated. A firing squad is all very well in military cases but death tends to be rather messy and doesn't seem to be an appropriate option to me. At least it should in theory be painless. Beheading, well, I think that in a civilised society that has probably seen its day, particularly now experts tell us that a severed head is still able to function, in other words feel, hear and see for six or seven seconds after decapitation. No matter what a man or woman has done, two wrongs do not make a right. An execution ought to be painless. The knowledge that death is imminent is surely sufficient punishment. The gas chamber is probably the most humane method, providing a painless gas is used. It would certainly be the most spectator-friendly method of execution for those chosen to witness such an event.

In writing this book about London murders I have in part achieved one of my goals, to condense enlightening information about a particular crime into a concise account of each case. I now look forward to my next seemingly insurmountable challenge, to successfully cancel a subscription to *Reader's Digest*. It's going to be a long hard slog but I'll get there in the end. No matter what other reservations I might hold, I have no reservations or doubts that while ever man exists, the continued perpetration of murderous acts will exist alongside him.

An early nineteenth century execution at Newgate. Author's collection

A–Z Listing

A

ACID BATH MURDERS, THE – see HAIGH, JOHN GEORGE

ANDREWS, JANE

Born in Cleethorpes, Lincolnshire in 1967, after answering an advertisement for a lady's dresser in 1998 she secured the post. Her new employer was none other than HRH The Duchess of York. During the nine years she spent in the Duchess' service she married a man twenty years her senior, but the marriage failed after six years, due to her adultery, ending in divorce in 1996. In 1997, Andrews lost her job, when the royal household was reorganised, although she remained on friendly terms with the Duchess. She later worked for the Knightsbridge jeweller Annabel Jones, Claridge's, and finally for the jewellers Theo Fennell. Not long after she had lost her royal post she met Thomas Cressman at a party in Chelsea. Later, they became lovers. Wealthy American-born businessman Thomas Cressman, who ran several companies supplying high quality motor accessories, was the son of American millionaire Harry Cressman. Before he met Andrews, Cressman had several long-term girlfriends. The couple moved into a £400,000 house in Bagley's Lane, SW6. They became engaged and Andrews was looking forward to marriage but as one of Cressman's friends said: '...Tommy was ready for marriage but not with Jane'. The couple went on holiday to France, staying with Cressman's mother near Cannes. Shortly before they returned to England, Andrews telephoned her former husband, Christopher Dunn-Butler, and told him that Cressman didn't want to marry her. On Monday 18 September 2000, after concerns were raised at Cressman's absence from work, a colleague, who had a set of keys, went to Bagley's Lane to investigate. In the master bedroom he discovered thirty-nine-year-old Cressman, wearing only his blue boxer shorts, dead on the floor, with a knife in his hand. It was later determined that Cressman had been knocked unconscious with a cricket bat then stabbed in the chest with a 18cm kitchen knife, which had cut through his rib-cage, entered a lung and pierced his heart, damaging vital blood vessels. A letter found in the wastepaper basket at their Fulham home from Cressman to Andrews showed evidence of their deteriorating relationship. Cressman's fiancée, thirty-three-year-old Jane Andrews was nowhere to be seen. She had not turned up for work and soon became the prime suspect. Once it emerged that Andrews had at one time been a member of the Duchess of York's household, the tabloid newspapers had a field day. An extensive search was made and a little before 7.00am on Wednesday 20 September, Andrews was discovered in a distressed state, lying under a blanket in a white VW Polo, parked in a lay-by on the A38, near Liskeard in Cornwall. She had taken an overdose of the painkillers Nurofen. She was taken to hospital and after she had sufficiently recovered was questioned by police. She told them that she had stabbed Cressman in self-defence after he had attacked and raped her. The police were not convinced as to her innocence and she was charged with murder. Jane Andrew's trial began at the OLD BAILEY on Monday 23 April 2001. Andrews' claims about Cressman's ill-treatment of her, on which her defence was based, were refuted by his previous girlfriends, all of whom testified to his gentle and caring nature, whereas Andrews was described by some of her previous boyfriends as manipulative, lying and jealous. Some went as far as to say that she had stalked them. The jury found by a majority of 11-1 that she had killed her lover in a jealous rage. Judge Michael Hyam, the Recorder of London said: 'In killing the man you loved you ended his life and ruined your own. It is evident that you made your attack on him when you were consumed with anger and bitterness. Nothing could justify what you did to him… It was a brutal attack and even if you felt yourself wronged and you were emotionally vulnerable, you were attacking an unarmed man who had possibly been asleep only a few minutes before you attacked him…there is only one sentence which I can place upon you and that is one of life imprisonment.'

ANTIQUIS MURDER, THE

A little after 2pm on 29 April 1947, father of six Alec de Antiquis, a thirty-four-year-old mechanic who ran a motor repair shop in Colliers Wood, South London, was in the West End on business, when he saw a robbery in progress at Jay's Jewellers, situated at 73-75 Charlotte Street. The robbery had been a violent one, in which shots were fired. As he tried to foil the robbers' escape at the junction of Tottenham Street, by driving his motorcycle in front of the fleeing three masked raiders, one of the gang shot him through the head. The robbers made their escape among the crowds and traffic. The police were quickly on the scene, led by Superintendent Robert Fabian ('Fabian of the Yard'). Mr Antiquis died in the ambulance before he reached hospital. The murder weapon was found by a schoolboy on the Thames foreshore at Wapping at low tide. Another gun found nearby was also identified as being used in the robbery. A taxi driver reported seeing two masked men entering a building in Tottenham Court Road. A search produced a raincoat and a scarf, folded to create a mask. The raincoat was traced to twenty-three-year-old Charles Henry Jenkins, who had a criminal record (younger brother of Thomas Jenkins, involved in the killing of Commander Ralph BINNEY), two of his associates were also picked up. Christopher James Geraghty, aged twenty (who had been in borstal with Jenkins) and Terence Peter Rolt, aged seventeen, and both incriminated themselves. All three were members of a gang of young thugs who styled themselves the 'Elephant Boys'. They were charged with the murder of Alec de Antiquis. The trial of Geraghty, Jenkins and Rolt began at the Central Criminal Court, OLD BAILEY, on Monday 21 July 1947, before Mr Justice Hallet. It lasted a week. The jury took fifteen minutes to arrive at a verdict in all three cases. Sentence of death was pronounced on Geraghty and Jenkins. Although it was Geraghty who fired the gun that killed Mr Antiquis, Jenkins was an accessory engaged in a joint enterprise of armed robbery. Rolt, who was too young to be hanged, was sentenced to be detained during His Majesty's Pleasure. Geraghty and Jenkins were hanged at PENTONVILLE PRISON on Friday 19 September 1947 by Albert PIERREPOINT. After serving less than nine years, Rolt was released from prison on licence in June 1956.

ARCHER, RICHARD – see PRINCE, RICHARD ARCHER

AUBREY, MARY

In 1687, Mary Aubrey, a midwife, murdered her husband and chopped off his head and limbs, in Long Acre, Covent Garden. She was found guilty of PETTY TREASON and sentenced to death. Her young son who had assisted her was acquitted as he was considered to have only acted under his mother's coercion. Mary Aubrey was hanged and then burned at TYBURN.

B

BALCOMBE STREET SIEGE, THE

An IRA cell of four highly trained operatives came to the UK mainland early in 1974. All were crack shots and experienced bomb-makers. Martin O'Connell, Harry Duggan, Edward Butler and Hugh Docherty were responsible for a whole series of terrorist outrages, believed to number as many as fifty, between August 1974 and December 1975,

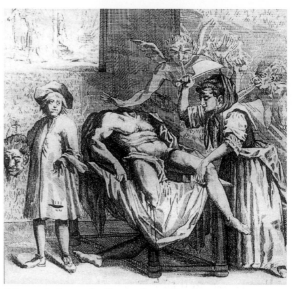

Mary Aubrey, the Long Acre Murderess.
Author's collection

which resulted in the murder of at least ten people and the wounding and maiming of scores of others, in bomb and gun attacks. They set up three London bases: in Fairholme Road, Hammersmith, Crouch Hill, Hornsey and Milton Grove, Stoke Newington, where they made their lethal shrapnel bombs, packed with ball bearings, large nails, and heavy carriage bolts. For fourteen months the gang carried out attacks in London and the South of England, the first was on a public house in Caterham. On 11 October, bombs were thrown at the Victory Club in Edgeware Road and the Army and Navy Club in Pall Mall. On 20 December 1974, a bomb discovered on Aldershot Station, designed to kill military personnel, was defused. Fingerprints found on the mechanism later proved to match the terrorists in the Balcombe Street Siege. Two days later former prime minister Edward Heath's Belgravia home in Wilton Street was attacked. A bomb was thrown through a window, which blew out the front of the building. Fortunately, Mr Heath was out. A later attempt was also made on Mr Heath's life, when a bomb was placed beneath his Rover motor-car. The device failed to go off. Other atrocities included the murders of off-duty policeman Stephen Tibble and Professor Gordon Hamilton-Fairley, an eminent cancer research specialist, killed in Campden Hill Square, Holland Park, by a bomb intended for his neighbour, Conservative MP Hugh Fraser. On 29 August 1975, bomb disposal expert Captain Roger Goad was sent to defuse a device found in a shop doorway in Kensington High Street. The IRA gang had been foiled several times in recent weeks and this particular bomb was expressly made to kill the person defusing it. It had been fitted with a booby trap. Captain Goad was killed instantly. On 5 September, the gang placed a bomb in the foyer of the *Hilton Hotel* in Park Lane. Casino Manager, Robert Lloyd and Dutch tour party manager Mrs Gesiena Loohuis were killed and sixty-three hotel guests and staff were injured, some of them losing limbs. On 9 October, the gang tried to bomb the *Ritz Hotel* but security being tight, they left the bomb a little further down Piccadilly, outside Green Park Underground Station, where it exploded, killing twenty-three-year-old Graham Tuck. The gang then turned their attention to restaurants. A bomb intended for *Locketts* restaurant in Marsham Street, Mayfair, failed to detonate but on 29 October one exploded at the *Trattoria Fiori* in South Audley Street, where there were several casualties. On 12 November, *Scott's Oyster Bar* in Mount Street, Mayfair was targeted, businessman Frank Batey was killed and fifteen customers wounded. On 18 November, the gang killed jeweller Theodore Williams and Ruth Edgson with a shrapnel bomb, which they threw through the window of *Walton's Restaurant* in Walton Street, Chelsea. Ross McWhirter, journalist, broadcaster and publisher, who along with his twin brother, Norris, published the *Guiness Book of Records* was targeted by the gang after he had personally offered a £50,000 reward for the capture of the IRA unit. On 27 November 1975, Mr McWhirter was shot by Harry Duggan, as he answered his door at his country home near Enfield. By 6 December, when matters came to a head, over a thousand police were deployed in the West End of London alone, searching for the gang. The gang, whose identities up to that point were still unknown, were eventually spotted on Saturday 6 December, after undercover Flying Squad detectives, patrolling in a London taxi cab saw them shooting at the windows of *Scott's Restaurant*. This second attack on the Mount Street restaurant was to be their last. The terrorists fled the scene in their stolen Ford Cortina. The taxi gave chase and was soon joined by other units of armed police. As the gang fled, they peppered police vehicles with gunfire and sped a mile north to Marylebone, abandoning their car in Rossmore Road, before fleeing on foot to nearby Balcombe Street, closely pursued by police, where they randomly rang the doorbell of No. 22B, the home of Post Office supervisor John Matthews and his wife Sheila, who had just settled down for a night's TV viewing. As John Matthews answered the door he was confronted by four men carrying pistols and a machine gun. He was pushed inside and the men entered the building, where the Matthews were taken hostage in their first floor flat and the Balcombe Street Siege began. Gang leader Martin O'Connell, aged twenty-five, immediately rang Scotland Yard. He told the operator who they were, gave the location, telephone number and the name of their hostages, before demanding a plane to fly them to Ireland, finishing the call with the words: 'Do as we say or the hostages will die.' During the six-day siege, which saw the terrorists barricading themselves in the lounge frantic negotiations took place. The police, who were not willing to give in to the terrorists' demands, knew that they could watch TV from the Matthews' lounge. Scotland Yard saw to it that the media became aware that the SAS were about to be called in. This was broadcast on the television news, which the terrorists saw, resulting in them being prepared to talk terms. The terrorists offered to release fifty-three-year-old Sheila Matthews in exchange for a hot meal. The exchange took place at midday. By 4.00 pm, the terrorists called the police to ask how they could surrender without being shot. They gave themselves up in pairs by stepping onto the balcony unarmed. Mr Matthews followed them out. Overwhelming forensic evidence was found which linked the gang to a host of atrocities and their trial began at the OLD BAILEY in January 1977. Although they were charged with twenty-five offences, including seven murders, police believed the true count of terrorist offences were much higher. The trial lasted thirteen days and at its conclusion the jury took seven hours to find the gang guilty of almost all the charges they had been brought up on. The four were given a total of forty-seven life sentences. A further 616 years were added for other offences. They were told they would have to serve a minimum of thirty years. Twenty-two years later, O'Connell, Duggan, Butler and Docherty were released as part of the Good Friday Agreement.

BARNEY, ELVIRA DOLORES

A celebrated case in which a highly-born socialite did not have to answer for her crime. She was acquitted of both murder and manslaughter, solely due to the skill of her defending counsel. In the early hours of 31 May 1932, neighbours in William Mews, situated between Belgravia and Knightsbridge, heard a shot and when they went to investigate, could hear Mrs Barney at No. 21, sobbing and calling out: 'Don't die, chicken, don't die.' The neighbours misheard Mrs Barney, the resident, as what she was actually saying was: 'Don't die, Mickey.' They were, however, used to being awakened by quarrels at No. 21. Twenty-seven-year-old Mrs Elvira Barney had already shocked her neighbours and polite society, when, after her husband had left her, she set up home with her twenty-four-year-old lover, Michael Scott Stephen, an ex-public schoolboy, who described himself as a dress designer. He was the son of a London bank manager. Stephen lived largely by sponging off wealthy women. Elvira Dolores Barney was the daughter of Sir John Mullens, a former government broker, whose London residence was a house in nearby Belgrave Square. Elvira and her lover belonged to the set known as the 'Bright Young Things', who lived carefree lives around London, and provided fodder for Evelyn Waugh in several of his early novels. Antics reminiscent of the characters in PG Woodehouse's Wooster novels were the order of the day, although their exploits extended further than mere riotous parties and absurd practical jokes, to the depths of decadence and promiscuous sex. When a doctor arrived at William Mews he discovered Michael Stephen had been shot dead. The police were called and a .32 Smith and Wesson revolver was found lying close to the body. There were two empty chambers. Mrs Barney said that she and Stephen had been to a nightclub with guests from a cocktail party the previous evening. After they returned home they began to quarrel, and Stephen picked up her pistol to shoot himself. As she struggled to stop him the gun went off. Police were not convinced by Mrs Barney's statement. Home Office pathologist Sir Bernard Spilsbury carried out a post-mortem. He discovered that Stephen had been shot at close range and that the bullet had passed through a lung and lodged against a rib. As a result of the downward flow of blood, Sir Bernard was able to ascertain that Stephen had been standing when shot, and had remained so for several minutes afterwards. Sir Bernard stated that in his opinion an accidental shooting was 'improbable'. On 3 June, Mrs Barney was arrested at her parents' home and charged with murder. Her reply to the police when told she was to be arrested was: 'I'll teach you to arrest me, you bloody swine!' She was remanded in Holloway. The trial opened at the OLD BAILEY on 4 July 1932, before Mr Justice Humphreys. The prosecution was led by Sir Percival Clarke and the defence by Sir Patrick Hastings. Mrs Barney stuck to her story that the gun had gone off accidentally and never wavered. She didn't change a word of her statement. Despite convincing evidence to the contrary from expert witnesses who demonstrated as to the likelihood of the gun going off accidentally, when a fourteen pound force needed to be exerted to fire the trigger, her society lawyer Sir Patrick Hastings, by skilfully twisting the words of witnesses, sowed seeds of doubt in the minds of the jury and managed to get her off; even in the light of what her neighbours said; that late one night, Mrs Barney appeared naked at her bedroom window and fired her pistol at Stephen in the mews below, as she called out to him: 'Laugh, baby, laugh, for the last time!' Elvira Barney did not survive long to enjoy her freedom. On 13 December 1936, she went to Paris. After a night of revelry on Christmas Eve, she was found dead in her hotel bedroom on Christmas Day, aged thirty-one. Cause of death was a cerebral haemorrhage.

BARTLETT, ADELAIDE – see PIMLICO POISONING CASE, THE

BARTON, RONALD WILLIAM

On Saturday 10 August 1985, fourteen-year-old Keighley Barton was abducted whilst out walking her dog, near her home in Sebert Road, Forest Gate, London E7, and later murdered by her violent, domineering, sexually-abusing, stepfather Ronald Barton, a mini-cab driver. Barton was aged forty-five at the time of his arrest for Keighley's murder. An evil sex fiend, with a string of sexual offences dating back to 1959, as well as convictions for violence and grievous bodily harm, Barton had moved in with Keighley's twenty-two-year-old mother, Theresa, when Keighley was just five months old. The couple were married two years later in 1974. Theresa had two children by him, both of them boys. In 1980, when Keighley was eight, Ronald Barton was given a one year suspended sentence for acts of gross indecency with her. Both Keighley and her mother gave evidence against him. Theresa Barton was to reveal much later that both she and Keighley were forced to submit to sexual acts, often being compelled to do so at the point of a gun barrel. Terrified of what Barton might do to her, Theresa Barton allowed the abuse to continue, until she accused him once again of abuse in 1982, but at the last minute, following threats from Barton, Keighley refused to testify against him. However, as a result of the accusations made against Barton, Keighley was placed in a hostel. Keighley was so worried about what might happen to her mother that she ran away, returning to the family home. The situation did not improve and there were numerous incidents culminating in Theresa Barton asking her husband to leave and early in 1985, she secured a court order banning her husband from going within a quarter of a mile of the family home in Sebert Road. Barton went to live in a flat in Mildenhall Road, Clapton. Shortly afterwards, Theresa Barton became involved with another man and her husband made several abusive telephone calls to them. He was also spotted spying on them. On the rainy morning of Saturday 10 August 1985, Keighley took the family Alsatian, Rex, out for a walk to nearby Wanstead Flats. The dog came home alone. Keighley was never seen alive again. The police were called and, owing to his past record, suspicion immediately fell on Ronald Barton, who denied any knowledge of his stepdaughter's disappearance. Convinced that he was involved, police arrested Barton on 17 August. He was immediately bailed. A few days later, two letters arrived at Sebert Road in Keighley's handwriting, one for Mrs Barton, the other, for Ronald Barton. Both letters said that she had lied about her stepfather's abuse of her. Although there had been several reported sightings of Keighley, none of them proved fruitful. Police were convinced that she was dead and that Barton had murdered her, most probably after she had written the two letters that had been received after her disappearance. On 23 October 1985, Ronald Barton was charged with the abduction and murder of Keighley Barton. Whilst he was on remand in Brixton prison he was brazen enough to boast to another inmate that he had disposed of her body by putting it in the boot of his old Peugeot, which had then been put in a car-crusher. Barton said: 'I paid a mate of mine in the scrap business £50 to do it. When that block is smelted down her body will come to the top as dross. There will be no other trace.' His claims and also his attempt to secure a false alibi from another prisoner were immediately reported to the police. Like so many other murderers have been, Barton was under the mistaken apprehension that without a body he could not be convicted. A trial date was set for 25 February 1986, but evidence having been brought by Barton's defence that Keighley had been sighted by several witnesses in the preceding months, the trial did not go ahead. No further evidence of Keighley having been alive, the case finally came to court before Mr Justice Turner, at the OLD BAILEY on 7 October 1986. The defence claimed that Keighley was almost certainly alive as sightings of her had been reported by over twenty witnesses; and in his closing speech for the defence, Mr Robin Grey QC told the jury: 'Thank heaven we are not in the days of capital punishment when this man could hang if you convict him and then Keighley turns up alive and well. There is a real possibility that Keighley is alive...' On 29 October, the jury retired to consider their verdict. On 30 October they gave it, finding Ronald Barton guilty, by a majority of ten to two. In summing up, Mr Justice Turner said: 'I am satisfied that you for many years abused a girl who should have been entitled to regard you as her father. You started to gratify

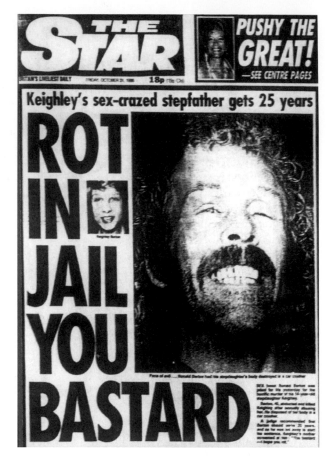

The Star.

your unnatural desires when that girl was only eight years old... There is no question that you are an evil, cynical and depraved man, whom society – including your wife and family – are entitled to be and will be protected from for many years.' Barton was sentenced to life imprisonment, with the stipulation that he should serve a minimum of twenty-five years. Following sentencing, probably in order to secure some protection from the rough justice that awaits many child abusers in prison, Barton requested to see the Governor. He admitted his guilt and retracted his story that he had disposed of Keighley's body in a car crusher. Detective Superintendent Charles Farquahar and Detective Inspector Norman MacNamara went to see him, both had been instrumental in bringing Barton to justice. He told them that he had buried the body in Abney Park Cemetery, Stoke Newington. A search of the cemetery was made and a skirt, cardigan and shoe were found in thick undergrowth. Keighley's body, identified by a Mexican ring on one of the decomposing fingers, was found nearby. Pathologist Dr Peter Vanezis was able to ascertain that Keighley had been stabbed to death. He identified eleven stab wounds to the chest and arms. Keighley was finally laid to rest on 25 February 1987 in Manor Park Cemetery, Forest Gate.

BATTERSEA FLAT MYSTERY

Mr T. W. ATHERSTONE
Leading Character Actor,

14 Gt. Percy Street, W.C.

Forty-seven-year-old Thomas Weldon Atherstone, as this particular murder victim was known, was the stage name of Thomas Weldon Anderson, an accomplished leading character actor, who had performed chiefly in provincial companies. In London he appeared on the same bill as Belle Elmore at both the Bedford Music Hall and the Euston Palace (see CRIPPEN, DR HAWLEY HARVEY) during an artistes' strike, when they were both booed off the stage for being blacklegs. He had for many years been happily married and had four children, who were well provided for. At the time of his murder Atherstone was separated from his wife and was living alone in Great Percy Street, Finsbury. Eight years previously, in 1902, he met the actress Miss Elizabeth Earle and as a love affair developed he became besotted with her. She left the stage to become a teacher at the Academy of Dramatic Art in Gower Street. For four years she had lived in the ground-floor flat at 17 Prince of Wales Road, Battersea but after the flat had been burgled in the Spring of 1910 she moved to the first floor flat immediately above. During his attachment to Miss Earle, Atherstone had shown himself to be of a jealous disposition. In 1909, he sustained a head injury after being knocked over by a motor-car, after which his jealousy became more pronounced; convincing himself she was romantically linked to every man Miss Earle was even vaguely acquainted with. He began to quarrel with her and struck her on more than one occasion. In an attempt to pacify him she even gave up the male pupils to whom she gave private lessons.

Such was Atherstone's jealousy, unbeknown to Miss Earle, he took to spying on her by watching her activities from the empty ground-floor flat. So convinced was he that she was having an affair that he had fashioned an improvised life preserver, made from a 17 inch length of electrical cable wrapped with brown paper and bound with string, with which it is believed he intended to threaten Miss Earle's would-be admirer. On the night of 16 July 1910, Atherstone had secreted himself in the ground floor flat and police believed from the evidence found at the scene and nearby that he found himself confronted by a burglar, who had gained entry via the adjacent gardens. Various witnesses came forward with descriptions of a man aged between twenty and thirty climbing over walls in the vicinity both shortly before and immediately after two shots had been heard. It became apparent that a violent struggle had taken place before Atherstone was shot twice in the head. He was found mortally wounded on the stairs from the scullery door at the back of the empty flat. His improvised life preserver was found in his pocket. He died later that evening at 10.20pm. Atherstone's conviction that his mistress was involved with another was confirmed by some of the entries in the red memorandum book found in his pocket, which indicated that he had been keeping a diary. Some of the entries showed his extreme jealousy and it was apparent that he had been keeping a close watch on Miss Earle's flat, using the empty flat on the ground floor for that purpose. One entry read:

If he had kept away from her, if he had broken from the spell of her fascination and remained out of reach, this would never had happened. He has no one to thank but himself. We all reap what we sow.

Despite extensive police enquiries, the murderer was never caught; and no evidence was found of Miss Earle being romantically linked with anyone other than Atherstone.

BATTLE OF STEPNEY, THE – see SIDNEY STREET, THE SEIGE OF

BELLINGHAM, JOHN

At about a quarter past five on the evening of 11 May 1812, Prime Minister and First Lord of the Treasury, the Right Honourable Spencer Perceval, was on his way to the House of Commons. As he and his associates passed through the Lobby (which in the old houses of Parliament was opposite the south end of Westminster Hall), a thin-faced man, aged about forty stepped forward, drew a pistol and shot the Prime Minister in the left breast. As he fell to the ground, he called out: 'Murder!' The assassin was quickly overcome and taken into custody by the Sergeant-at-Arms. His name was John Bellingham. Meanwhile, Spencer Perceval was carried into the office of the Speaker's Secretary, where he shortly died. Bellingham was recognised as a man who had in recent days made frequent visits to the Commons and had enquired about the identities of various Members. When asked what his motive was for shooting the Prime Minister, Bellingham replied: 'It was want of redress and denial of justice on the part of the government, Bellingham had in recent weeks petitioned his MP, General Gascoyne, Member for Liverpool, concerning his grievances with the Government over injustices he said he had received in Russia, where his business dealings had landed him in trouble through no fault of his own. Bellingham's trial took place at the Sessions House, OLD BAILEY, on 15 May 1812, just four days after Perceval's death, before Lord Chief Justice Mansfield. Bellingham made a speech to the jury and rambled on for two hours. Although it appears by his actions that Bellingham was insane, and some witnesses said as much, he apparently showed no visible signs of insanity. Unless a person was obviously out of his mind, then a jury would have no alternative but to find a prisoner guilty, if they believed he had committed the crime for which he was being tried. The jury found him guilty after just fourteen minutes of deliberation. Sentence of death was passed on the prisoner. Bellingham was executed on Monday 18 May 1812 outside

John Bellingham [top image]. *Bellingham shooting Spencer Perceval in the lobby of the House of Commons 11 May 1812.*
Author's collection

NEWGATE GAOL before an enormous crowd. The executioner was William Brunskill. Bellingham's body was afterwards conveyed on a cart to St Bartholomew's Hospital, where it was dissected in the anatomical theatre before many spectators. Not everyone was content with Bellingham's fate, as this contemporary account shows:

> *Bellingham has been convicted of murder and hanged, but some unease is now felt, since his wits had apparently been turned by the wrongs he suffered, and it is not the mark of a civilized society to execute lunatics.*

John Bellingham. Author's collection

BENEFIT OF CLERGY

Benefit of clergy was a medieval privilege originally applied to the exemption of Christian clerics from secular courts and it extended only to the commission of felonies. In the process of time a much wider and more comprehensive criterion was established. Benefit of clergy could be claimed by anyone who could read a passage from the Bible. In some cases even those who were unable to read could satisfy the criterion if they were taught by a literate person to memorise a passage, and in doing so could automatically claim benefit of clergy. Benefit of clergy had its origins in Psalm 51:

> *Have mercy upon me, O God, after thy great goodness: according unto the multitude of thy tender mercies blot out my transgressions.*

Henry Vll decreed that non-clergymen could only claim benefit of clergy once. In 1512 he further restricted benefit of clergy by removing certain offences as being 'unclergyable'. In 1547, the privilege of claiming benefit of clergy more than once was extended to peers of the realm. The ecclesiastical courts lost their jurisdiction over all criminal matters in 1576 and under statute law were either discharged, branded on the thumb or sentenced to one year's imprisonment. With the decrease in capital offences in all but the most serious cases, benefit of clergy was abolished in 1827, it being deemed to be no longer necessary.

BENSON, MARY – see PHIPOE, MARIA THERESA

BERRY, JAMES (executioner)

James Berry (1852-1913) was born in Heckmondwike (now West Yorkshire), the son of a wool stapler. He joined the West Riding Police force in Bradford at the age of twenty-two and, before he was appointed executioner in 1884, worked briefly as a boot salesman. Berry perfected and developed the 'long drop' method developed by William

MARWOOD, who had become a personal friend. His improvements became standard practice in British executions. He had calling cards printed: 'James Berry, Executioner, Bilton Place, Bradford, Yorkshire.' He disliked anyone referring to him as 'hangman', insisting on being called executioner. Unlike his predecessors who died in office, Berry resigned from his post. He published his memoirs, *My Experiences as an Executioner,* in 1892.

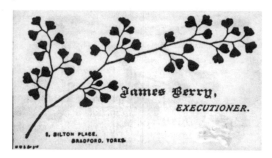

One of James Berry's Visiting Cards.
John D Murray collection

BILLINGS, THOMAS – see HAYES, CATHERINE

BILLINGTONS, THE (executioners)

James Billington (1847-1901) came from Bolton in Lancashire and before being appointed executioner had worked as a wrestler, coalminer and millhand, after which he had settled down to work as a barber, a job he continued to hold when he was not doing 'government work'. When carrying out executions, Billington wore a dark suit and black skullcap. His barbers shop was just outside Bolton, in Market Street, Farnworth. Having been an abstainer from strong drink for eight years, he forsook the temperance movement, abandoned barbering and became the landlord of the *Derby Arms* in Bolton. When James Billington died on Friday 13 December 1901, aged fifty-four, he had executed 147 men and women. His older son, Thomas, also carried out executions. He died shortly after his father, on 10 January 1902, at the age of twenty-nine. John, his second son, Thomas and his youngest William or Billie, also worked as executioners, but little has been recorded about them as they were not as high profile as their father and even he, unlike CALCRAFT and MARWOOD, left no memoirs. What is known is that the Billington brothers sometimes turned up to carry out executions in the provinces that their father had been engaged for and even impersonated one another when carrying out work as assistant or chief executioner. The Billingtons were soon to be replaced by a new breed of executioners on the Home Office List: John ELLIS and the PIERREPOINTS. William lived until he was over sixty, dying on 2 March 1952.

BINGHAM, RICHARD JOHN – see LUCAN, THE SEVENTH EARL OF

BINNEY MURDER, THE

On 8 December 1944, a smash-and-grab robbery in the City of London at Frank Wardley Ltd, a jeweller's, situated at 23 Birchin Lane, had tragic consequences for a have-a-go hero. At 2.30pm a car roared down the street and stopped outside Wardley's shop. Three men got out and while one smashed the window with an axe, the other two snatched as much jewellery as they could hold. As the car made its getaway from Birchin Lane into Lombard Street retired naval officer, fifty-six-year-old Commander Ralph Binney CBE, RN, stepped out in front of the car to try to bring it to a halt but the driver drove straight at him. Commander Binney was driven over and his clothing became caught on the underside of the vehicle as it sped off dragging him along for a full mile, until he was flung free by London Bridge Station with appalling injuries, as the car turned east into Tooley Street. Taken to Guy's Hospital, he died later that afternoon. Dr Keith Simpson performed an autopsy that evening:

He had various fractures and lacerations, but the principal cause of death was crushing and penetrating of the lungs by the broken ends of his ribs as the car ran forwards and then backwards over him.

The car was found abandoned near the Elephant and Castle. Police enquiries led them to a gang of young criminals known as the 'Elephant Boys' (see ANTIQUIS MURDER, THE). Only two of the gang of jewel thieves were identified by witnesses, the driver, twenty-six-year-old Ronald Hedley and Thomas Jenkins.

At the OLD BAILEY Jenkins was found guilty of manslaughter and sentenced to eight years. Hedley was convicted of murder and sentenced to death. Although his appeal against both his conviction and sentence was dismissed, a few days before his scheduled execution Hedley was reprieved, his sentence being commuted to one of life imprisonment. He was released after serving just nine years. On Sunday April 23 1954, an article appeared in the *Sunday Pictorial* captioned 'FREED KILLER GOES BACK TO MURDER CORNER' and illustrated by a photograph of Hedley standing at the spot where Commander Binney was run down.

Since 1945 an annual award, known as the Binney Medal, has been given for the 'bravest action in support of law and order' by a person who is not part of the police force, within the City of London and Metropolitan Police areas.

BLAKE, DANIEL

In the summer of 1762, twenty-year-old Daniel Blake, the son of a butcher at Bunwell, Norfolk came to London to seek employment as a gentleman's servant. He had a fondness for loose women and spent what money he had in low company. He obtained a position with Lord Dacre and had been in his Lordship's employment for about ten weeks, when in order to provide him with the means to satisfy his insatiable lust for carnal pleasures, he committed murder and robbery.

At the dead of night he entered the room of John Marcott, Lord Dacre's butler and repeatedly struck him on the head with a poker. He then slit his throat from ear to ear and, after removing twenty guineas

Sir John Fielding the blind magistrate, who reputedly was able to remember criminals simply by the sound of their voices.
Author's collection

from Marcott's breeches, returned to his room. On the day after the murder Blake discharged several small debts. Under questioning Blake broke down and confessed his guilt. He was taken before Sir John Fielding who committed him to NEWGATE. Blake was tried at the next Sessions at the OLD BAILEY and hanged at TYBURN on 28 February 1763.

BODIES IN THE CAR KILLER, THE – see SHOREY, MICHAEL

BOOTHE, MICHAEL (victim)
At 12.40am on Sunday 29 April 1990, forty-nine-year-old actor Michael Boothe was found barely conscious with appalling injuries, outside the public conveniences in Boston Road, on the edge of Elthorne Park, Ealing. Mr Boothe was clinging to the park railings. Before he lapsed into unconsciousness he said he had been attacked by a gang of six young men. He was taken to hospital where he died a few hours later. Michael Boothe lived alone in St Margaret Road, Hanwell. The previous evening he had been drinking with friends at a gay pub in Earls Court. At about 11.00pm he went to the home of one of his friends in Jersey Road, Hanwell. He left sometime between 12.15am and 12.30am to walk home. His journey took him past the spot where he was attacked.

The pathologist who examined Mr Boothe said his injuries were the worst of their kind he had ever seen. Michael Boothe had been kicked, punched and stamped on so violently that one of his feet had almost been severed from his leg. Despite an extensive enquiry by local police in which 147 witnesses were interviewed, nobody was ever charged. Six young men known locally were suspected of the murder but there was insufficient evidence to bring charges. In May 2002 the case was reopened but as yet nobody has been brought to justice.

BOROSKY, GEORGE – see VRATZ, STERN AND BOROSKY

BOURDIER, LOUIS
Louis Bourdier, a thirty-two-year-old Frenchman, a currier by trade, murdered thirty-three-year-old Mary Anne Snow (with whom he cohabited and had three children), on Tuesday 10 September 1867, at 3 Milstead Terrace, Old Kent Road, slitting her throat. She had threatened to leave him and he couldn't bear to part from her. Mary lived for some time after she had been attacked and was quite sensible when a doctor arrived but died about two minutes afterwards from the six inch gash to her throat, which was between one and two inches deep in places and had severed

HOUSE IN MILSTEAD TERRACE.   PORTRAIT OF THE PRISONER.   THE MURDER OF EMMA SNOW.

Louis Bourdier slit Emma Snow's throat.
Illustrated Police News

veins and arteries on both sides of her neck. Found guilty of murder, Bourdier was hanged at HORSEMONGER LANE GAOL on 15 October 1867 by William CALCRAFT.

BOW STREET RUNNERS

Originally founded by the novelist and magistrate Henry Fielding in 1749, the year his novel *Tom Jones* was published, and often referred to as London's first professional constables, the Bow Street Runners were attached to Fielding's office and court at 4 Bow Street, Covent Garden. The Runners with their distinctive blue greatcoats travelled nationwide to serve writs and arrest felons on the authority of the magistrates. Henry Fielding was succeeded at Bow Street by his half-brother Sir John FIELDING who refined the Runners into London's first effective police force. In 1805, the Bow Street Horse Patrol was created by Richard Ford. These officers wore scarlet waistcoats beneath their blue greatcoats, which led to them being nicknamed 'Robin Redbreasts'.

Henry Fielding (1707-54).
Author's collection

BRAIN, GEORGE

Thirty-year-old prostitute Rose Muriel Atkins, commonly known as 'Irish Rose', was murdered on the night of 13 July 1938. She had been stabbed with a cobbler's knife, beaten over the head with a starting handle and afterwards run over with a motor vehicle, which left tyre marks on her body – found in Somerset Road, Wimbledon the following morning, close to the All England Lawn Tennis Club. The tyre marks left on her legs were identified as coming only from certain models of either Austin or Morris motor-cars. Twenty-seven-year-old van driver George Brain was employed by a wholesale boot suppliers and repairers in St Pancras. He lived with his parents in Paradise Road, Richmond. Irish Rose was reported as being seen getting into a green van at about 11.30pm the previous night. When, two days later, Brain's employers reported to the police that both their green Morris Eight van and Brain had gone missing having first embezzled £30 from them, a possible link was established. The van was soon traced to one of Brain's workmate's garages. There were bloodstains in the van and a bloodstained knife was found in the garage. The tyres also matched the tyre marks on the victim's legs. After Brain's photograph was published he was spotted by a schoolboy at Sheerness on the Isle of Sheppey and arrested on 25 July. He claimed that Rose Atkins had tried to blackmail him threatening to reveal to his employers that he was using the firm's van for pleasure. He said he had lost his nerve and hit her with the starting handle but had then suffered a blackout and had no recollection of subsequent events. Tried at the OLD BAILEY, it took the jury just fifteen minutes to find Brain guilty. He was hanged at WANDSWORTH PRISON on 1 November 1938.

BRAVO CASE

This famous Victorian murder case involved the poisoning by antimony of thirty-year-old barrister Charles Delauny Turner Bravo. Charles Bravo and his wealthy twenty-five-year-old wife, Florence, lived at The Priory, Balham. Charles was Florence's second husband. She had married at the age of nineteen Alexander

Ricardo, a hopeless drunk, who had died of alcoholism, or so it was believed at the time. No significance was attached to the discovery of traces of antimony in Ricardo's body. Florence was also inclined to overindulge where drink was concerned. Not long before Alexander's death the Ricardos had gone to Malvern to take the waters at Dr James Manby Gully's hydropathic establishment. Florence had an affair with Dr Gully, who much to her parents' disapproval, helped her to secure a separation from her husband. Obligingly, Alexander died. On her husband's death Florence became a wealthy woman, inheriting over £40,000. She went to the continent with Dr Gully, a married man who was estranged from his much older wife. After she suffered a miscarriage, Florence grew tired of Dr Gully and took a widowed female companion, Jane Cox, before they all returned to England. Florence took a lease on a fifteen-room house, The Priory, Bedford Hill, Balham, with an army of servants to look after her. Mrs Cox moved in and Dr Gully, now no longer her lover but still on friendly terms, moved into a house nearby.

In order to satisfy her parents' sensibilities and gain their favour once again, Florence decided to marry. Mrs Cox suggested Charles Bravo, as a suitable match. They were married in December 1875. Bravo was noted for his parsimony, which galled Florence, as it was 'her' money he was being mean with. They occupied separate bedrooms. On 18 April 1876, Charles came home badly shaken after his horse had bolted. He dined with Florence and Mrs Cox. Florence retired at 9.15pm. She was feeling unwell and had only recently suffered a miscarriage. Charles retired shortly afterwards with toothache. At 9.45pm he came out of his room and shouted for hot water to drink. He collapsed and lapsed into unconsciousness. A doctor was called and he suspected poisoning. When Charles Bravo came round he said he had been rubbing

The inquest on the body of Charles Bravo. Illustrated Police News

laudanum into his gums and may have swallowed some. The eminent surgeon Sir William Gull was called in by Florence. He confirmed that Bravo was dying from poison. He died on 21 April.

A post-mortem revealed that Bravo had died from antimony poisoning, administered in a single dose of between 20-30 grains. In her evidence at the inquest, Mrs Cox said that Mr Bravo had admitted to taking poison. The coroner urged the jury to return an open verdict but a public outcry resulted in the Attorney General ordering a second inquest, which was tantamount to putting Florence Bravo and Mrs Cox on trial. Although the affair between Dr Gully and Florence Bravo was revealed, it was not possible to pin the administration of poison on either Gully or Florence Bravo. The jury concluded that Charles Bravo had been wilfully murdered but 'there was not sufficient proof to affix the guilt upon any person or persons'. Florence Bravo continued to drink heavily and died on 17 September 1878.

BRAYBROOK STREET MASSACRE, THE

On 12 August 1966, three plain clothes policemen stationed at Shepherd's Bush police station assigned to patrol car Q, a Triumph 2000, were patrolling London's 'F' Division, which covered Hammersmith Fulham and Shepherd's Bush. The policemen were DS Christopher Head, aged thirty, DC Stanley Wombwell, aged twenty-seven and PC Geoffrey Fox, aged forty-one. At 3.10pm they received a call to pick up DI Ken Coote from Marylebone Magistrates Court, to which they replied they would be there in twenty minutes. En route to Marylebone something prompted them to pull a blue Vauxhall Standard Vanguard van over in Braybrook Street, Shepherd's Bush close to Wormwood Scrubs Prison. The Triumph came to a halt a short distance in front of the van. DS Head and DC Wombwell got out of the car and walked over to the van to talk to the three men inside. Within moments the two policemen had been gunned down. A man got out of the van and rushed over to the car and shot PC Fox, who was sitting in the driving seat, with the engine running. As he was shot in the temple the Triumph lurched forward and ran over the dying DS Head. A male witness who saw the van reversing at speed down Braybrook Street and Erconwald Street, thinking it might be a prison break, noted the registration number PGT 726. The van was found in a railway arch garage in Lambeth, rented to thirty-six-year-old unemployed lorry driver, John Witney, with some spent cartridges inside. He was arrested at his Paddington flat and gave the name of his accomplices, John Duddy, a thirty-seven-year-old Glaswegian, and thirty-yeas-old Harry Roberts, from Wandsworth, the gang's leader. They had been planning to steal a car and rob a rent collector. Duddy was arrested in Glasgow on 16 August but Roberts remained at large. On 11 November, four days before the trial of Witney and Duddy was due to begin, a gypsy reported he had seen a tent, concealed in Thorley Wood, situated near Bishop's Stortford in Hertfordshire. Roberts was run to ground nearby in a deserted barn at about noon on 15 November, shortly after his accomplices' trial had begun. It was abandoned and a new trial scheduled for Tuesday 6 December, before Mr Justice Glyn-Jones at the OLD BAILEY. It lasted five days. The jury took thirty minutes to find all three guilty of murder. The judge told the prisoners:

> My recommendation is that you should not be released on licence, any of the three of you, for a period of thirty years...

BRIDES IN THE BATH MURDERS, THE – see SMITH, GEORGE JOSEPH

BROWN, DELANO – see CARTY AND BROWN

BROWNRIGG, ELIZABETH

Elizabeth Brownrigg, wife of James Brownrigg, by whom she had sixteen children, after having lived the first seven years of married life in Greenwich, moved to Fleur de Lys Court, Fleet Street. She practiced midwifery and became an overseer at the workhouse of St Dunstan-in-the-West. Mary Mitchell, a poor girl from Whitefriars was apprenticed as a servant to Mrs Brownrigg in 1765, likewise Mary Jones, a child of the Foundling Hospital was also placed with her; she also had other apprentices and increased her income by allowing pregnant women to lie-in at her home. She treated her apprentices cruelly, keeping them at near starvation levels and whipping them mercilessly. Mary Jones managed to escape one night and returned to the Foundling Hospital, where she was examined by the surgeon. The governors directed their solicitor to write to James Brownrigg threatening prosecution if he could give no proper reason for this ill treatment. The letter was ignored but fortunately Mary Jones was discharged from her apprenticeship. Mary Mitchell, having been with the Brownriggs for a year, also resolved to quit their service but she was prevented from escaping by the Brownriggs' younger son and her ill-treatment increased. The elder son, John, directed Mary to put up a half-tester bedstead, which she was unable to do so he beat her savagely, and continued with the beating until he had exhausted himself. Mrs Brownrigg would sometimes seize Mary by the cheeks and pull them so violently that blood gushed from her eye sockets. Mary was often tied to a chain suspended from the ceiling and beaten and sometimes chained by the neck in the cellar and given only bread and water to eat. On the morning of 13 July, Mrs Brownrigg went into the kitchen and

Elizabeth Brownrigg. Author's collection

made Mary Clifford strip naked and, although she was already bruised and sore, whipped her so violently that blood streamed down her body. Mary was then made to wash herself in a tub of cold water. While she was doing so Mrs Brownrigg struck her on the shoulders with the butt end of her whip. Mrs Brownrigg treated Mary Clifford five times similarly that same day. The parish authorities being made aware of this ill treatment saw to it that James Brownrigg was arrested but Elizabeth and her son escaped. The girls were taken to St Bartholomew's Hospital, where Mary Clifford died of her injuries within a few days. Mrs Brownrigg and her son moved address several times before they went to lodge with Mr Dunbar, who kept a chandler's shop in Wandsworth. Mr Dunbar read a newspaper report on 15 August which so clearly described his lodgers that he was certain they were the wanted murderers. He brought a constable to the house and mother and son were arrested and taken to NEWGATE.

James and Elizabeth Brownrigg and their son John, were indicted for the murder of Mary Clifford at the next OLD BAILEY Sessions. After a trial lasting eleven hours Elizabeth Brownrigg was found guilty of murder and sentenced to

The Kitchen where the floor Girls were employ'd & often whipped and tortured. | The Colender the Stairs where one of the Girls lay & where both were confined on Sundays.

Elizabeth Brownrigg. Author's collection

death. Her husband and son were acquitted of murder but were detained and charged with various misdemeanours for which they each received six months' imprisonment. Elizabeth Brownrigg was hanged at TYBURN on 14 September 1767. Afterwards her body was taken to Surgeons' Hall, dissected and anatomised, and there her skeleton was later exhibited.

BULSARA, BARRY – see GEORGE, BARRY

BUSH, EDWIN ALBERT

On 3 March 1961, fifty-year-old Mrs Elsie May Batten, wife of renowned sculptor Mark Batten, was found stabbed to death in a shop situated at No.23 Cecil Court, the narrow walkway which straddles Charing Cross Road and St Martin's, Lane, occupied then, as it is today, mostly by second-hand book, antique print and curio shops. For the past two years Mrs Batten, who lived in Castletown Road, Fulham had been helping out as a part-time shop assistant, mostly to fill her days while her husband, who usually spent four days a week out of London, worked at his studio in Dallington, Sussex. No. 23, an antique and curio shop was owned by Louis Meier and run by his manageress Mrs Marie Gray; both were often away attending auctions.

On the morning of the murder, Mrs Batten unlocked the iron gates outside the shop and began arranging the display. When Mr Meier arrived after midday to pay Mrs Batten's wages, he found that the usual outside display was incomplete, and when he entered the shop the light was on but Mrs Batten was nowhere to be seen. He discovered her body in a curtained off area towards the rear of the shop, when he noticed Mrs Batten's legs sticking out from beneath the thick brocade drapes. An eighteen-inch antique dagger was protruding from her chest and another from her neck. There was a wound to her shoulder and another to her back. She had also been hit over the head with a heavy stone vase, which was found nearby. A piece of board under Mrs Batten's body had the imprint from the heel of a man's shoe. Neighbouring shopkeepers remembered having seen a young coloured man who had been making enquiries about dress swords. Mr Meier remembered that the previous day a young Indian-looking man had expressed interest in a dress sword costing £15 and also several daggers. The same man had also tried to sell a sword at an adjacent shop, which was subsequently proven to have been stolen from Meier's shop that morning and had been used to inflict some of the injuries on the murder victim.

With so many witnesses, the police used a technique for the first time in England, the Identikit picture. Although the concept had been introduced to Scotland Yard in 1959, this was the first time it had been put to practical use. This first Identikit picture was widely circulated. On 8 March, PC Cole was on duty in Old Compton Street, when he saw a young man who looked very similar to the Identikit picture. He was taken into custody and picked out in an identity parade. His name was Edwin Albert Bush, a twenty-one-year-old Eurasian. The heel of one of his shoes was an exact match for the heel mark found at the murder scene. He was charged with murder. He admitted killing Mrs Batten in order to steal the sword. At his trial which began at the Central Criminal Court, OLD BAILEY on 12 May, Bush tried to play the race card, saying he had killed Mrs Batten after she had made an offensive remark about his colour but this contradicted his earlier statement when he admitted he had killed her in order to obtain the sword. He was found guilty of murder on 13 May. An appeal failed and he was hanged at PENTONVILLE PRISON on 6 July 1961.

A present-day view of 23 Cecil Court.
The Author

BUTLER, EDWARD – see BALCOMBE STREET SIEGE, THE

BUTTON AND BADGE MURDER, THE – see GREENWOOD, DAVID

BYRON, EMMA (KITTY)

In 1902, twenty-three-year-old milliner's assistant Kitty Byron was infatuated with City stockbroker Arthur Reginald Baker, known as Reggie, with whom she lived in lodgings in Duke Street, off Oxford Street. The couple frequently quarrelled and Baker, who was known to be a heavy drinker, when drunk often beat Kitty. He also used to take her meagre earnings, and according to witnesses although he generally treated her harshly, amounting to physical and mental cruelty, she seemed to be very much in love with him. After a violent row on the evening of 7 November 1902, which went on well into the night, the following morning the landlady, Madame Liard, told them they would have to leave. Baker was overheard by the maid, who was friendly towards Kitty, talking to Madame Liard. He told her that Kitty would go but he would like to keep the room. Madame Liard refused. When the maid told Kitty what had happened, she was very angry and said: 'I'll kill him before the day is out.'

On 10 November, the day of the Lord Mayor's Show, Kitty bought a strong-bladed knife, which has been suggested may have been for the purpose of killing herself. She went to the City and in the early afternoon sent an express message from Lombard Street Post Office to Baker's office near the Stock Exchange, asking him to meet her as a matter of urgency. He went to the Post Office to meet her and customers noticed they were involved in a heated discussion. As they left the building and entered Post Office Court, possibly having been goaded by Baker, Kitty produced a knife from her muff and stabbed him twice. As he fell to the ground and died almost immediately, Kitty collapsed over him in a fit of passion, sobbing with great vehemence. At her trial in December 1902 at the OLD BAILEY, before Mr Justice Darling, she did not go into the witness box. In her defence, Sir Henry Dickens (son of Charles Dickens), made a moving speech. In finding her guilty of murder, the jury in delivering its verdict added a strong recommendation for mercy. She was given a life sentence, which in 1907 was reduced to ten years. Kitty was released from prison after serving six years. The money for Kitty's defence was provided by Baker's fellow members of the Stock Exchange.

BYRON, WILLIAM (THE FIFTH LORD BYRON)

William Byron, the fifth Lord Byron, known as the 'Wicked Lord', is often mentioned in accounts about his more illustrious great-nephew and heir, the poet, George Gordon Byron, the sixth Lord Byron. Lord Byron's country seat, Newstead Abbey, in Nottinghamshire, was bounded by a neighbouring estate surrounding Annesley Hall, owned by his cousin William Chaworth. These country landowners habitually went to London where they met once a month in the *Star and Garter* tavern in Pall Mall. On 26 January 1765, the two men quarrelled over the quantity of game on their respective estates. Following this heated exchange of words a waiter was asked to show them to a private room. A short while later a bell rang and the innkeeper went to see what was required. When he entered the room he found Lord Byron and Mr Chaworth 'at grips'. Mr Chaworth was severely wounded. He was carried to his lodgings, where he died the next day.

Before he died, Mr Chaworth said that he, himself had made the first thrust. A charge of murder was brought against Lord Byron. A peer accused of murder could only be tried by the House of Lords. Once preparations for the trial had been made, Lord Byron was invited to place himself in custody in the Tower of London. He was taken to his trial in Westminster Hall by coach, escorted by mounted guards. The executioner's axe was placed before him with the blade facing towards him. The hall was packed and seats were being sold for six guineas each. Lord Byron pleaded not guilty. Although a surgeon explained how his lordship's sword had penetrated Mr Chaworth's naval and made a wide gash in his stomach, the wound having caused the death, the fact that William Chaworth had drawn his sword first was in Lord Byron's favour. The customary vote was taken, starting with peers most recently created and ending with the princes of the blood. Lord Byron was found not guilty of murder, but guilty of homicide. Under a special statute affecting peers of the realm, Byron could plead BENEFIT OF CLERGY and this amounted to acquittal. A first offender who could read one verse of the Bible was declared to be under the jurisdiction of the Church and released from punishment from the temporal courts.

Lord Byron returned to Newstead. It was made clear to him that he would not be welcome in London again. Thereafter, he lived as a scandalous recluse with 'Lady Betty', a servant girl, as he had driven his wife away through his wicked ways. To his dying day on 21 March 1798, the Wicked Lord kept the sword with which he had killed his cousin hung on his bedroom wall.

C

CALCRAFT, WILLIAM (hangman)

A boot and shoemaker by trade, born near Chelmsford in Essex, William Calcraft (1800-79) was made hangman in 1829. His appointment by the Court of Aldermen was reported in *Bell's Life in London* on 5 April. He was paid a guinea a week by the Corporation of London and the County of Surrey paid him a quarterly retainer of £5 5s. In addition he received a guinea for each execution he carried out. He also received fees for officiating at executions in other parts of the country. At the time of Calcraft's appointment the hangman was still required to carry out public whippings, a duty which was soon to be taken over by prison officers, the whippings then being carried out inside the prisons. Calcraft began his career in punishing malefactors by flogging juvenile offenders at NEWGATE. He was noted for his swiftness in dispatching prisoners, at least to the point of them plummeting to their deaths, which at Calcraft's hands was not all too often an easy one.

Despite being a very inefficient hangman, even with the aid of the drop, his convict clients often suffering unspeakable agonies as they invariably choked to death, his methods rarely succeeding in breaking their necks, he continued to hold the post of hangman for forty-five years, until his enforced retirement at the age of seventy-four in 1874. Following his last hanging, that of James Godwin, a wife murderer, on 25 May, having been gently persuaded that in consequence of his advanced years, it would be better for him to resign, he obligingly, though reluctantly did so; and the Corporation of London paid him a pension of twenty-five shillings a week, until his death five and a half years later, at his home in Poole Street on 13 December 1879, his wife of forty-five years having predeceased him in 1870.

William Calcraft (1800-79). A cobbler by trade, Calcraft was appointed hangman at Newgate in 1829. He served as executioner until he was seventy-four. He retired on a pension of twenty-five shillings a week. Author's collection

CAMDEN RIPPER, THE – see HARDY, ANTHONY JOHN

CAMDEN TOWN MURDER, THE

The Camden Town Murder is considered to be one of the most sensational unsolved murders of the twentieth century. Railway chef Bertram Shaw's job took him to Sheffield each evening and he returned to London the following morning. On the morning of 12 September 1907 he came home from work as usual to his lodgings at 29 St Paul's Road (now Agar Grove), Camden Town. He discovered that his sitting-room had been ransacked and when he forced open the locked bedroom door he found the naked body of his common-law wife, twenty-three-year-old Phyllis Dimmock, with her throat savagely cut.

Like Bertram, Phyllis worked the night-shift. She was a prostitute and was well known throughout the area. The *Rising Sun* in Euston Road was a regular haunt of hers, as was *The Eagle* in Camden Town. A letter and a postcard found in her rooms and written in the same hand led police to a young man who had been seen with her at both public houses. Robert Wood was a talented artist who worked as an engraver at a glassmaker's in Grays Inn Road, and also earned money as a freelance cartoonist. He lived in a comfortable home in St Pancras with his father. He was arrested on circumstantial evidence and charged with murder. The trial began at the OLD BAILEY on 12 December. Wood was defended by the brilliant SIR EDWARD MARSHALL HALL. This case is significant for Wood being the first person accused of murder to be acquitted after giving evidence at his own trial (until the Criminal Evidence Act of 1898, the accused had previously not been allowed to give evidence in the witness box). Wood completely charmed the jury, stuck to his original story concerning his version of events as told to the police and they acquitted him. Nobody else was ever implicated in this murder.

CANNICOTT, WILLIAM

William Cannicott, from his youth had been a livery servant. When he was twenty he married a fellow servant, Dorothy Tamlyn, who was almost twice his age; and soon afterwards set her up in a haberdasher's shop in Boswell Court. About ten years later, Cannicott, having been the servant of the late Admiral Matthews, leased a house for Dorothy in East Street and furnished it to be let out as lodgings. One day, without his knowledge, Dorothy sold two of William's best suits of clothes. He had been extremely generous to his wife and when he discovered his clothes missing, he swore he would never come home to her any more. He took lodgings some distance away, although he continued to send Dorothy money. In his new surroundings he was regarded as a single man and he was hired by a gentleman in Cavendish Square, exactly for that reason. He fell in love with his new master's nursery maid, whom he called Nanny, and shortly after taking up a new position with the Earl of Darnley on 3 June 1754 he married his new love at Marylebone Chapel. A man named Hobson was employed as Lord Darnley's coachman. He knew Cannicott from several years previously and also knew his first wife. Although Cannicott made every effort to shield her from finding out, the first Mrs Cannicott went to acquaint her with the facts. Nanny reproached Cannicott with such tenderness 'as showed less anger than love' and told him he must not attempt to see her again but must leave her to struggle alone with her misfortunes.

Hobson and his wife made mischief and told Dorothy Cannicott her husband had received his wages and that she should try to get them from him. This she did, making threats of prosecution if he refused, saying that she could and would hang him for having two wives. He arranged to meet her at the *Red Lion* in Berkeley Square. They took a walk as far as Tottenham Court, but had to take shelter from a violent thunderstorm in a public house. She asked him for money and when he refused she began to threaten him, which threw him into a dreadful rage. As they left the building he saw a chord hanging over the banister rail. He took it, and walking ahead of his wife fashioned a noose, which he threw over her head and tightened. She seized it with her hands and struggled so hard that the cord broke and fearing that she would overpower him, for she was a mightily strong woman, pulled his scissors from their sheath and stabbed her many times in the throat, from which injuries she died. He was soon arrested but would admit to nothing. It was only after Nanny was arrested and confined upon suspicions of being an accessory, that he admitted to everything in order that she might be discharged. Tried at the OLD BAILEY, William Cannicott was hanged at TYBURN on 20 September 1756.

CARR, FRANCES, COUNTESS OF SOMERSET – see OVERBURY, SIR THOMAS

CARR, ROBERT, EARL OF SOMERSET – see OVERBURY, SIR THOMAS

CARROLL, PATRICK
This case is notable for being the first trial of a prisoner at the court constituted as the Central Criminal Court. Patrick Carroll from Ballihoy, Ireland enlisted in the 7th Regiment of Fusiliers at the age of twenty-two. Seven years later, he switched regiments to the Marines and was stationed in Woolwich. There he frequented the *Brittania*, a public house kept by a widow, Mrs Browning. He repeatedly asked her to marry him and although she was not entirely averse to the idea, she refused to entertain his advances any further after he had abused her on more than one occasion while in a state of intoxication.

On Sunday 26 April 1835, Carroll went to the *Brittania* and, on finding she had invited some friends for tea, without having extended an invitation to himself, some angry words ensued and he was forcibly ejected from the house. He returned next morning and insisted on seeing Mrs Browning in private. Having been told she would not see him he forced his way into the bar and repeatedly struck her with his hand before drawing his bayonet and stabbing her. She died. On Friday 15 May, Patrick Carroll was tried at the Central Criminal Court, OLD BAILEY, for murder. Found guilty, he was hanged outside NEWGATE on Monday 18 May 1835.

CARTY, DONNEL – see CARTY AND BROWN

CARTY AND BROWN
Nineteen-year-old Donnel Carty and eighteen-year-old Delano Brown, two black teenagers, part of a gang known as the Kensal Green Tribe, who carried out a seven-month mugging campaign, were given life sentences at the OLD BAILEY on 28 November 2006 for the murder of thirty-one-year-old solicitor, Tom Ap Rhys Pryce, great-grandson of General Sir Henry Edward Ap Rhys Pryce DSO, aide-de-camp to King George VI. On 12 January 2006, at about 11pm, Mr Pryce was walking home from Kensal Green station when he was fly-kicked to the ground and stabbed twice in the

chest. His attackers took his Oyster Card and mobile phone. Police found a trail of blood from the station to where he collapsed just yards from his front door in Bathhurst Gardens. Carty and Brown were tracked down after police viewed CCTV footage of Carty using Mr Pryce's Oyster Card at Kensal Green station following the murder. On Monday 14 May 2007 the Court of Appeal ruled that the seventeen year term handed to Brown was 'unduly lenient' and raised it to twenty years. The twenty-one year minimum tariff handed to Carty was found to be perfectly appropriate.

CHAPMAN, GEORGE

George Chapman was the name adopted in 1892 by Severin Klosowski, the son of a Polish carpenter. He came to London aged twenty-three, in 1888, and found work as a barber's assistant in Whitechapel High Street. He married Lucy Baderski in 1899 but, shortly afterwards, a woman arrived from Poland and claimed to be his wife. A lawsuit was settled in Lucy's favour and in 1891 she and her husband emigrated to America. He returned alone the following year and took up with a woman named Annie Chapman, with whom he lived for about a year. He adopted her name and claimed to be an American. He later lived with a married woman, Elizabeth Spink, who had parted from her railwayman husband, Shadrach, and using her money firstly set up in business in Hastings as a barber before returning to London, where as Mr and Mrs Chapman, they ran the *Prince of Wales* in Bartholomew Square near Old Street. Mrs Chapman became ill with vomiting and abdominal pains. In December 1897, she died.

In 1898, Chapman, having become acquainted with Bessie Taylor, they moved to run *The Grapes* in Bishop's Stortford before returning once again to London in 1900 to *The Monument Tavern*, in Union Street, Lambeth, where Bessie became ill and died in February 1901. Chapman next moved to *The Crown* in Borough High Street, where Maud Marsh came into his life. She became ill. Her mother suspected poisoning. When Maud died on 22 October 1902, the doctor refused to grant a death certificate. When a post-mortem revealed that she had died of antimony poisoning, the bodies of Elizabeth Spink and Bessie Taylor were exhumed. Their bodies were remarkably well preserved, characteristic of antimony poisoning, which was confirmed as the cause of death. When it was discovered Chapman had purchased tartar emetic from a local chemist, he was charged with the murder of Maud Marsh. Tried at the OLD BAILEY, he was hanged at WANDSWORTH on 7 April 1903. Chapman was one of the many possible candidates suggested as being the unidentified JACK THE RIPPER, the theory being that he had changed his modus operandi for fear of detection.

CHARING CROSS TRUNK MURDER –
see ROBINSON, JOHN

CHIVERS, ELIZABETH

Elizabeth Chivers lived in Stepney. She went into service aged fourteen. When she was thirty she became

Elizabeth Chivers drowning her baby.
Author's collection

pregnant by her employer, Mr Ward, an attorney. She moved to private lodgings paid for by Ward but three months after the baby was born, her former mistress, Mrs Ward, discovered her whereabouts and exposed her shame to all and sundry. This so enraged Chivers that she decided to get rid of the child. Several witnesses saw her throw the baby into a pond near Hackney but were too late to save it from drowning. Chivers was immediately taken into custody and found guilty of murder at the OLD BAILEY Sessions in July 1712. She was hanged at TYBURN on 1 August.

CHRISTIE, JOHN REGINALD HALLIDAY

By 1953, the one-time neat, three storey houses of well-to-do Victorian families in Rillington Place, Notting Hill, had become run down and most were divided into flats, many of them being occupied by members of London's growing immigrant community. On 24 March 1953, new tenant Beresford Brown, recently arrived from Jamaica, was examining the kitchen on the ground floor of No.10. The previous tenants, an Irish couple, the Reillys, had been evicted by the landlord after just one day's occupancy as they had taken over the tenancy from John Christie who had lived there with his wife since 1938; but Christie, who took £7 deposit from the Reillys had no right to sub-let and had disappeared owing several months' rent. Beresford Brown noticed there was a strange mixture of unpleasant smells, which were being partially disguised by disinfectant. These smells were most potent in the kitchen and seemed to originate from a section of wall, which he tapped. It had a hollow sound and further investigation revealed a papered over door. He peeled back the wallpaper and shone his torch into a cut out section. In the torchlight Brown could see what appeared to be the body of a woman.

The local police being summoned were quick to call in Scotland Yard and Detective Chief Inspector Griffin and pathologist Dr Francis Camps were soon on the scene. When the door had been fully opened a largish alcove was revealed. The dead woman was in a sitting position with her back towards the room. When the body was removed two more dead women were found wrapped in blankets. A fourth body was discovered beneath the floorboards in the front room. The first body was

Daily Mirror.

identified as twenty-six-year-old Hectorine MacLennan, the others in the alcove were Kathleen Maloney, also twenty-six and Rita Nelson, aged twenty-five. All three women were prostitutes. The body beneath the floorboards was Christie's wife, Ethel, who had not been seen for over three months. While these bodies were being examined, the police concentrated on the small garden at the rear of the house. There they unearthed a large quantity of bones, which turned out to be those of Ruth Fuerst, aged twenty-one, who had disappeared in July 1943 and Muriel Eady, a woman in her early thirties, who was reported missing in October 1943.

During their search the police discovered a tobacco tin which contained four locks of pubic hair. One lock matched that of Ethel Christie. The former occupant of the flat, fifty-five-year-old office worker John Reginald Halliday Christie had already been at the centre of a murder enquiry, when in 1949 he was principal prosecution witness at the trial of fellow resident TIMOTHY JOHN EVANS, who was hanged for murder. Evans' wife and baby daughter had been strangled and their bodies found in the ground-floor washhouse at 10 Rillington Place. Evans accused Christie of carrying out the murders. Christie was born in Halifax, Yorkshire, in 1898 and was known in his teens, due to his sexual inadequacy, as 'Reggie-no-dick'. He served in the First World War, where he was gassed in France in 1918, which affected his voice and left him softly spoken thereafter. He married Ethel Waddington in 1920 but according to several accounts his sexual inadequacies continued and he often visited prostitutes. He had a criminal record for various petty offences including in 1929, assaulting a woman with a cricket bat. His wife left him but by the late 1930s he had settled down to work as a stock clerk and the Christies were reunited. Christie also professed some medical knowledge and was eager to advise anyone willing to listen to him. During World War Two he concealed his criminal record and joined the police force as a special constable.

Following the gruesome discoveries in Rillington Place a nationwide hunt for Christie was instigated. On the morning of Tuesday 31 March Christie, who had been staying at a nearby doss house made his way to Putney Bridge, where he was spotted staring into the River Thames by police constable Thomas Ledger, who arrested him. Once in custody Christie did not deny his guilt and at his four-day trial at the OLD BAILEY before Mr Justice Finnemore, despite having confessed to the murders of seven women, including Evans's wife, Beryl (but not to the murder of the baby, Geraldine Evans), was charged only with the killing of his wife. Christie spoke quite candidly about how he had enticed the women home and, having plied them with alcohol, rendered them unconscious with coal gas before strangling them. Evidence suggested that he also had sexual intercourse with them, indulging a taste for necrophilia. His occasional lapses into vagueness were seen as an attempt to bolster up his plea of 'not guilty by reason of insanity' but the jury thought otherwise, after the judge, in his summing-up asked them to measure Christie's behaviour against the McNAGHTEN RULES, which he acquainted them with. They found him guilty of murder after less than an hour and a half's deliberation. An enquiry into his mental state upheld their views. Christie did not appeal. He was hanged at PENTONVILLE on 15 July 1953.

CHRISTOFI, STYLLOU PANTOPIOU

In 1954, the ground floor and first floor of 11 South Hill Park, Hampstead were occupied by the family of a Greek Cypriot named Stavros Christofi, who worked as a wine waiter in the West End at London's famous *Café de Paris*. Stavros lived with his

11 South Hill Park, Hampstead.
The Author

German wife Hella and their three children. After about fifteen years of marriage, the family were joined in 1953 by Stavros's mother, Mrs Styllou Christoffi. Styllou Pantopiou Christofi was illiterate even in her native language. Unable or unwilling to learn either English or German, she had great difficulty communicating with her daughter-in-law, who became the object of her hatred and obsessive jealousy.

On the evening of 29 July 1954, while Stavros was at work and the children in bed, Mrs Christofi murdered Hella by hitting her on the head with a cast-iron ash plate, then strangling her. She then set about burning the body in the garden. John Young, a neighbour, witnessed Mrs Christofi poking what appeared to be a tailor's dummy. Some time later, Mrs Christofi stopped a passing motorist and in broken English told a pathetic tale. She said: 'Please come, fire burning, children sleeping.' When the police came, the blood and other evidence in the kitchen told an entirely different story. There is no doubt that Mrs Christofi was a horrible woman to have as a mother-in-law. In 1925, while two fellow villagers had held open the mouth of her own mother-in-law, Mrs Christofi had rammed a blazing torch down her throat, killing her. On that occasion she was acquitted. However, this time she was not so lucky. She was tried at the Central Criminal Court before Mr Justice Devlin. Christofi refused to plead insanity and was found to be sane by three doctors. On 28 October, she was found guilty of murder. Mrs Christofi was hanged at HOLLOWAY by Albert PIERREPOINT on 13 December 1954. By coincidence, the last two women to be hanged in Britain committed murder in the same street just nine months apart. A stone's throw away from the Christofi house, RUTH ELLIS shot David Blakeley in April 1955.

CIANTAR, DENNIS

Thirty-four-year-old, knife carrying, unemployed, crack cocaine addict Dennis Ciantar was jailed for life on Monday 19 July 2004 for the cowardly lunchtime killing of bricklayer Gavin McGrath, also aged thirty-four. The murder took place on 14 September 2003, following a petty argument over queue jumping in the fast food outlet

McDonald's in Seven Sisters Road, Nag's Head, Holloway. After an argument over who should be served first, Mr McGrath left McDonald's with his purchases and Ciantar, who did not wait to collect the cheeseburger and fries he had ordered, followed him up the street and without any provocation or warning stabbed him in the back. Mr McGrath died at the scene. The crime was caught on CCTV. On sentencing him to life imprisonment Ciantar was told it would be at least fifteen years before he could be considered for parole. Judge Richard Hawkins said: 'You stabbed him without mercy with a large kitchen knife. He came to an end in that sudden and brutal way. I conclude you intended to kill.'

CLAPHAM COMMON MURDER, THE – see MORRISON, STINIE

CLARKE, CAPTAIN

Captain Clarke RN, commander of the *Canterbury*, a sixty-four gunner under Admiral Knowles, had distinguished himself in battle against the Spanish fleet. There was some discontent about Admiral Knowles' conduct during the battle and he was brought to answer before a court martial, at which Captain Knowles was a witness in his defence. Captain Innis, commander of the *Warwick* took exception to Clarke's evidence and called him 'a perjured rascal', accusing him of giving false evidence. At every opportunity in the days that followed, Innis vilified Clarke, which culminated in Clarke giving Innis a verbal challenge. A little after dawn on 12 August 1749, the two captains, attended by their seconds, met in Hyde Park. They were not more than five yards apart when Captain Clarke fired before Captain Innis had levelled his pistol. Innis was struck by a shot in the chest and died of his wound about twelve o'clock that night. A coroner's jury found a verdict of wilful murder against Clarke. The captain was apprehended, brought to trial at the OLD BAILEY, found guilty and sentenced to death. However, the King, in consideration of Captain Clarke's distinguished service granted him a free pardon. On the last day of the sessions at the OLD BAILEY on 1 June 1750, Captain Clarke, along with several other convicts was brought to receive sentence of death. On presenting His Majesty's pardon, which was duly recorded, he was discharged.

CLEFT CHIN MURDER, THE

At 2.30am on Saturday 7 October 1944, nightwatchman Bill Hollis was at work at a Chiswick car depot. He heard the distinct sound of a single gunshot. At about 8am, apprentice electrician John Jones found several items scattered along the grass verge of the Great Southwest Road. They included an identity card, cheque book and driving licence, all belonging to George Heath. Jones handed them into the police. Not long afterwards, a man's body was found in a ditch at Knowle Green near Staines. He had been shot in the back at close range. The body was quickly linked to the items found by the roadside in Chiswick and the dead man identified as thirty-four-year-old freelance cab driver, cleft-chinned George Heath. His missing Ford V8 saloon was found in Lurgan Avenue, Fulham on 9 October. The car was placed under observation and within a short time of its discovery a dark haired young man came out of a house and got into it. Three policemen quickly moved in and the man was discovered to have a Remington automatic pistol in his possession and several rounds of ammunition. He was arrested and taken to Hammersmith police station.

The man, an American, gave a false name, claiming to be Second Lieutenant Richard Allen. Under the *Visiting Forces Act* a potential serious diplomatic problem emerged. An officer from the American Army Criminal Investigation Department interviewed Allen and after several hours of questioning he broke down and confessed to being Private Karl Gustav Hulten, aged twenty-two, who was absent without leave. He claimed to have found the car near the army barracks where he was stationed in Newbury and said at the time of the murder he was with a girl, Georgina Grayson. She was tracked down to a bedsit at 311 King Street, Hammersmith and brought in for questioning. Eighteen years old, her real name was Elizabeth Jones. She hailed from Neath in South Wales and worked as an exotic dancer at the *Blue Lagoon Club* in Carnaby Street, using the stage name Georgina Grayson. She said she did not know a man named Hulten, but after being shown a photograph she confirmed that she knew Hulten as 'Ricky' and they had met the previous week in a café, since when they had been out on several dates. She also said he had spent the entire night of 7 October with her, in her flat. Satisfied with her answers, the police allowed her to leave. On her way home she bumped into an old acquaintance, Henry Kimberley, who happened to be a Reserve Constable. He said she looked tired. She told him about being questioned by police and he told her not to worry if she had nothing to do with the murder. However, his suspicions were aroused when she remarked:

> It's no wonder I look tired. If you'd seen someone do what I've seen done, you wouldn't be able to sleep at night either.

Kimberley went with police officers to bring Jones in for questioning once again, and this time she told in detail how Hulten had shot George Heath and also how from 3 October she had accompanied him on a campaign of crime and violence in the army vehicle he had commandeered. She said he had told her he was connected with Chicago gangsters and she, according to Hulten had incited him to commit robbery and murder as she said she wanted 'to do something exciting'. They had hailed Heath's taxi near Olympia and Hulten had shot him in Chiswick – to impress her. The US Government waived its right and allowed Hulten to be tried in a British court. Hulten and Jones' trial commenced at the OLD BAILEY on Tuesday 16 January before Mr Justice Charles. It lasted six days and both were found guilty of murder and sentenced to death. Jones was reprieved two days before her scheduled execution and her sentence commuted to life imprisonment. She was released in January 1954. Hulten was hanged at PENTONVILLE on 8 March 1945.

CONWAY AND RICHARDSON

Peter Conway and Michael Richardson were two would-be robbers, who during their first attempt at robbery committed murder. On Saturday 26 May 1770, Conway and Richardson purchased a pair of pistols. The next day they went to Whitechapel where they drank until dusk. They then ventured out into the streets and stopped a gentleman's servant but he having no money they allowed him to pass. Earlier that afternoon, Mr Venables, a butcher, had been walking with his friend, Mr Rogers, a carpenter and they were returning through Whitechapel to the City. Both men had the appearance of being well-to-do and they were held up by Conway and Richardson and another man named Fox. The two men resisted and were immediately shot dead by Conway and Richardson. The murderers took no booty with them and all three villains headed off towards Stepney, then to Ratcliffe Highway and on to Wapping, where they robbed a man of eighteen shillings and a watch. Conway and Richardson were soon apprehended as a result of the pewter shot they used, traced to Robert Dun's shop near Ratcliffe Highway, and through Conway's attempt at pawning the watch in Jermyn Street, after descriptions of the watch and culprits had been circulated. Witnesses were able to identify them as the murderers and Sir John FIELDING committed them both to NEWGATE. They were tried at the next Sessions at the OLD BAILEY and hanged at TYBURN on 19 July 1770. Afterward their bodies were put in chains and hung on a gibbet on Bow Common, where it was said more than fifty thousand people visited the spot within the first five days.

CONWAY, PETER – see CONWAY AND RICHARDSON

COOPER, THOMAS

In 1842, Hornsey Wood covered what is now the park itself in the part of the capital known as Finsbury Park. A hostelry known as the *Hornsey Wood Tavern* once stood close to the site of the present-day boating pond. Near this pub, on 5 May 1842, Thomas Cooper, a twenty-two-year-old bricklayer-turned-thief, was surprised by policeman Charles Moss while he was engaged in some felonious act. Without hesitation Cooper shot and wounded Moss. The sound of gunfire attracted the attention of another policeman called Mallet, and a baker called Mott, who was walking in the woods nearby.

Mallett and Mott gave chase as Cooper headed off in the direction of Highbury. Meanwhile, another baker, named Howard, was driving his post chaise down Hornsey Road. He saw Cooper being chased and raced after him. Cooper headed for Highbury Barn. As another policeman, Timothy Daly, closed in on Cooper near Highbury Cottage, Cooper jumped over a hedge into a short cul-de-sac called Black Ditch. This area was bounded by a paling fence which hemmed Cooper in long enough for Daly and Howard to catch up. Cooper, who was carrying two large horse pistols, fired both of them. One hit its target and Daly died instantly, but Hudson was unscathed and with the help of two gardeners was able to overcome Cooper and hold him. Cooper was tried at the OLD BAILEY, found guilty of murder and hanged outside NEWGATE on 4 July 1842.

COPELAND, DAVID

In April 1999, David Copeland, who is now more usually referred to as 'The London Nail Bomber' directed his intense hatred against his most loathed members of the community, ethnic minorities and gay men. He planted three nail bombs. The first exploded on 17 April in Brixton and was principally directed at the black community there. This bomb injured forty people. The second bomb exploded in Brick Lane in the East End on Saturday 24 April and was directed at the Asian community. Fortunately, the bag in which the bomb had been hidden was spotted by a passer-by who put it in the boot of his car believing it to be lost property. It exploded shortly afterwards and ten people suffered minor injuries. Then on Friday 30 April Copeland left a sports holdall in the *Admiral Duncan*, a pub frequented by gay men in Soho's Old Compton Street. The bomb it contained exploded at 6.30pm when about seventy people were in the pub. In such a confined space its effect was devastating. Nick Moore, Andrea Dykes (who was pregnant) and John Light were killed and many other victims suffered dreadful injuries. A little over an hour before the bomb went off a work colleague of Copeland's recognised him from a CCTV image shown on the news of the suspected

An early nineteenth century engraving showing Hornsey Wood Tavern, *which was situated where the present day boating lake is in Finsbury Park.* Author's collection

bomber taken shortly before the Brixton bomb went off. Copeland was quickly traced and arrested at 9pm that evening. Found guilty of murder at the OLD BAILEY in June 2000, he was given six life sentences. In March 2007, a High Court judge ruled that Copeland must serve at least fifty years behind bars.

COURVOISIER, FRANCOIS BENJAMIN

What is today's Dunraven Street, running parallel with Park Lane and lying between North Row and Wood Mews, Mayfair, was, in 1840, Norfolk Street. It was there, at No. 14, a small but elegant three-storied house, that Lord William Russell a seventy-three-year-old widower, lived with his staff of three servants; a cook, maid and valet, Francois Benjamin Courvoisier, who was Swiss. Lord William was by all accounts, an irascible, tetchy, somewhat peevish old gentleman, a younger son of the Duke of Bedford and uncle of the then Secretary of State for the Colonies.

On the morning of 6 May 1840, the housemaid, on coming downstairs from her quarters on the top floor, found the principal rooms in disarray. In the dining room, furniture had been turned upside down, the drawers of the escritoire were open and had been rifled, there was a bundle lying on the floor, as though thieves had been interrupted. It appeared that a burglary had taken place. She summoned the cook and they then called Courvoisier, who, much to their surprise came from his room already dressed. This was unusual in itself, because he was habitually late in the morning. Together they went upstairs to their master's bedroom. While Courvoisier opened the shutters, the housemaid saw that Lord William was lying dead on his bloodstained bed.

Help soon arrived and despite the general mayhem elsewhere in the house, it was first assumed that Lord William had committed suicide. His throat had been cut from ear to ear, a towel had been placed over his face and this was soaked with blood, which also covered the pillows and bedding. However, it soon became apparent that this was no suicide, when it was discovered that some silver and other valuable items were missing. Suspicion was aroused by the bundle in the dining room, which contained small items of plate and jewellery that a thief would normally have put into his pocket, leading those investigating the crime that the scene had been staged, but fortunately for them, not with any degree of expertise. In this the police were not wrong.

In his Lordship's bedroom several items were missing, including money. The futile efforts of the real murderer to throw suspicion on burglars had been amply proved to the satisfaction of the police, who were convinced the culprit was from within the household. Courvoisier was taken into custody and the cook and maid placed under surveillance. Three days later a search of the butler's pantry provided further circumstantial evidence against the valet and Courvoisier was committed for trial. He was first held in Tothill Fields

Francois Benjamin Courvoisier.
Author's collection

prison. A subscription was raised from foreign servants in London, to provide funds for his defence.

The trial opened at the OLD BAILEY on 18 June. Courvoisier pleaded not guilty. Madame Piolaine, a Frenchwoman, gave evidence. She had, unbeknown to Courvoisier, already been taken to Tothill Fields and identified him. Louis Piolaine and his wife's cousin, Joseph Vincent, ran a small hotel, the *Dieppe*, in Leicester Place. Several years before the murder, Courvoisier had worked there for about a month. Six weeks before the murder Courvoisier had called on Madame Piolaine and a few days later returned with a brown paper parcel which he asked her to look after for him. When her husband read about the murder case the parcel was opened and it was found to contain items of silver belonging to Lord William Russell. The jury had no difficulty in deciding upon a guilty verdict and Courvoisier was sentenced to death. After he had been taken to NEWGATE following sentencing, he admitted that he had been justly convicted.

Courvoisier was only prevented from suicide by the vigilance of his captors and he said he intended to open a vein with a bit of sharpened stick, which had been taken away from him when his mattress was changed. The execution took place outside NEWGATE on 6 July 1840. The executioner was William CALCRAFT.

COWLAND, JOHN

In November 1700, Sir Andrew Slanning was in the company of John Cowland and several other gentleman at the Theatre Royal, Drury Lane, when he arranged an assignation with a willing orange-woman. She accompanied Sir Andrew and the other gentlemen from the theatre as soon as the play was over. When Mr Cowland put his arm around the woman's neck, Sir Andrew asked him not to do that, as she was his wife. Mr Cowland knowing otherwise wanted the woman for himself and began to quarrel.

Swords were drawn but were soon put up again. The party then went to the *Rose Tavern*, where Captain Waggett attempted to reconcile the two men. As they were going upstairs to take a glass of wine Cowland drew his sword and stabbed Sir Andrew in the belly. Sir Andrew called out: 'Murder!' One of Lord Warwick's servants disarmed Cowland, whose sword was smeared with Sir Andrew's blood to a depth of five inches. Cowland was taken as he tried to flee the scene. Sir Andrew was dead within minutes. John Cowland was tried at the OLD BAILEY on 5 December and executed at TYBURN on 20 December 1700.

CREAM, DR THOMAS NEILL

Known as the Lambeth Poisoner, profoundly cross-eyed Dr Cream was born at 61 Wellington Lane, Glasgow on 27 May 1850. Four years later the Cream family emigrated to Canada. Thomas Cream studied medicine graduating from McGill College, Montreal in 1876. Earlier, in 1874, he had insured his lodgings for $1,000, within a fortnight of graduation, as a result of a mysterious fire, Cream had put in a claim for almost the full amount. At first his insurers refused to pay but eventually forked out £350 for what they believed was a case of arson. Before long Cream met the daughter of a wealthy hotelier, Flora Elizabeth Brooks, who shortly became pregnant.

Dr Thomas Neill Cream, 'The Lambeth Poisoner'. John D Murray collection

The pregnancy was terminated by Cream and almost resulted in Miss Brooks' death. Her father insisted they marry and Cream was virtually marched up the aisle on 11 September 1874. The day after the wedding Cream took to his heels and headed for England and didn't get in touch again until he heard Flora had died of consumption just over a year later, and that was only to demand $1,000 from her father for her marriage settlement. He got $200 for his cheek.

On his arrival in England Cream enrolled as a postgraduate student at London's St Thomas's Hospital. During this further period of study he also received honours from the Royal College of Physicians and Surgeons at Edinburgh and afterwards returned to Canada, where from premises in Dundas Street, London, Ontario, he began to earn a considerable income as an abortionist. However, after the deaths of two of his patients under very dubious circumstances his practice was ruined and he moved to the USA and set up practice in Chicago, where he was later arrested on a charge of murder but acquitted through lack of evidence. Then, also in Chicago, in 1881, he was charged with poisoning a patient, Daniel Stott, found guilty of murder in the second degree and imprisoned for life in the Illinois State Penitentiary at Joliet. Bizarrely, he incriminated himself by the self-advertising of his crime through a series of anonymous letters. With the assistance of his family his sentence was reduced on appeal to seventeen years; and on 31 July 1891, taking into account his good behaviour, he was released. His father had died in 1867 and having collected his $16,000 inheritance, Dr Cream boarded the *Teutonic* for Liverpool.

On Monday 5 October 1891, Dr Cream, now calling himself Dr Neill, checked into *Anderton's Hotel* in Fleet Street. On 6 October he went to Ludgate Circus where he met prostitute Elizabeth Masters and spent the evening with her drinking before going back to her rooms at 9 Orient Buildings, in Lambeth's Hercule Road. This sordid district of London obviously took his eye because the following day he moved into lodgings at 103 Lambeth Palace Road. From there this suave, silk hatted, bespectacled, sexual deviant, known to his victims as 'Fred', went on a rampage of killing south of the River Thames that rivalled the JACK THE RIPPER murders in the East End. He, like the Ripper, chose prostitutes as his prey, plying them with poison, administered in pills containing strychnine. Ellen Donworth, Matilda Clover, Emma Shrivell and Alice Marsh all fell victim to Cream. Just as he had done in Chicago he began sending anonymous letters, which put himself into the frame and with the help of prostitute Louisa Harvey, who had managed to elude the doctor's attempts to poison her, Cream was arrested on 3 June 1892 in Lambeth Palace Road by Inspector Tunbridge. Seven bottles of strychnine were found at his lodgings.

Dr Cream's trial began at the OLD BAILEY on 17 October 1892, before Mr Justice Hawkins. He was charged with the murder of Matilda Clover and, three days later, with overwhelming evidence against him, the jury found Cream guilty.

On 24 October 1892, the *St James's Gazette* included a report of Dr Neill (Cream) by 'one who knew him':

Women were his preoccupation, and his talk of them far from agreeable. He carried pornographic photographs, which he was too ready to display. He was in the habit of taking pills, which he said, were compounded of strychnine, morphia, and cocaine, and of which the effect, he declared, was aphrodisiac. In short, he was a degenerate of filthy desires and practices...

Cream never confessed or gave any indication what had driven him to murder. He was hanged at NEWGATE on 15 November 1892 and buried in Dead Man's Walk.

CRIPPEN, DR HAWLEY HARVEY

This case is notable for the murderer being the first to be caught by wireless telegraph. Hawley Harvey Crippen was born in Coldwater, Michigan. When he met his future wife he was a thirty-one-year-old widower. Doctor Crippen was 5ft 4in tall, with piercing blue-grey eyes, which due to an affliction bulged slightly. Compelled to wear thick-lensed glasses, he constantly blinked. He married his colleague's secretary, Brooklyn-born Cora Turner (of Polish descent who had changed her name from Kunigunde Mackamotzki and was fourteen years his younger), on 1 September 1892. Cora had aspirations to become an opera singer but the American stage did not welcome her.

In 1900, Crippen was given the opportunity to go to London for Munyon's Remedies, a patent medicine outfit on a salary of £3 a week. The Crippens took rooms at 37 Store Street, off Tottenham Court Road, Bloomsbury. While the doctor was dispensing quack medicines, the wife was visiting theatrical agents. Doctor in name only, his professional qualifications did not allow him to practice in England, so he knuckled down to work as a glorified salesman. If Cora was not quite Covent Garden material, London and the provinces had the Music Halls. She managed to get some periods of regular employment under her new stage name Belle Elmore, which meant on occasions she was away from home, sometimes for several weeks, which enabled her to indulge her nymphomaniac inclinations. Not a great success on stage, in off-stage theatrical activities, she became something of a personality, rising to become Honorary Treasurer of the Music Hall Ladies Guild, enabling her to befriend such stars as Marie Lloyd and Vesta Tilley. Her constant entertaining and her

39 Hilldrop Crescent. Author's collection

expensive tastes in stage attire and gowns were a drain on the Crippens' finances. In September 1905, they moved to a large semi-detached house in Holloway. 39 Hilldrop Crescent was rented for £52 10s a year. To supplement their income the Crippens took in paying guests. A delivery of clothing to the Crippens' household in January 1909 was carefully documented by Jones Brothers, of Holloway, who delivered three suits of pyjamas.

In September 1908, Miss Ethel Le Neve became Crippen's secretary at Albion House, 61 New Oxford Street. She was tiny, dark, attractive, demure and genteel – almost the exact opposite of what Cora had become. Ethel and Doctor Crippen found that they were soul mates and fell deeply in love.

On 17 January 1910, Crippen went to the chemists Lewis and Burrows in New Oxford Street and asked for five grains of hyoscine hydrobromide for Munyon's Remedies and put down the use for which he wished the drug in the Poison Register, 'homeopathic preparation'.

The last people to see Cora Crippen alive were retired mime artistes Paul and Clara Martinetti. They were invited to Hilldrop Crescent on the evening of 31 January 1910. The little dinner party broke up at about 1.30am. On the afternoon of 2 February, Belle Elmore failed to appear at a meeting of the Music Hall Ladies' Guild, held in a room at Albion House, loaned by her husband. Two letters were delivered by the hand of Ethel Le Neve, both were signed 'Belle Elmore', but neither was in her handwriting. The letters informed the Guild that she was resigning her membership, owing to an urgent visit to America due to a family illness.

It was on the 20 February when Crippen took Ethel to the Music Hall Ladies' Guild annual ball, at the Criterion, that Belle's friends began to take a little more

Illustrated Police News Author's collection

interest in the doctor. Ethel was wearing one of Belle's brooches. Crippen told Belle's friends that his wife had developed pneumonia in California and was dangerously ill. On 24 March, Doctor Crippen and Ethel Le Neve went on a five-day Easter holiday to Dieppe as Mr and Mrs Crippen. Before they left, Crippen sent a telegram to the Martinettis saying 'Belle died yesterday at six o'clock...'

On their return from France, Belle Elmore's friends bombarded him with questions. 'She passed on of pneumonia, up in the high mountains of California,' he told them. A friend of Lil Hawthorne happened to be Detective Superintendent Froest, of Scotland Yard. He was in charge of the recently formed Serious Crimes Squad and since Hawthorne was suspicious that something was amiss, he promised to look into the matter. Chief Inspector Walter Dew was assigned to make general enquiries. Inspector Dew explained the reason for the visit and Crippen told him: 'I suppose I'd better tell the truth.' A lengthy statement was taken over five hours. Crippen stated that by the time he came home from work on 1 February his wife had gone. She had run off with another man and to add insult to injury had left most of her clothes and the jewels he had given her, and left him with no clue as to her whereabouts. He said he tried to explain his wife's disappearance without causing a scandal, and conceal the fact that he had been cuckolded. Crippen and Ethel accompanied Inspector Dew and Sergeant Mitchell to Hilldrop Crescent, where they looked around. They were satisfied nothing was amiss. However, Crippen must have felt uneasy about this police attention. He panicked and fled with Ethel to Rotterdam.

On Monday 11 July, Chief Inspector Dew returned to Albion House to clear up some final points. Crippen's associate, Doctor Rylance, informed Dew that on Saturday 9 July, he had received a letter from Crippen instructing him to wind up his affairs. Included in the letter was the ominous sentence: 'In order to escape trouble I shall be obliged to absent myself for a time.' A dental mechanic employed at Albion House told Dew that Doctor Crippen had sent him out to purchase clothing for a boy of sixteen.

When the inspector visited 39 Hilldrop Crescent, he discovered only the French maid. The house was searched from top to bottom once again, and again, during 12 and 13 July. On a third inspection of the coal cellar after Dew had been prodding the floor with a fire-poker, he discovered that there were some loose bricks. The presence of quicklime urged him to dig deeper. It was not long before the gruesome discovery of what little remained of Cora Crippen was made. Just a stinking heap of human flesh, viscera and hair, wrapped in a pyjama jacket.

The remains were examined by

Daily Graphic Author's collection

Doctor Pepper and Doctor Bernard SPILSBURY. Tests were carried out on tissue samples by the toxicologist Dr William WILLCOX. The discovery of hyoscine hydrobromide led them to conclude that poisoning by the same was the cause of death and that the remains were those of a stout female, who bleached her hair. Part of the flesh from the abdomen showed a scar consistent with the ovariectomy undergone by Cora Crippen. A warrant was issued on 16 July for the arrest of Doctor Hawley Harvey Crippen and Ethel Le Neve for murder and mutilation.

Meanwhile, Crippen and Le Neve were in Belgium and were staying at the *Hotel des Ardennes* in Brussels. On Wednesday 20 July, having boarded the SS *Montrose* at Antwerp, as Mr John Philo Robinson and

Crippen in the witness box. Author's collection

Master John Robinson, they set sail for Quebec. Crippen had shaved off his moustache and removed his spectacles. His failure to refrain from being over affectionate towards his 'sixteen-year-old son', with whom he shared a double cabin, aroused the suspicion of Captain Kendall, who quickly came to the conclusion that Master Robinson was a woman. Kendall, who had seen a police notice about the fugitives, communicated the news to Scotland Yard, via the new Marconi Electric Telegraph.

Chief Inspector Dew and his sergeant, made arrangements to travel to Quebec by a faster ship. They set sail from Liverpool on 23 July aboard the SS *Laurentic,* and arrived in Quebec ahead of the SS *Montrose*. Dr Crippen and Ethel Le Neve were arrested on Sunday 31 July and brought back to London after three weeks' detention in Canada, aboard the SS *Megantic.*

Cora Crippen's remains were interred at Finchley Cemetery on 10 October 1910. A few bits of flesh were retained for the trial, where they were passed round in a soup plate. Crippen's trial began on Tuesday 18 October 1910, at the OLD BAILEY, before the Lord Chief Justice, Lord Alverstone. Ethel Le Neve was to be tried separately with being an accessory after the fact. Mr Richard, for the defence suggested that the remains had been buried in the cellar at 39, Hilldrop Crescent, sometime before September 1905, when the Crippens had moved into the house. However, the tell-tale label on the pyjama jacket, bearing the words 'Jones Brothers Ltd.' in which the remains had been wrapped, proved they could only have been buried there after the Crippens' occupancy, as Jones Brothers did not become a Limited Company until 1908. On the fifth day of the trial, having heard all the evidence, the jury retired and returned after only twenty-seven minutes, with a guilty verdict. Sentence of death was pronounced.

The trial of Ethel Le Neve began on 25 October and lasted one day. She appeared before the same judge and had the same prosecutor as her lover. She was defended by Mr F E Smith, KC, afterwards, 1st Earl of Birkenhead. She gave no evidence but was acquitted and set free. Doctor Crippen's appeal was heard on 5 November. It failed. He was hanged on the morning of 23 November 1910 at PENTONVILLE by John ELLIS.

CROSSMAN, GEORGE

Serial bigamist and murderer. In 1904 William Dell rented part of a house from George Crossman in Ladysmith Avenue (later renamed Wrentham Avenue), Queens Park. He complained to Mr Crossman about the appalling smell that was coming from a cupboard under the stairs. Crossman attributed the smell to a box of size (a gelatinous substance used to prepare plaster for decoration, amongst other things) that had gone bad. He assured his tenant he would have it removed. The box was in fact a tin trunk. Mr Dell was not convinced by Crossman's explanation and thought there might be something sinister occurring. He reported the matter to the police and, coincidentally a constable called to investigate just as the trunk was being carried out by some workmen, while Crossman puffed on a cigar to mask the stench. When he saw the policeman, Crossman panicked and ran off, leaving behind a bemused constable and Mr Dell. They followed him, but as they closed in, he took a razor out of his pocket and cut his throat, dying where he fell. The trunk was opened and found to contain the remains of Ellen Sampson, encased in cement, which had cracked and released noxious smelling gases. Crossman had bigamously married her more than a year previously, she being the fifth of seven women to have become his wife.

CUMMINS, GORDON

Twenty-eight-year-old, 5ft 7ins tall, multiple murderer Gordon Cummins horribly mutilated and killed four women in six days after picking up his unsuspecting victims in West End pubs and clubs in wartime London. Born in New Earswick, North Yorkshire, Cummins was well educated but not industrious. He moved to London and before World War Two worked in a laboratory. In 1936, he married a theatre producer's secretary. He was called up in 1941 and joined the RAF, training for the air-crew. In 1942, he was billeted in St John's Wood, where his colleagues nicknamed him 'The Duke' on account of his phoney Oxford accent. On Saturday 8 February 1942, Cummins left his RAF billet and went to see his wife, from whom he borrowed money. He then went to the West End.

The following morning the body of forty-two-year-old pharmacist, Miss Evelyn Margaret Hamilton, was discovered in the doorway of a brick air raid shelter in Montagu Place, W1. She had been strangled and her handbag, containing the sum of £80, had vanished. Cummins repeated the pattern of taking money and small items of little value from his victims. On 10 February, an ex-actress and Windmill Theatre showgirl, turned prostitute, thirty-five-year-old Nita Ward (real name Mrs Evelyn Oatley), was found almost naked and dead on the bed, in her flat at 153 Wardour Street, W1. She had first been strangled, then her throat cut and the lower part of her body crudely torn open with a tin opener. On Thursday 13 February, another prostitute, forty-three-year-old Mrs Margaret Florence Lowe (known as Pearl), was found murdered in her flat, Flat 4, 9-10 Gosfield Street, W1. She had been strangled on her divan bed with one of her silk stockings and her body cut and disfigured by a razor and a knife, which had been left nearby. In the kitchen was a half empty bottle of stout: a crucial piece of evidence, as the bottle had Cummins' fingerprints on it from his left hand, and it had been established that the murderer was left-handed, by the pressure exerted during strangulation, evident by the bruising on the neck of his victims.

Chief Inspector Greeno, Detective Inspector Higgins and Home Office pathologist Sir Bernard SPILSBURY were attending the crime scene, when news came of yet another murder. Thirty-two-year-old Mrs Doris Jouannet (also known as Doris

Robson) of 187 Sussex Gardens, Paddington, the wife of an elderly hotel manager, a naturalised Frenchman, who at the time of the murder was on duty at a West End hotel. Mrs Jouannet led a double life, working as a prostitute when her husband was at work. She had been killed in the early hours of that morning and had been strangled by a scarf, which was still wrapped round her neck and her body slashed several times with a razor blade. Later that evening, Cummins picked up Mrs Greta Heywood near Piccadilly and had a drink with her at the *Trocadero Hotel*. When Cummins became what Mrs Heywood described as 'unpleasantly forward', she decided to leave. Cummins followed her and eventually caught up with her in Alban's Street, where he forced her into a doorway and tried to strangle her. She passed out and fortunately, before death overcame her, Cummins was disturbed by a delivery boy taking some bottles to the nearby *Captain's Cabin*. Cummins panicked and fled, leaving his gas mask behind. It had his service number printed on the case. Cummins tried to murder again that night, picking up a prostitute named Mrs Mulcahy. He tried to strangle her, but she freed herself and screamed. Cummins fled, leaving behind his RAF webbing belt.

Through the serial number on the gas mask case Cummins' involvement in the four murders was quickly established and items belonging to his victims were found amongst his possessions. His trial began at the OLD BAILEY on Monday 27 April 1942 before Mr Justice Asquith, with overwhelming and conclusive evidence against him, it ended the next day. The jury took just thirty-five minutes to find him guilty. He was executed at WANDSWORTH on 25 June 1942. Cummins is believed to have committed at least one other murder. Police suspect that he strangled nineteen-year-old prostitute, Maple Church, in October 1941, as the pattern of the bruising corresponded with that of his other victims, indicating that the killer was left-handed. The killer had also rifled her handbag.

D

DE BUTTE, LOUIS – see MERCIER, FRANCIS

DE VERE, EUGENE – see STITCHELL, EWEN

DOBKIN, HARRY
Wartime fire-watcher Harry Dobkin, working in Kennington for a firm of solicitors, had in his youth been obliged to undergo a marriage arranged by a matchmaker, at Bethnal Green Synagogue in 1920. Rachel Dubinski was not to be the wife of his dreams and after three days the newlyweds parted forever but not before a baby had been conceived. A son was born nine months later and Harry, having supported him into adulthood, was now expected to continue supporting Rachel through a £1 a week maintenance order, which he resented. On 17 July 1942, demolition workers were clearing the site of a Baptist church near the Oval Kennington in St Oswald's Place that had been bombed in 1940. In the cellar beneath what had once been the vestry they prised up a large slab of stone and revealed a human skeleton, with a small amount of flesh clinging to the torso. The head had been severed but was partially intact and the arms and legs were missing; lime was also present in the soil surrounding the skeleton indicating foul play, not just another bomb victim. The remains were examined by Professor Keith Simpson and identified through dental records as being Rachel

Dobkin, who had been reported missing by her sister Polly on 12 April 1941. Sufficient flesh remained in the neck to show strangulation as the cause of death. Rachel had gone to meet her husband on 11 April 1941 to discuss the late payment of her maintenance. Harry Dobkin was arrested and charged with murder. His trial commenced at the OLD BAILEY on 17 November 1942. He was found guilty and hanged at WANDSWORTH on 27 January 1943.

DOCHERTY, HUGH – see BALCOMBE STREET SIEGE, THE

DONOVAN AND WADE
On 12 October 1904, half-brothers Conrad Donovan and Charles Wade decided to rob a newsagent and tobacconist's shop at 478 Commercial Road, Stepney run by Miss Matilda Emily Farmer. Unknown to them, the two men had been seen acting suspiciously outside the premises two days previously by a Sunday school teacher, who was later able to identify them. Miss Farmer was well known in the area for owning and wearing jewellery. During the course of the robbery she was bound and gagged. When she was discovered the following day she had choked to death on the gag and her jewellery was missing. The two culprits were quickly apprehended and brought to trial. As the judge pointed out, accidental homicide consequent on robbery is murder. Donovan and Wade were hanged at PENTONVILLE on 13 December 1904.

DROMELIUS, GERALDIUS – see VAN BERGENS, THE AND DROMELIUS

DUDDY, JOHN – see BRAYBROOK STREET MASSACRE, THE

DUELL, WILLIAM
Hanged at TYBURN on 24 November 1740, for the ill treatment and murder of Sarah Griffin at Acton. After being executed, along with convicted burglars and felons Thomas Clock, William Meers, Margery Stanton and Eleanor Munoman, Duell's body was taken down and removed to Surgeons' Hall to be anatomised. His body was stripped and washed by servants. One of them noticed signs of life. The hanged man's breathing gradually increased in strength. A surgeon was summoned and he took several ounces of blood from Duell, who soon recovered his senses. Within two hours he was able to sit up in a chair and was well enough that evening to be taken back to NEWGATE. Sentence of death was commuted to transportation.

DUFFY AND MULCAHY
John Duffy and David Mulcahy were childhood friends both born in 1959. Between 1982 and 1986 London's suburban

Contemporary engraving of William Duell. Author's collection

railway stations were the focus of a major police investigation, during which time one man was believed to have been responsible for at least thirty rapes, three of them resulting in murder. The first rape took place in June 1982. The first murder on 29 December 1985, when nineteen-year-old Alison Day was raped and strangled and her body dumped in the canal near Hackney Wick Station, where it was found seventeen days later. On 17 April 1986, the body of fifteen-year-old Maartje Tamboezer was found in a copse near the Horsley to London railway line and on 19 May 1986 the body of twenty-nine-year-old Anne Lock was found near the railway line at Brookmans Park in Hertfordshire. In all three cases the victims had been raped then strangled with string and a sock had been stuffed down their throats. A massive police investigation resulted in a list of 4,874 suspects, one of which was John Duffy. Professor David Canter provided a psychological profile of the murderer. Out of seventeen characteristics Professor Canter highlighted Duffy matched thirteen perfectly. Duffy was charged with all the rapes and the three murders. He did not admit to anything. In 1988 Duffy was convicted of two of the murders but acquitted of the rape of Anne Lock due to insufficient evidence. He was sentenced to thirty years' imprisonment. In 1997 Duffy began to recount his crimes to prison psychologist Dr Jennie Cutler. During sessions over several years he confessed to eight additional rapes between 1975 and 1986 and admitted his involvement in the rape of Anne Lock. Crucially, he put his accomplice David Mulcahy, a builder from Chalk Farm, in the frame, naming him as his partner in fifteen attacks. Mulcahy, a married father-of-four, was convicted at the OLD BAILEY in February 2001 of the murder of the three women, seven more rapes and five counts of conspiracy to rape. He was jailed for twenty-four years.

DUGGAN, HARRY – see BALCOMBE STREET SIEGE, THE

DUNN AND O'SULLIVAN

On 22 June 1922, Field Marshall Sir Henry Wilson was gunned down on the front doorstep of his Belgravia home by two English-born members of the IRA. Sir Henry Hughes Wilson (1864-1922) was born in Edgeworthtown, County Longford. After serving in Burma and the Boer War, he was commander of the Staff College (1910-14), rising to chief of the Imperial General Staff (1918-22). He was made a baronet in 1919. When he left the army in early 1922 he entered politics, as MP for North Down, Ulster. He had recently returned from Belfast, where he had been advising the Northern Irish authorities on how to deal with bomb outrages perpetrated by Southern Republic terrorists, when, on 22 June, Sir Henry unveiled the War Memorial at Euston Station. Afterwards he returned home in full dress uniform to 26 Eaton

36 Eaton Place, Belgravia, site of the assassination of Sir Henry Wilson.
The Author

Place, where Reginald Dunn and Joseph O'Sullivan, both ex-servicemen, were waiting for him. Sir Henry drew his dress sword, the only weapon he had to defend himself with but he was powerless against his assassins' bullets. As the two killers were chased down Ebury Street, not an easy feat for O'Sullivan as he had a wooden leg, they seized a cab, then a victoria (a two seat, four-wheeled carriage), firing as they fled at their pursuers; they injured two policemen. They were seized by the ever increasing crowd and it was only swift police intervention that prevented them being lynched. Sir Henry was buried in the crypt of St Paul's Cathedral. Dunn and O'Sullivan were hanged at WANDSWORTH on 10 August 1922.

DYSON, GEORGE – see PIMLICO POISONING CASE, THE

E

EATON, ROADES AND SWIFT

The Revd John Talbot had been chaplain to a regiment in Portugal before he returned to London, where he preached for three months at St Alphage in the Wall. He then became curate at Laindon in Essex, where he was involved in a lawsuit with several parishioners, on account of which he returned to London. A group of friends became acquainted with this curate and believing him to be a man of fortune decided to waylay, rob and murder him. On Friday night, 2 July 1669, Talbot was followed to Gray's Inn by Stephen Eaton, a confectioner; George Roades, a broker; Henry Pritchard, a tailor, and Sarah Swift, who might reasonably be described as an opportunist; and according to Talbot, at least two others, who remain unknown. The clergyman felt ill at ease at being followed, for what purpose he had no idea. He spent some time writing letters and after taking a little refreshment, assuming the danger to be over, took the back way home, through Old Street and over the fields to Shoreditch. It was at about eleven o'clock that he was seized by his pursuers, who began to pick his pockets. They took about twenty shillings and also his knife with which they attempted to kill him by cutting his throat. They first cut out a piece of flesh from his throat without touching the windpipe, then stabbed him so deep that the point almost reached his lungs. However, they did not sever any nerves, which would have prevented him speaking; and having stripped him of his coat and doublet, fled the scene. Talbot was given assistance by some nearby brickmakers and the Watch at Shoreditch was summoned. He received medical attention from a surgeon, Mr Litchfield and it appeared he might recover. Other physicians also attended him free of charge. Four of the culprits were quickly apprehended and identified by Talbot and taken to NEWGATE. The Revd John Talbot died on Monday 11 July, as a result of the injuries he received in the attack, after a violent fit of coughing seized him and broke his jugular vein. The four culprits were taken to NEWGATE and tried at the next sessions at the OLD BAILEY, where they were all found guilty of murder and sentenced to death. Henry Pritchard received a pardon upon some favourable circumstances that were produced. On Wednesday 14 July 1669, Stephen Eaton, George Roades and Sarah Swift were taken in a cart from Newgate to the dreaded triple tree at TYBURN, where they were hanged. The two men confessed but Sarah Swift remained obstinate to the last.

EDMONDSON, MARY

Mary Edmondson was the daughter of a farmer from near Leeds in Yorkshire, who in 1757 was sent to lodge with a widowed aunt, Mrs Walker, at Rotherhithe. One winter evening two years later Mary called out from the open door of the house: 'Help! Murder! They have killed my aunt!' Assistance soon came and Mrs Walker was found lying on her right side near the kitchen table with her throat cut. Mary's account was that four men had entered the house by the back door and seized her aunt by the throat. She herself, had received a cut to the arm, as a result, she said of one of the men having jammed it in the door. Mary claimed her aunt had been killed during the course of the robbery that followed. Mrs Walker's executors caused the house to be thoroughly searched and several items Mary had said were stolen, were not missing at all. Mrs Walker's watch and other valuable items were discovered under the floorboards of the 'necessary house' [lavatory]. Mary was committed to the New Jail, Southwark, and tried at the next assizes for Surrey at Kingston. Although circumstantial, the evidence left the jury in little doubt that she was guilty of murder. Mary Edmondson was hanged on 2 April 1759 on Kennington Common. Before she died she made a short speech to the large crowd:

It is now too late to trifle either with God or man. I solemnly declare that I am innocent of the crime laid to my charge. I am very easy of mind, as I suffer with as much pleasure as if I was going to sleep. I freely forgive my prosecutors, and earnestly beg your prayers for my departing soul.

EDWARDS, EDGAR

On 23 December 1902, Edgar Edwards was apprehended after assaulting John Garland, a grocer, from Godrell Road, Victoria Park, with a lead window weight, at 89 Church Road, Leyton. Mr Garland had gone to meet Edwards to discuss the purchase of his grocery business. Later, police discovered a business card in the name of John W Darby, a Camberwell grocer, in the bedroom. When police went to Camberwell to talk to Mr Darby they discovered Mr Darby, his wife Beatrice and their ten-month-old baby, Ethel, were nowhere to be found and most of the contents of their living quarters had disappeared. A bloodstained window weight was also found. The shop was being managed on behalf of Mr Edwards by a dwarf and his wife. When attention was turned to the garden of Edwards' recently acquired house in Leyton, a grim discovery was made. The remains of the Darby family had been buried in six sacks, having being brought there in wooden crates from Camberwell by a hired horse-drawn van along with some furniture. Evidence suggested that Edwards was intent on building up a chain of grocery shops without having to pay for the businesses he had planned to take over. He

The Darby family. Illustrated Police News

Edgar Edwards [seated right] *in the condemned cell at* WANDSWORTH. Illustrated Police News

had lined up several potential prospects. Edwards' trial began at the Central Criminal Court within the OLD BAILEY before Mr Justice Wright on Thursday 12 February 1903. The jury retired just before twelve o'clock on Friday 20 February and returned after half an hour with a guilty verdict. Edwards was hanged by BILLINGTON on Tuesday 3 March 1903 at WANDSWORTH. His last words were: 'I've been looking forward to this lot.'

ELBY, WILLIAM

On 2 August 1707, William Elby, along with an unknown accomplice broke into the house of James Barry at Fulham, intending to burgle it. Mr Barry heard a noise in the house sometime after midnight and went to investigate along with his wife and servant Nicholas Hatfield. They found a window had been broken open and saw two men outside. As Mr and Mrs Barry ran upstairs to arms themselves, Hatfield, on stepping into the kitchen was met by Elby, who drove him into the pantry and stabbed him in the breast. He died twelve hours later. During the scuffle the other thief had fired a pistol that had wounded Elby in the leg, which led to him being quickly apprehended as he tried to flee. The accomplice got clean away. Elby was imprisoned in NEWGATE and tried at the next OLD BAILEY Sessions. As he received sentence of death, Elby called out: 'God damn you all!' He was hanged at Fulham on 13 September 1707.

ELLIS, JOHN (executioner)

John Ellis (1874-1932), during the course of twenty-three years executed 203 men and women including Dr Hawley Harvey CRIPPEN, Frederick SEDDON and George

Joseph SMITH. When he resigned his post in 1924 later that year Ellis tried to commit suicide. After drinking heavily, he attempted to shoot himself through the head. He bungled it and succeeded only in fracturing his jaw. The magistrate he appeared before following this failed suicide attempt told him: 'I'm sorry to see you here, Ellis, I have known you for a long time. If your aim was as true as some of the drops you have given, it would have been a bad job for you.' He was bound over to keep the peace and to stay away from strong drink and thoughts of suicide. Ellis became very depressed. His health was not good and he continued to drink heavily. In September 1932, he attempted suicide again by slitting his throat with a cut-throat razor. This time he did not bungle it. The coroner's verdict was 'Suicide while of unsound mind'.

ELLIS, RUTH

This case is noted for the subject being the last woman to be hanged in Great Britain. Ruth Ellis was a 5ft 2in tall, twenty-eight-year-old, bleached platinum blonde, night-club manageress and mother of two, who shot her twenty-four-year-old racing car driver lover, David Blakely, outside the *Magdala Tavern*, Hampstead on Easter Sunday, 10 April 1955. Ruth was born in the North Wales seaside resort of Rhyl. The name on her birth certificate was Ruth Neilson, her father being Arthur Hornby, a musician, who worked professionally as Arthur Neilson. Ruth had a peripatetic childhood and the remainder of her relatively short life was crammed full of incident. She became pregnant aged seventeen, giving birth to an illegitimate son, Clare Andrea Neilson, in

A present-day view of the Magdala Tavern, *South Hill Park, Hampstead, externally unaltered since Ruth Ellis shot David Blakely there in 1955. The shop on the right was once Hanshaw's newsagents. Ellis waited there until Blakely emerged from the* Magdala.
Paul T Langley Welch

September 1945, who in early life was mostly looked after by her sister, Muriel, while Ruth moved to London's West End, where she worked as a model and later as a night-club hostess, experiencing both the high life and the seedier aspects that such occupations can bring.

She married an alcoholic dentist, George Ellis in November 1950, producing a daughter, Georgina, in October 1951, who was later adopted. Her marriage ended in divorce. Ruth embarked on a social life full of drink, high living and sex. The abuse and deceit she endured from her younger lover David Blakely, who promised her marriage and stability in her troubled life, only brought sadness, disappointment and jealousy, which resulted in Ruth's last desperate act. She neither denied or tried to justify her actions; and during her trial which began in the No.1 Court at the OLD BAILEY on Monday 20 June 1955, before Mr Justice Havers, when asked by the leading prosecuting counsel, Mr Christmas Humphreys, 'Mrs Ellis, when you fired that revolver at close range into the body of David Blakely, what did you intend to do?' her fate was sealed when she replied: 'It is obvious that when I shot him I intended to kill him.' Some less generous-spirited commentators have said that had this 'ice-cool' murderess not been a young woman with undoubted physical attractions, then the case would not have warranted so much media attention, nor indeed prompted the degree of public indignation following her conviction for murder and subsequent execution.

The story of Ruth Ellis and David Blakely has continued to arouse considerable public curiosity. There is so much that remains unexplained about this tragic case, a story of love, uncontrolled passion, violence, jealousy and hatred. Albert PIERREPOINT in his autobiography *Executioner Pierrepoint* commented:

> *When I left Holloway after the execution of Ruth Ellis, the prison was almost besieged by a storming mob. I needed police protection to get me through. I knew I would have walked out of Strangeways* [where a forty-year-old woman, described by some as a harridan, had just been reprieved] *a week earlier into an empty street. At Euston Station a crowd of newspapermen were awaiting me. I shielded my face from the cameras as I ran for my train. One young reporter jogged alongside me asking, 'How did it feel to hang a woman, Mr Pierrepoint?' I did not answer. But I could have asked: 'Why weren't you waiting to ask me that question last year, sonny? Wasn't Mrs Christofi a woman too?'* [See CHRISTOFI, Styllou Pantopiou].

Ruth Ellis was executed on Wednesday 13 July 1955.

ERSKINE, KENNETH

During the late spring and hot summer of 1986 a serial killer was on the loose in South London. The killing spree began in West Hill Road, Wandsworth, with a seventy-eight-year-old spinster, Nancy Emms. Her body was discovered in bed by her home help on 9 April. Death was at first attributed to natural causes. It was only after her portable TV was discovered missing that a post-mortem was ordered. She had been strangled and bruises on her chest suggested that her killer had knelt on her during the process of strangulation and probably got in through the bedroom window which Miss Emms habitually left open. More killings followed; all the victims were strangled and all were elderly. On each occasion the killer had entered by an open window. Sixty-seven-year-old widow, Janet Cockett, was found dead in her flat at Stockwell's Overton Estate on 9 June. On 27 June retired engineer, Fred Prentice, was attacked in his sleep in a council-run old people's home called Breadmead, in Cedars Road, Clapham. As he was been strangled he managed to trigger an alarm, which sent his attacker fleeing into the night. Mr Prentice survived.

The next night, 28 June, the Stockwell Strangler, as he became known, struck again, killing two male victims in one night, eighty-four-year-old Valentine Gleim and ninety-four-year-old Zbigniev Stabrava, who had adjoining rooms at an old people's home, Somerville Hastings House in Stockwell Park Crescent. The Stockwell Strangler was believed to be white until a pubic hair found at a crime scene identified the strangler as being African or Caribbean. The strangler's fifth victim took him north of the River Thames to Islington, where at Sybil Thorndike House, on the Marquess Estate, he killed eighty-two-year-old widower, William Carmen. Home Office pathologist Dr Iain West concluded that all the victims had been strangled by the use of just one hand. There were other marks on the victims' bodies and money and other items of value had been stolen. On 12 July, seventy-five-year-old Trevor Thomas was found dead in the bath at Jeffreys Road, Clapham and on 20 July the strangler returned to the Overton Estate where he killed seventy-four-year-old William Downs.

Gradually, clues to the strangler's identity had been building up. A palm print found at the home of the strangler's second victim matched one found at the home of Mr Downs but unlike fingerprints, which were being computerised, no data base was then available. A painstaking search of records by hand eventually resulted in a match and just as the breakthrough came the killer struck again. His final victim was eighty-year-old, widow, Florence Tisdall, killed at her Ranelagh Gardens flat, close to Putney Bridge, on 23 July.

It was discovered that the palm prints matched those held on record of twenty-four-year-old petty criminal and burglar, Kenneth Erskine, a drifter, who had had no permanent home since he was sixteen. Police searched for him and discovered he was due to pick up his unemployment benefit in Southwark on 28 July. As he joined the queue for his cheque police swiftly moved in and arrested him. Fred Prentice picked out Erskine at an identity parade without a moment's hesitation and a public appeal brought in further evidence. Erskine's eighteen-day trial was held at the OLD BAILEY. Sentencing Erskine, Mr Justice Rose jailed him for seven life terms and recommended that he serve a minimum term of forty years.

EVANS, TIMOTHY JOHN

This double murder occurred at what was soon to become one of London's most notorious addresses, 10 Rillington Place, Notting Hill. On 2 December 1949 the bodies of nineteen-year-old Beryl Evans and her fourteen-month-old baby daughter, Geraldine, were found by police, dumped in the outside washhouse. At this same address the notorious serial killer John Reginald Halliday CHRISTIE lived on the ground floor. The Evans family lived in the top floor flat. On 30 November Timothy Evans, a twenty-four-year-old illiterate van driver, had visited Merthyr Tydfil police station and made a voluntary statement, in which he said he had returned home from work on 8 November and found his wife, Beryl, dead. He also said he had disposed of the body down a drain.

After the discovery of the bodies in the washhouse Evans made a new statement, in which he accused John Christie of killing his wife while carrying out an illegal abortion. Then, after the pathologist, Dr Teare found no evidence of an abortion, Evans changed his statement again and confessed to both murders. Evans was known to quarrel violently with Beryl and to beat her up. The violent arguments were often about money. At the OLD BAILEY on 11 November 1950, Evans retracted his confession and blamed Christie for both murders. However, the prosecution's chief witness was John Christie and at the conclusion of Evans's trial, it took the jury just forty minutes to find him guilty of murder. Evans was hanged on 9 March 1950 at PENTONVILLE. After the dreadful events of 1953 when Christie himself was charged with murder, some doubt was cast on Evans' guilt but Dr Francis Camps, pathologist in the Christie case, entertained no doubt about Evans' guilt. Christie admitted to killing Beryl but not to the baby and various scenarios have been suggested for both killings. Timothy Evans was posthumously pardoned on 8 October 1966.

F

FAHMY CASE

During the evening of Monday 9 July 1923, the orchestra leader in the Savoy Grill at the *Savoy Hotel*, situated in London's famous thoroughfare the Strand, asked the elegantly dressed, petite and pretty French lady in her native language, as she spoke very little English, if she would care to hear any special piece of music. 'Thank you very much,' she said in a low voice, 'my husband is going to kill me in twenty-four hours and I am not in the mood for music.' The orchestra leader smiled and said: 'I hope you will still be here tomorrow, Madame.'

The lady concerned, described by some as a strikingly beautiful Parisienne brunette, was none other than Marie-Marguerite Fahmy, aged thirty-two, wife of Egyptian Prince Ali Kamel Fahmy Bey, described by one commentator as the wastrel heir to a great industrialist, he had no need to work at anything but pleasure. At twenty-three he had an income of £100,000 a year, a palace on the Nile, yachts, a racing car and four Rolls Royces. It was widely believed he enjoyed a homosexual relationship with his secretary, Said Enani. Prince Fahmy had fallen violently in love with the former Marguerite Laurent, shortly after she had divorced her previous husband. He pursued her to Deauville and after she agreed to become a Moslem, they married on 26 December 1922.

On Tuesday 10 July 1923 the *Daily Telegraph* reported on one of the worst storms London had experienced in many years. At about two-thirty am, as the storm continued to rage outside, John Beattie, a night porter, was wheeling a luggage trolley along the corridor at the back of the fourth floor of the *Savoy*, when the Prince, dressed in mauve silk pyjamas and green velvet backless slippers, came out of one of the doors of his suite, approached him and said:

Look at my face! Look what she has done!

Beattie did as he had been instructed but saw only a slight pink mark on Fahmy's left cheek. Then the other door of the suite was flung open and Madame Fahmy stepped into the corridor, wearing a low-cut evening gown, fashioned out of shimmering white beads. She began to speak loudly to her husband in French and Beattie was obliged to politely ask the couple to return to their suite so as not to disturb other guests. Beattie continued on his journey, and as he pushed the trolley round the corner towards the front of the hotel, he heard a loud bang, then another and then a third. The porter ran back to the Fahmys' suite and when he reached it, he saw Madame Fahmy throwing down a pistol. Prince Fahmy was laying on the floor, bleeding from the head. Madame Fahmy had fired three bullets into her husband, from a Browning .25 automatic pistol,

THE DAILY MIRROR, Tuesday, September 11, 1923.

GERMANY SEEKING NEW CONFERENCE WITH FRANCE

The Daily Mirror

NET SALE MUCH THE LARGEST OF ANY DAILY PICTURE NEWSPAPER

No. 6,194.   Registered at the G.P.O. as a Newspaper.   TUESDAY, SEPTEMBER 11, 1923   One Penny.

SAVOY SHOOTING: MME. FAHMY'S TRIAL OPENS

Mme. Said, sister of the dead man, with her husband, Dr. Said (centre), and Abdul Faath Razal Bey, an Egyptian lawyer, representing Mme. Said.

Sir Henry Curtis Bennett, K.C., one of the counsel engaged for the defence.

Mr. Cecil Whiteley, K.C., who held a watching brief, arriving at the Old Bailey.

Said Enani, the dead man's secretary, said the couple were not very happy.

A new portrait, received from Paris last night, of Mme. Fahmy, who is charged with the murder of her husband, Ali Kamel Fahmy Bey (inset), a wealthy young Egyptian.

The large crowd that waited outside the Old Bailey in the hope of gaining admittance for the opening of the trial. Many fashionably-dressed women were present

Daily Mirror. Author's collection

one of a matching pair (His and Hers) that the couple always kept by their bedsides. A few hours later Prince Fahmy died in Charing Cross Hospital and Madame Fahmy was arrested.

The trial of Madame Fahmy was held in No.1 Court in the OLD BAILEY, before Mr Justice Rigby Swift. It lasted for six days and commenced at ten o'clock on the morning of Monday 10 September 1923. The prosecution was lead by Percival Clarke, eldest son of a more famous father. Madame Fahmy was defended by the formidable Sir Edward MARSHALL HALL, who used Madame Fahmy in the witness box to great effect by getting her to reveal her husband's perverted sexual practices. Marshall Hall was able to extract information from Said Enani which showed Fahmy in a bad light. Enani said that he remembered an incident when the Prince struck his wife a violent blow and dislocated her jaw. Shortly after the honeymoon, a cruise along the River Nile on Fahmy's largest yacht, Madame Fahmy wrote a statement. This was an exhibit at the trial. Headlined 'THE SECRET DOCUMENT' in newspapers throughout the world, translated into English, the statement ran:

> I, Marie Marguerite Alibert, of full age, of sound mind and body, formally accuse, in the case of my death, violent or otherwise, Ali Fahmy Bey, of having contributed in my disappearance.
> Yesterday, 21 January 1923, at three o'clock in the afternoon, he took his Bible or Koran – I do not know how it is called – kissed it, put his hand on it, and swore to avenge himself upon me tomorrow, in eight days, a month, or three months, but I must disappear by his hand. This oath was taken without any reason, neither jealousy, bad conduct, nor a scene on my part.
> I desire and demand justice for my daughter and for my family.
> Done at Zamalik, at about eleven o'clock in the morning, 22 January 1923.
> M. MARGUERITE ALIBERT
> P.S. Today he wanted to take my jewellery from me. I refused; hence a fresh scene.

Marshall Hall suggested that the Prince was a man of vicious and eccentric sexual appetite. He revealed to the jury that Fahmy's homosexual relationship with his secretary, Said Enani, was a well-known fact in Egyptian society. He told the jury:

> We know that women are sometimes very much attracted to men younger than themselves, and he went out of his way, with all his Eastern cunning to make himself agreeable and acceptable to her. But this was a man who enjoys the sufferings of women. He was abnormal and a brute. After marriage all restraint ceased and he developed from a plausible lover into a ferocious brute with the vilest of vile tempers and a filthy perverted taste. It makes one shudder to consider the conditions under which this wretched woman lived.

The Prince's proclivity for anal sex with his wife having been raised, suggested that he used his wife sexually as though she were some unnatural male lover. These unnatural sexual acts caused her to have distressing ailments in an embarrassing place, and it had been Madame Fahmy's hope that during their stay in Europe, she would be able to return to Paris for surgery. However, her husband denied her request, telling her that he preferred the operation to be carried out in London. It was Madame Fahmy's repeated request that she should be allowed to return to Paris in order that her injured fundament could receive the necessary attention that culminated in the tragic events of 10 July. Marshall Hall's legendary use of theatrical effect in the courtroom was never more so clearly demonstrated than in the closing stages of the trial, when he brandished the gun with which Madame Fahmy had killed her husband, before the jury. He set the scene of the fatal events by crouching in imitation of Prince Ali Fahmy, demonstrating the threat he posed as he advanced towards his wife. Marshall Hall told the court:

...she turned the pistol and put it to his face, and to her horror the thing went off.

The jury were almost spellbound by this demonstration and while he was talking Marshall Hall pointed the gun at the jury, then, to add greater effect, he threw the pistol down on the courtroom floor, the sound of which startled the entire courtroom, and he uttered the words:

Was that deliberate murder? Would she choose the Savoy Hotel for such an act?

Then there came a female voice from the gallery:

No.

And then another:

Of course not!

Mr Justice Swift concluded his summing-up by saying:

A person who honestly believes that his life is in danger is entitled to kill his assailant if that is the only way he honestly and reasonably believes he can protect himself. But he must be in real danger, and it must be the only way out of it.

The jury took less than an hour to acquit. After her acquittal Madame Fahmy said: 'It is terrible to have killed Ali, but I spoke the truth.'

FIELD, FREDERICK HERBERT CHARLES

This thirty-two-year-old Royal Air Force deserter, twice confessed to the murder of two different women, on each occasion withdrawing the confessions at his trial. On 2 October 1931 Nora Upchurch, a twenty-year-old prostitute, was found by some workmen, strangled in the basement of 173-9 Shaftesbury Avenue, an empty shop backing onto New Compton Street. One of the men, Frederick Field, the last person known to have visited the premises prior to discovery of the body, came under suspicion due to a statement he made regarding a key to the premises, which he claimed to have given to a man who had a gold tooth and was wearing plus fours. However, insufficient evidence meant no charges were brought against anyone and at the inquest the coroner's jury brought in a verdict of murder by a person or persons unknown.

Then in July 1933 Field sold his story to the newspapers claiming that he had murdered Nora Upchurch. He was arrested, but his story was not consistent with the facts, as he claimed he had strangled her with his bare hands, when in fact the victim's own belt had been used as a ligature. He was nevertheless put on trial at the OLD

BAILEY and, having previously retracted his confession, the judge directed the jury to acquit. Field then decided to join the Royal Air Force but he eventually deserted. When in 1936 he was arrested for desertion from the armed services, he immediately confessed to the murder of Beatrice Sutton, a middle-aged prostitute, found strangled in her flat at Elmhurst Mansions, Elmhurst Road, Clapham, on 4 April 1936. On this occasion the police made sure that the statement he had given them contained incontrovertible evidence, concerning what was in the flat and exactly how the victim had died. Despite once again attempting to evade justice by withdrawing his confession, the jury found him guilty of murder and he was hanged at WANDSWORTH on 30 June 1936.

FLETCHER, WPC YVONNE (victim)

In 1984, the former town house of Nancy, Viscountess Astor (1879-1964), the first woman to be elected to the House of Commons, at 5 St James's Square, was occupied by the Libyan People's Bureau. In April that year ant-Gadaffi Libyans demonstrated outside, protesting against the Colonel's regime. The police were marshalling the rival factions in an attempt to prevent them clashing. On Tuesday 17 April, a burst of automatic fire came from a first floor window. Several anti-Gadaffi demonstrators were injured and WPC Yvonne Fletcher, who was on crowd control duty, was killed outright. The diplomatic status of those responsible for murdering WPC Fletcher meant that the occupants of the Libyan People's Bureau were flown back to Libya. A memorial to the fallen policewoman was erected at the spot where she fell, the first such monument of its type.

FOLAN, PATRICK

On 2 June 1999, a body found buried in a shallow grave beneath the concrete foundations of the modern extension of the Royal Northern Hospital, in Tollington Way, Upper Holloway, was later identified as that of Mrs Michele Folan, who had disappeared some eighteen years previously, in October 1981. Michele Folan, aged twenty-four and her twenty-six-year-old husband, Patrick, had been seen arguing in the *Half Moon,* a public house situated in Holloway Road, opposite the main

The spot where WPC Yvonne Fletcher fell in St James's Square. The Author

building of the hospital, on the night she is believed to have last been alive. Demolition men, clearing the site of the extension to build a housing development found Mrs Folan's fully clothed remains encased in concrete, her head was shrouded with a plastic bag and the rope garrotte used to strangle her was still twisted around her neck.

Folan, a bricklayer by trade, had been working as a labourer on the building site when his wife disappeared. Michele Folan's disappearance had baffled police, who had questioned her husband and reopened the case several times, having at one point dug up the patio in Folan's garden, although no charges were brought against Folan. With the help of relatives, including Mrs Folan's mother, Folan brought up the couple's two children at their Upper Holloway home in Bovington Close. Martin and Nicola Folan were aged three and sixteen months respectively, at the time of their mother's disappearance. It emerged that Michele Folan had begun divorce proceedings against her husband, after two years of marriage, only days before she disappeared. Folan admitted that he had been violent towards his wife but maintained that she had run off, always trying to change the subject whenever the matter came up at family gatherings.

Folan was tried at the OLD BAILEY, where one witness remembered him as the quiet Irish bricklayer who helped to concrete the foundations of the hospital. Another witness, a close friend of Michele Folan told the court: 'I thought she was being emotionally and physically tortured by him.' William Boyce, prosecuting, said: 'The body was concealed in a shallow grave dug in a place the person knew would soon be covered with a concrete floor. The person must have had inside knowledge of what was about to happen to the site.' Despite his continued denial, Folan was found guilty of his wife's murder and given a life sentence on 7 December 2001. In November 2006, Folan's case was reviewed at the Royal Courts of Justice. Mr Justice Jack ruled Folan must serve a tariff of at least fifteen years before being considered for parole and only then if he can persuade the parole board that he poses no danger to the public could be released on a perpetual life sentence, subject to recall to gaol if he breaks his licence in any way.

FOSTER, GEORGE

1n 1802, George Foster lodged with Joseph Bradfield in North Row, Grosvenor Square. He worked for coachmaker James Bushwell and was described as being diligent and good natured. Foster was estranged from his wife but she called on him from time to time with their infant daughter. Foster's wife and daughter were last seen alive when they spent part of the afternoon of Sunday 5 December 1802 with him at the *Mitre* tavern, situated near the canal at Paddington. Their bodies were found in the canal by boatman John Atkins about a mile from the *Mitre*, the baby's on Monday, the woman's on Thursday. There was sufficient circumstantial evidence against Foster for him to be charged with their murders.

Foster was tried at the OLD BAILEY on 14 January 1803. On being found guilty of the murders the recorder passed sentence on the prisoner: which was, that he be hanged by the neck until he be dead, and that his body be delivered to be anatomised, according to law in that case made and provided.

Before his execution, Foster admitted to the murders. He said he so hated his wife that he was determined to rid the world of a being he loathed. He said he had taken her twice before to the canal with the intention of killing her but his courage had failed him. He regretted the loss of the baby. Foster was executed outside NEWGATE on 18 January 1803. Then:

After hanging the usual time, his body was cut down and conveyed to a house not far distant, where it was subjected to the galvanic process by Professor Aldini…On the first application of the process to his face, the jaws of the deceased criminal began to quiver, and the adjoining muscles were horribly contorted, and one eye was actually opened. In the subsequent part of the process the right hand was raised and clenched and the legs and thighs were set in motion.

FRANKLIN, JAMES – see OVERBURY, SIR THOMAS

FREEDMAN, MAURICE

Ex-policeman Maurice Freedman had hopes of marrying young typist Annette Friedson. However, Freedman was already married and Miss Friedson's family were not impressed by the unemployed Freedman's hand-to-mouth existence. He pawned his clothes to raise money for gambling and even Annette wondered when he would divorce his wife as promised. Realising that he was a hopeless case she told Freedman that she wished to end the relationship. His reaction to this severing of ties frightened Annette and each day her brother took her to the office where she worked in the City of London. On the morning of 26 January 1932 Freedman waited inside the building and cut her throat with a razor. When he was arrested Freedman claimed he had intended to kill himself and that Annette had died accidentally. He also claimed he had thrown the razor in the canal. However, the razor was found on a bus. As well as her blood group it had also traces of fibres from Annette's coat. The bus conductor was able to identify Freedman. He was found guilty at the OLD BAILEY and hanged at PENTONVILLE on 4 May 1932.

FRIZER, INGRAM

Christopher Marlowe, poet and dramatist, the son of a shoemaker, was born in Canterbury in 1564. His early education locally was followed by Cambridge. He rose to prominence as a dramatist with such works as *Tamburlaine the Great*, *The Jew of Malta*, and *The Tragical History of Dr Faustus*. Kit Marlowe, as he was known to many, was well acquainted with the leading men of the day including Sir Walter Raleigh but his atheism and outspoken opinions meant that he was often in danger of being arrested. Believed to be involved in covert activities under the auspices of Elizabeth I's spymaster Sir Francis Walsingham, on 31 May 1593 Marlowe was in the company of three men at a widow's house in Deptford, (some commentators call it a tavern but contemporary accounts suggest the lady rented rooms for meetings and provided food and drink) Ingram Frizer, Robert Poley and Nicholas Skeres.

Ingram Frizer was in the employ of Sir Thomas Walsingham, a relative of the spymaster, who was also a patron of Christopher Marlowe; Robert Poley and Nicholas Skeres (or Skiers, who hailed from landed gentry at Skiers Hall in Hoyland township in Yorkshire's West Riding) were both in the employ of spymaster Walsingham, and both had been involved in the uncovering of 'The Babbington Plot', a scheme to assassinate the Queen and replace her with the imprisoned Roman Catholic Mary Queen of Scots. Apparently by the evening all four men were the worse for drink and an argument ensued regarding settling the bill. Marlowe and Frizer drew their weapons and Marlowe was stabbed through the eye with Frizer's dagger, dying instantly. Much more sinister motives are believed to have been behind Marlowe's tragically early death, shortly before his thirtieth birthday. He was buried in an unmarked grave on 2 June in St

Mary's churchyard, Deptford. Two weeks later Ingram Frizer was pardoned by Elizabeth I.

FURNACE, SAMUEL JAMES

On the evening of Tuesday 3 January 1933, a garden shed at 30 Hawley Crescent, Camden Town, was the scene of a murder the perpetrator had attempted to disguise as his own suicide. Inside the partially burned shed, sitting at a desk, were the charred remains of a man's body. The shed, which was divided into two portions, had been rented as an office by unsuccessful businessman, builder and decorator, forty-two-year-old Samuel Furnace. A suicide note meant to create the impression that the body was that of Furnace read: 'Goodbye all. No work. No money. Sam J. Furnace.'

However, suspicion was aroused when a bullet wound was discovered in the corpse's back and the teeth of the deceased were of a man considerably younger than Furnace. A most-mortem examination revealed that the dead man had been shot twice. Further investigation showed him to be a twenty-five-year-old rent collector, Walter Spatchett, who lived with his parents in Dartmouth Park Road, Highgate. Enquiries revealed that Furnace and Spatchett were well acquainted and often met socially to play billiards. On the day before the fire Spatchett had collected £36 in rent payments.

A nationwide hunt was instigated for Furnace. Walter Spatchett was buried at Highgate Cemetery on 11 January. Furnace was caught after he contacted his brother-in-law, Charles Tuckfield, by letter, date stamped 14 January, requesting that he bring some clean shirts and other items of clothing to a location in Essex. The police were informed immediately and that same day, 15 January, Furnace was apprehended at a lodging house at 11 Whitegate Road, Southend. Furnace was brought back to Kentish Town police station. He claimed that the killing had been accidental. Locked in a cell overnight he asked if he could have his overcoat, as it was particularly cold. When the coat was brought to him he took out a phial of hydrochloric acid which he had secreted in the lining and drank the contents. He was taken to St Pancras Hospital where doses of morphine were administered to ease his suffering, but he never regained consciousness and died about twenty-four hours later on Tuesday 17 January. His body was taken to St Pancras Mortuary where a post-mortem examination was carried out by Home Office pathologist Sir Bernard SPILSBURY. On Friday 20 January a coroner's jury concluded that Walter Spatchett's death was not accidental and that Samuel James Furnace was guilty of his murder.

G

GARDELLE, THEODORE

Theodore Gardelle was a Swiss painter who specialised in miniatures. He lodged on the western side of Leicester Fields, today's Leicester Square, with his landlady, Mrs King, close to the home of Sir Joshua Reynolds. From available accounts he appears to have been an otherwise inoffensive man. Some say he killed Mrs King in order to rob her, others because she spurned his attempts to seduce her and, by his own admission, he killed her following a quarrel after she repeatedly poured scorn on a miniature portrait of her which he had executed. He was goaded into this fit of frenzy early in February 1761. Gardelle maintained that Mrs King came into the parlour and began to verbally abuse him about the miniature. The quarrel continued to the adjacent bedroom. When

Gardelle told Mrs King that she was a very impertinent woman, she struck him a violent blow on the chest. He pushed her away and Mrs King's foot caught in the floor-cloth and as she fell backwards, her head hit a sharp corner of the bedstead with great force. As blood streamed from her mouth, Gardelle went to assist her. Mrs King threatened him with charges of assault and continued to rant and rage, at which point Gardelle panicked, picked up a sharp-pointed ivory comb and drove it into her throat. Her cries faded away and she died.

Horrified at what he'd done, Gardelle said he covered Mrs King's body with the bedclothes, before swooning away and hitting his head on the wainscot, which raised a bump over his right eye. A maid-servant who lived in the house was out on an errand. The only other residents, another lodger and his servant, were out of town. When the maid returned he paid her wages on behalf of Mrs King and discharged her, telling her that her mistress had gone to the country and would be bringing back another servant with her. When he eventually summoned up the courage several days later, Gardelle stripped the body and laid it out on the bed. He disposed of the bloodstained bedclothes by putting them in soak in a tub in the back washhouse. He then carved up Mrs King's body, disposing of blood and some pieces of flesh in various sinks. He

burned several body parts and laid other pieces out in the cock loft. Callers to the house were informed that he expected Mrs King to return any day. He hired a woman to help him clean up but on finding a quantity of 'meat' in blocked up sinks and the blood-soaked bed linen, she reported her suspicions that foul play was afoot to the BOW STREET RUNNERS.

When the house was properly searched conclusive evidence was found, both in the cock loft and elsewhere in the house. Gardelle was committed to the New Prison at Clerkenwell, where he attempted to commit suicide twice, firstly by taking forty drops of opium, then by swallowing twelve halfpennics, hoping the verdigris would kill him.

Theodore Gardelle attempting to dispose of Mrs King's remains.
Author's collection

It only resulted in severe stomach pains. For greater security, he was removed to NEWGATE and closely watched. Theodore Gardelle was tried at the OLD BAILEY and found guilty of murder. He was hanged on a specially erected scaffold in the Haymarket near its junction with Panton Street, close to the scene of his crime. Afterwards, his body was gibbeted on Hounslow Heath.

GATEHOUSE, THE

The Gatehouse was built in 1370 by Walter Warfield, Cellarer to Westminster Abbey. It had two wings built at right angles to each other. Both had gates and gaols. Being close to Westminster Hall it was convenient for holding state prisoners. Sir Walter Raleigh spent the last night of his life there. In November 1727, Richard SAVAGE, William MERCHANT and James GREGORY were imprisoned there following the murder of James Sinclair. In 1761, Dr Johnson wrote the Gatehouse was 'so offensive that, without any particular reason, it ought to be pulled down, for it disgraces the present magnificence of the capital, and is a continual nuisance to neighbours and passengers'. The Gatehouse was demolished on the orders of the Dean and Chapter of Westminster in 1776.

The Gatehouse. Author's collection

GEORGE, BARRY

Barry George, alias Barry Bulsara, was convicted of the murder of popular TV presenter Jill Dando, aged thirty-eight. George had just turned thirty-nine at the time the murder took place. Miss Dando was shot on the doorstep of her Hammersmith home at 29 Gowan Avenue, a little after 11.30am, on the morning of 26 April 1999. She was killed by a single shot to the head. The bullet had entered her left temple and exited above her right eye. Miss Dando had announced her wedding to Alan Farthing, a gynaecologist, earlier in the year. The wedding was due to take place on 25 September.

Various theories about motives for killing Jill Dando were expounded in the media and at first the police thought that the killing might have been the result of a personal vendetta or grudge, possibly connected to her involvement with the BBC TV programme *Crimewatch*. There was one theory that Jill Dando had been killed by Serbian agents, linked to her fronting a TV programme for the Kosovars. By the beginning of 2000 enquiries led police to a man calling himself Barry Bulsara. It emerged that Bulsara's surname was in fact George and that he had adopted the surname Bulsara, the family name of the late rock star Freddie Mercury, with whom he claimed kinship. It transpired that George had also called himself Paul Gadd (the real name of pop star Gary Glitter), when at the age of sixteen, he had taken a job as a delivery boy at the BBC, using that name, during which time he claimed to be the pop star's cousin. George had also adopted other aliases in the ensuing years. He was never in regular employment and had a criminal record, having been given a three-month suspended sentence for indecent assault in 1980 and in 1983 had been arrested in the grounds of Kensington Palace, carrying a knife. He later served a thirty-month sentence for attempted rape, at which time he was using the name Steve Majors, claiming kinship with the American actor Lee Majors. In 1989, he was briefly married to a Japanese student but she left him after he allegedly ill treated her.

Since 1985, George had lived in a council flat at 2B Crookham Road, situated a little over five minutes walk from Jill Dando's house. Investigations revealed that he had once belonged to a gun club. Magazines about firearms were found in his flat, as were copies of the BBC's in house magazine, *Ariel*, which gave reports of the Dando killing. Gun magazines found in George's flat, microscopic bullet fragments found in his clothes and fibres from his polyester trousers, which matched one found on Jill Dando's coat, led to Barry George being charged with her murder. George's trial began at the OLD BAILEY on 2 May 2001. At its conclusion, the jury, having deliberated for almost five days found George guilty of the murder of Jill Dando. An appeal was dismissed in July 2002. Much doubt has been expressed as to his guilt.

GERAGHTY, CHRISTOPHER JAMES – see ANTIQUIS MURDER, THE

GODFREY, SIR EDMUND BERRY (victim)

Sir Edmund Berry Godfrey was the victim of what has often been described as the greatest unsolved murder of the seventeenth century. His death was surrounded by mystery, intrigue and deceit, and it is marked by a false confession that resulted in the execution of three innocent men for a crime they neither committed nor played any part in. Born into an ancient Kentish family on 23 December 1621, he was educated at Westminster School and Christ Church, Oxford. In 1640 he entered Gray's Inn at the Inns of Court. He abandoned his legal career and became a woodmonger and coal merchant, and became considerably wealthy. By the late 1660s he was spending some of his time in politics and was becoming well known as a justice of the peace. As a result of the assistance he gave through his business enterprises during the plague, he was held in high regard. Similarly, his reaction following the Great Fire of London in 1666, during which he suffered personal injury while helping others, made him a notable figure at court, and he was rewarded for his services with a knighthood.

Godfrey's death appears to have come about as a result of his involvement, in his capacity as a magistrate, in the swearing of documents concerning the conspiracy known to history as the 'Popish Plot'; which was later proven to be completely false and was in fact the invention of Dr Titus Oates, clergyman, and Dr Israel Tonge, Presbyterian minister and scientist. Just as the details of the plot were being openly discussed, the killing of the highly regarded Protestant magistrate Sir Edmund Berry Godfrey caused panic on the streets of London.

Witnesses reported having last seen Godfrey on 12 October 1678. On the evening of Thursday 17 October, his body was found in a drainage ditch on Greenberry Hill (now known as Barrow Hill), one of the slopes at the southern edge of Primrose Hill. Sir Edmund was lying face down, impaled on a sword. The hilt was beneath the body and the blade pointed upwards. He had also been strangled and beaten about the body. In December 1678, Catholic silversmith, Miles Prance, then detained for conspiracy confessed under torture to complicity in Godfrey's murder. His evidence was corroborated by the informer William Bedloe. Three men were named in the plot – Robert Green, Henry Berry and Lawrence Hill. They were arrested and convicted on the flimsiest circumstantial evidence and hanged. Prance's confession was afterwards declared false and he pleaded guilty to perjury. Was it simply coincidence that the surnames of the three executed men spelled out the exact spot where Sir Edmund Berry Godfrey's body was found, Greenberry Hill?

Sir Edmund Berry Godfrey.
Author's collection

GRAYSON, GEORGINA – see JONES, ELIZABETH MARINA

GREENSTREET, ROBERT

Robert Greenstreet had been apprenticed to a fishhook-maker, a Mr Souch, in Crooked Lane, London. He was such a kindly employer that he had continued to employ Greenstreet as a journeyman. However, Greenstreet was constantly badgering his master for an increase in wages. The elderly Mr Souch on one occasion declined to increase Greenstreet's pay and he was immediately felled to the ground under repeated blows, while Mr Souch called out:

Bob, you are a rogue to use me thus.

At hearing these words Greenstreet took out a knife and stabbed the old man in several parts of his body, shouting:

Damn your old soul!

This dreadful crime was carried out in front of the young apprentice who had succeeded Greenstreet, who in an effort to save his master received a stab wound through the hand. Greenstreet was quickly apprehended and a surgeon summoned but Mr Souch quickly bled to death. At his trial at the OLD BAILEY Greenstreet pleaded guilty. He was executed at TYBURN on 14 December 1761 and afterward dissected at Surgeons' Hall, where it was said that his eyes opened, though the body was dead.

GREENWOOD, DAVID

On the night of 9 February 1918, sixteen-year-old Nellie Trew did not return home after setting out to Plumstead library. She was reported missing by her father. Next morning her body was found on Eltham Common. She had been raped then strangled. A regimental badge used by the Leicestershire Regiment and a bone overcoat button with a piece of wire threaded through it, were found at the scene. It appeared that they had been lost by the murderer as he struggled with Nellie. This case became known as the 'Button and Badge' murder.

Twenty-one-year-old David Greenwood, who had been medically discharged from the army after serving in the trenches, worked as a machinist at Hewson's Manufacturing, Newman Street, W1. He lived just a hundred yards from where Nellie Trew's body was found. Photographs of the badge and button were widely circulated in newspapers. One of Greenwood's workmates, Ted Farrell, remarked on the badge's resemblance to the badge he wore but he said he had sold it. To satisfy his workmates, Greenwood went to Tottenham Court Road Police Station. When police questioned him they noticed his overcoat had no buttons. He said they had been missing for some time. His workmates refuted this. The wire attached to the button found at the murder scene was identified as being the same type as that manufactured by Greenwood's firm. Greenwood's trial began at the OLD BAILEY on 24 April 1918. He was found guilty and sentenced to death. Because of his good war record and also doubt being expressed

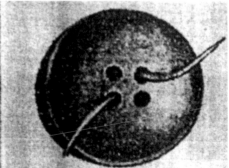

The Button and Badge Murder. This image of the badge and button was circulated widely in newspapers. Author's collection

that Greenwood was actually strong enough to have killed Nellie, the sentence was commuted to life imprisonment on the eve of his execution on 31 May. He was released from prison in 1933.

GREGORY, JAMES – see SAVAGE, RICHARD

H

HACKMAN, REVEREND JAMES

One of London's most famous meeting places, the piazza of Covent Garden, was the scene of arguably the most notorious West End murder in the last quarter of the eighteenth century. It was also notable for the swiftness of justice, which followed the tragic event. Martha Reay (or Ray), mistress of the Earl of Sandwich, was shot by Revd James Hackman, as she left the theatre on 7 April 1779.

Miss Martha Reay was born at Leicester Fields, Hertfordshire in 1742, the daughter of a staymaker, and at the age of fourteen was placed as an apprentice with Mrs Silver, of George's Court, St John's Lane, Clerkenwell, to be instructed in the business of a mantua-maker (maker of gowns). Attractive and highly accomplished, with a pleasant singing voice, Martha, in 1761, at the age of nineteen, caught the eye of the Earl of Sandwich (John Montagu, 4th Earl 1718-92, First Lord of the Admiralty), who took her as his mistress. Lord Sandwich had married in 1741 but Lady Sandwich's state of mental health had declined since the birth of their fifth child in 1751 and in 1755 the couple had parted forever. Her condition gradually declined until she was eventually formally declared insane by the Court of Chancery and made a ward of court. Lord Sandwich settled down to life with Martha. Martha and her children were referred to as Lord Sandwich's 'London family' and there was peace and harmony within the household.

There was to be a blight on this happy relationship. It came in the form of a young man named James Hackman. Hackman was born in Gosport, Hampshire of very respectable parents, who at the age of nineteen purchased him a commission in the 68th Regiment of Foot. Soon after he obtained his commission he was quartered at Huntington, where he was in charge of a recruiting party. He was invited by Lord Sandwich to his nearby country seat, Hinchbroke, where he first met Martha Reay, who was under Lord Sandwich's protection. Hackman fell desperately in love with Miss Reay, and she, flattered by the young man's attentions, did little to discourage his advances. Hackman took holy orders and was appointed to a parish in Norfolk in 1768. When in London, he would often attend the theatre and concerts with Martha and Lord Sandwich and the relationship between Martha and the amorous clergyman grew stronger. Hackman had every intention of marrying her. However, considering Martha's position in life, the mistress of a peer of the realm, with five illegitimate children, it is doubtful Hackman could really have secured a living, had they married.

By the beginning of 1779, Martha and Lord Sandwich had lived together, very happily, for over eighteen years and she had borne him nine children, five of which had survived. In March 1779, Martha decided to end the relationship with Hackman. On 7 April 1779, Hackman dined with his sister and brother-in-law, who was also his first cousin. The couple had married only five weeks previously. He left them promising he would return for supper. That evening Lord Sandwich was working late at the

Admiralty. Hackman, on seeing his lordship's coach with Martha Raey inside, concluded, quite correctly, that Miss Reay was going out to the opera, and would probably call on Signora Galli at her lodgings in the Haymarket (Catherina Galli was a retired *prima donna,* who amongst other fine singers had given Martha lessons. It was said that Martha Raey possessed a singing voice that could have earned her a high income, had she chosen a career on the stage). Hackman followed the two ladies into the theatre and there observed a gentleman talking to Miss Reay, who was later discovered to be Lord Coleraine. Hackman was seized with a fit of jealousy and at that moment decided to end his own life.

He left the theatre, went to his lodgings in Duke's Court, St Martin's Lane and returned a little while later with a brace of loaded pistols, intending to kill himself in Martha's presence. When questioned later why he had a brace of pistols, he replied that if one misfired on himself, he meant to use the other. When the play was over Martha, in the company of Signora Galli and Lord Coleraine, entered the lobby of the theatre, and it was there that Hackman first attempted to shoot himself, but the thickness of the crowd prevented him. He pursued Martha to the door of her coach. It was not until he beheld Martha's face that he thought of killing her at that instant. He took a pistol from each pocket and discharged the pistol in his right hand first, and immediately afterwards discharged the pistol in his left hand at himself. Martha was shot through the head. She, upon lifting her hand to her face, fell and died on the spot. Only slightly wounded, Hackman beat his head with the pistol and called out: 'Kill me! Kill me!' Martha was carried to the *Shakespeare Tavern* and Hackman with her. Her lifeless body was taken to a separate room within the tavern while Hackman's wounds were dressed in another. Hackman freely gave his name and was shortly afterwards taken before the magistrate, Sir John

Martha Ray. Author's collection

The Reverend James Hackman. Author's collection

FIELDING (the celebrated blind magistrate, half-brother of lawyer and novelist Henry Fielding) who committed him to Tothill Fields, Bridewell.

The Revd James Hackman was transferred to NEWGATE Gaol. During his incarceration he remained calm and composed and it is said that he spoke of the name and memory of Martha Ray with the highest rapture. On the morning of his trial at the OLD BAILEY Sessions, before Mr Justice Blackstone, Hackman ate a hearty breakfast in Newgate, with his brother-in-law, and two of his friends in attendance. He was found guilty of murder and sentenced to death. Following the verdict, Lord Sandwich wrote to Hackman:

17th April 1779

TO MR HACKMAN IN NEWGATE

If the murderer of Miss __ __ wishes to live, the man he has most injured will use all his interest to procure his life.

Hackman sent an immediate reply:

*The Condemned Cell in Newgate,
17th April 1779.*

The murderer of her whom he preferred, far preferred to life, respects the hand from which he has just received such an offer as he neither desires nor deserves. His wishes are for death, not life. One wish he has. Could he be pardoned in this world by the man he has most injured – oh, my lord, when I meet her in another world enable me to tell her (if departed spirits are not ignorant of earthly things) that you forgive us both, that you will be a father to her dear infants!

J. H.

There was to be no reprieve or pardon for the Revd James Hackman. Justice was swift, for there were only twelve days between the murder and the murderer's dissection. On 19 April 1779, the Revd James Hackman was hanged by Edward Dennis, and life, having at last been pronounced extinct, much as Hackman had wished, his body was left hanging for the customary one hour, before being taken to Surgeons' Hall for dissection. Martha Reay was taken back to her native Hertfordshire, where she lies buried in Elstree.

HAIGH, JOHN GEORGE

John George Haigh committed a series of murders, which became known as the ACID BATH MURDERS. Born in 1909, at Stamford, Lincolnshire, he was the son of an electrical engineer. Grammar School educated, Haigh worked in a second-hand car showroom, as an electrician in a cinema and as a salesman. He served several prison sentences, one when he was twenty-five, when he received fifteen months for obtaining money by false pretences. Then having set up under a false name as a solicitor, he defrauded his clients of over £30,000, for which he was sentenced to four years. Released on licence in 1940, he took to stealing from evacuated houses. In 1941 he was caught and sentenced to twenty-one months' hard labour. When he was released in the autumn of 1943 he went to work for an engineering firm in Crawley, Surrey, having by his own stealth managed to evade conscription.

In 1944, Haigh, who styled himself a businessman and inventor, lived at the *Onslow Court Hotel*, Kensington and rented the basement of nearby 79 Gloucester Road, which he used as a workshop, where he had a sideline business repairing one-armed bandits and pinball machines. Dapper in both manner and appearance, Haigh endeared himself to the mostly elderly, well-to-do female residents at the hotel. Haigh ordered several carboys of sulphuric acid and a forty-gallon tank, which were delivered to his workshop. On 9 September 1944, he killed an acquaintance, twenty-one-year-old Donald McSwan there, by hitting him over the head, then dissolved his body in acid. The following year he killed McSwan's parents after first luring them to his workshop on the pretext that their son, who was on the run for evading conscription, wanted to meet them. He likewise disposed of their bodies in acid. The forged power of attorney of the McSwans' property, which included four houses, netted Haigh a small fortune.

For greater secrecy Haigh gave his basement workshop up and rented premises in a more secluded location, situated behind Hurstlea Products in Giles Yard, Crawley. In 1947 he befriended Dr Archibald Lewis and his wife Rosalie, after he had expressed an interest in purchasing their house, situated at 22 Ladbroke Square. He later lured them to his 'factory' in Crawley and shot them both, before destroying their bodies in acid again Haigh gained financially from these killings. He managed to fend off enquiries from the Lewises' family and business associates by forging letters. By 1949, the meticulously well-mannered Haigh had all the accoutrements of a successful businessman, including Savile Row suits and an Alvis motor-car. One of the long-term residents at the *Onslow Court Hotel* was sixty-nine-year-old, Mrs Olive Durand-Deacon, a well-off widow. According to Haigh, she approached him about an idea she had for producing artificial fingernails. He was running short of money and had already been approached about his bill at the hotel (£5 15s 6d a week plus 10% service charges), which now amounted to almost £50. Mrs Durand-Deacon wore expensive jewellery and clothes, a ready source of money. He agreed to help with her enterprise and arranged to meet her outside the Army and Navy Stores in Victoria Street at 2.30pm on 18 February. She was never seen alive again.

The next day, Haigh asked another resident, Mrs Lane, about Mrs Durand-Deacon's whereabouts, as she had not turned up for her appointment with him. Later, to satisfy her, Haigh drove Mrs Lane to Chelsea police station to report Mrs Durand-Deacon missing. It later transpired that Haigh had driven Mrs Durand-Deacon to Crawley, shot her, then over a two-day period dissolved her body in sulphuric acid. When he reported her missing, his glib manner aroused police suspicion and on finding he had a record they went to Crawley to investigate. They found Mrs Duran-Deacon's false teeth and there were traces of blood in the workshop; and Home Office pathologist Dr Keith Simpson found a human gallstone in the gravel outside. Fragments of a left foot were also found, which when reconstructed and cast in plaster fitted Mrs Durand-Deacon's shoes exactly. Her plastic handbag (a unusual item at the time) and several other items linking Haigh to her were found. John Haigh was under the mistaken impression that without a body he could not be convicted of murder. When he realised otherwise he caved in and confessed to eight murders in total, three of which are believed to have been fictitious. He didn't do himself any favours when he asked police what chance they felt anyone had of being released from Broadmoor. They realised he was going for the insanity plea. They believed the three additional murders were his invention to add further weight to his later claim that he drank his victims' blood in an attempt to prove his insanity.

Haigh was tried for only the murder of Mrs Durand-Deacon. The trial opened at Lewes Assizes on 18 July 1949, before Mr Justice Humphreys. It lasted less than two days. Dr Yellowlees, an early exponent of forensic psychiatry, was the only one of nine doctors who examined Haigh prepared to speak in his defence. Dr Yellowlees later wrote about the 'sadly overrated Haigh case' describing Haigh as 'medically mad' but not 'McNaghten mad', referring to THE McNAGHTEN RULES. On the second day, the jury retired to consider their verdict at 4.23pm and returned to the court at 4.40pm with a guilty outcome. John Haigh was hanged by Albert PIERREPOINT at WANDSWORTH on 10 August 1949, seventeen days after his fortieth birthday.

HALLIWELL, KENNETH

On Wednesday 9 August 1967, at about 11.40am a chauffeur-driven car arrived outside 25 Noel Road, Islington, to take thirty-four-year-old playwright Joe Orton to Twickenham Studios. There was no reply to his knock on the door of Flat 4 on the second floor. He peered through the letterbox and saw a bald man lying on the floor. He knew it wasn't Mr Orton as he had driven him twice before.

When police officers broke into the flat, a cramped affair, just a studio with kitchen and bathroom – they found the naked body of the flat's owner forty-one-year-old Kenneth Halliwell. There were blood splashes on his chest, head and hands. Nearby on a divan bed was his flatmate and lover, Joe Orton, wearing only a pyjama jacket. Orton had severe head injuries inflicted by nine hammer blows to the skull. A bloodstained hammer was lying on his chest on the counterpane that covered his body. Brain matter had been spattered on both the wall and ceiling. On the desk in the

North London Press.

Author's collection

room in which they died, Halliwell had left a note placed on top of a red leather binder that held Orton's diary. It read:

If you read this diary all will be explained
KH
PS. Especially the latter part

Orton and Halliwell had been together since they were at RADA (Royal Academy of Dramatic Art). From the start Orton was heavily influenced by Halliwell's apparent sophistication and intellect. By the late 1950s they had all but abandoned any thoughts of acting and had decided on a literary career. Collectively their output was prolific, and Orton eventually developed a unique style far removed from the pretentious scribblings of the prematurely bald Halliwell. The support that each gave the other was to reach fruition in Orton's success as a dramatist. In 1962, Orton and Halliwell were given a six-month prison sentence for defacing library books. Halliwell removed 1,623 plates from art books, some of which were used in collages

25 Noel Road, Islington.
Paul T Langley Welch

adorning the walls of their flat. Orton had a penchant for writing false (and often very crude) blurbs and pasting them into the fly leaves. On their release they resumed writing and in 1963 Orton met with success. His rise as a highly successful dramatist was meteoric. Through humour he skilfully guided his audience around previously unthinkable territory.

Halliwell was viewed by many of Orton's new associates as having more pretensions than talent. Too wooden as an actor and with his writing skills never quite reaching the mark, the only part of his life he seemed to have developed into anything approaching an acceptable art form was collage but he lacked the self-assurance to try to promote himself and advance his efforts in this field. Orton encouraged him and, in 1967, arranged an exhibition of fifteen pictures in Chelsea. A few were bought by Orton's business associates but the general public showed no interest whatsoever.

Unlike Orton, who enjoyed a highly varied sex life with a large number of partners, Halliwell was by comparison less promiscuous. Orton used to tease him about his lack of success in attracting men and boys, and poked fun at his unadventurous approach to all things sexual. Not only were his meagre artistic efforts being overshadowed but he was failing miserably in the most intimate part of his life. To add to the anxiety, Halliwell was very self-conscious about his baldness. In an attempt to help him overcome this Orton bought him a wig out of the money he made from his play *Entertaining Mr*

Sloane. Halliwell's bouts of depression grew deeper and more frequent. Orton's diary mentions Halliwell's black moods, which were becoming more frequent, his violent outbursts and his rapid decline into self-doubt. Orton's fondness for Halliwell is apparent, as is his deep concern for his mental health and their deteriorating relationship. Halliwell had easy access to these diaries and as he read them it must have become apparent to him that his partner was slipping away from him. Halliwell was not prepared to let this happen. To prevent Orton leaving, Halliwell took a hammer and ended the life of one of the most gifted and finest post-war English playwrights. He then swallowed a massive dose of barbiturates. He emptied twenty-two capsules of Nembutal into a bucket and mixed it with a tin of grapefruit juice, which speeded the powerful drug into his system and caused death very quickly. Deputy Coroner for St Pancras Dr John Burton recorded the jury's verdict that Mr Orton was murdered by Mr Halliwell who then took his own life.

HAMBLETON, JOHN

At about nine o'clock on the evening of 17 August 1753, Mr Crouch, cook to the Earl of Harrington, was set upon in the King's Road, Chelsea, by two men, Hambleton and Lattie, who tried to rob him. They fired two pistols at him but missed. Mr Crouch took out a knife to defend himself and wounded Lattie in three places. Mr Crouch was disarmed and his belly ripped open with the knife, before he was then stamped upon and his body mangled. The two assailants fled. Mr Crouch was discovered early next morning still alive and was able to give a full description of the robbers. He died at his home in Green Street, Mayfair, three days later. The murderers were soon apprehended but Lattie died of the stab wounds he had received from Mr Crouch. Hambleton, a soldier of the Guards was tried at the OLD BAILEY, found guilty of murder and executed at TYBURN on 10 December 1753. His body was afterward dissected.

HAMMERSMITH NUDES MURDERS

Between February 1964 and February 1965 six prostitutes were murdered by a killer whose identity has never been revealed, but his methods earned him the name 'Jack the Stripper'. There may have been more victims but two other murders attributed to him did not fit his modus operandi. The six confirmed to have been murdered by the Stripper choked to death during forced fellatio. They were also found naked except for their stockings and four of the victims had paint flecks on them, identified as the type of paint used for spraying vehicles. Before the bodies had been dumped they had been stored near intense heat. Hannah Tailford, Irene Lockwood, Helene Barthelemy, Mary Flemming, Margaret McGowan and Bridget O'Hara, were all believed to have been killed by the Stripper. When the murders suddenly stopped police enquiries led them to a forty-five-year-old south London man who had committed suicide. Although his family were perplexed by his inexplicable suicide, he left a note saying he was 'unable to stand the strain any longer'. The man worked as a security guard on the Heron Trading Estate in Acton, whose round included a paint shop. With the prime suspect dead and no further murders the case was closed.

HARDY, ANTHONY JOHN

On 20 January 2002, police were called to a council flat in Royal College Street, Camden Town, after neighbours complained that fifty-year-old Anthony Hardy had been seen pouring battery acid through his neighbour's letterbox and writing obscenities on the door. Hardy was arrested and handcuffed. The police officers noticed that a bedroom door was locked. He claimed that the room was let to a lodger and he didn't have the key. The key was found in his possesion and when the door was opened there on the bed was a dead woman completely naked. Hardy was arrested on suspicion of murder.

The dead woman was thirty-eight-year-old prostitute and crack cocaine addict Sally Rose White. Although she had sustained cuts to her head and there were bite marks and bruising on her body, a post-mortem examination concluded that she had died of a heart attack; and death was attributed to natural causes. Hardy was charged with criminal damage for the other offences and examined by psychiatrists. When questioned about the dead woman he said he had drunk six litres of cider and a bottle of wine that day and had suffered an alcoholic blackout and had no knowledge of how the woman came to be in his flat.

On 30 December 2002, a vagrant was looking for discarded food in the bins behind the *College Arms* in Royal College Street, when he found a bag containing human remains. Police later found eight more bags containing body parts identified as coming from two different women who had both been killed within the previous few days. The hands and heads were never found. During their search police found a clear blood trail which led them to a block of flats and to Hardy's door. He was not at home. When they gained access police found a hacksaw, an electric jigsaw covered in blood and a woman's torso wrapped in bin liners.

A nationwide search for Hardy was launched. Next day he was caught on CCTV at University College Hospital where he had gone to get drugs to treat his diabetes. It was not until 2 January that he was seen again at Great Ormond Street Hospital where he was arrested at 9pm.

Newspaper reports referred to Hardy as the Camden Ripper. The body parts were identified as belonging to Elizabeth Selina Valad, aged twenty-nine, identified by the serial numbers on her breast implants and Brigitte MacClennan, aged thirty-four, identified by DNA testing. Both women were prostitutes with crack cocaine habits. On 6 January 2003 Hardy appeared at Hendon Magistrates' Court charged with all three murders. Initially Hardy claimed that he had not intended to kill anyone and that the women had died because of 'excessive force in the course of otherwise consensual but extreme sexual activity'. At his trial at the OLD BAILEY in November 2003 Hardy pleaded guilty to all three murders. On 23 November 2003 he was given three life sentences.

HAWKSWORTH, WILLIAM

William Hawksworth was a soldier in the Foot Guards. While Hawksworth was marching to relieve the guard in St James's Park, a man named Ransom, in company with a woman, jostled him and called out: 'What a stir is here about King George's soldiers!' Hawksworth broke rank and struck the woman on the face. Ransom called him a puppy and demanded to know why he had hit her, at which point Hawksworth knocked Ransom down with his musket and injured him so badly that he fractured his skull. Hawksworth's fellow soldiers marched on. A crowd gathered round and

Hawksworth slipped away to join his company. A surgeon was called to attend Mr Ransom, who concluded he was so badly injured he had no hope of recovery. When Ransom died a few hours later, a witness went to the *Savoy* and picked out Hawksworth who was promptly arrested and committed to NEWGATE. Although his colonel testified to his excellent character, Hawksworth was convicted of murder and sentenced to death. Shortly before his execution at TYBURN on 17 June 1723, Hawksworth made a speech to the crowd in which he advised them to keep a strict guard over their passion. He advised his fellow soldiers to submit with patience to the indignities that might be offered, and trust to the goodness of God to recompense their sufferings.

HAYES, CATHERINE

Catherine Hayes was born Catherine Hall of poor parents, in Birmingham in 1690. In 1705, when she was fifteen, she met some army officers and for a while became their collective mistress, until they moved on. Catherine then became maid to a Warwickshire farmer, named Hayes, who had a son named John, aged twenty-one, who was a carpenter. John fell in love with her and before long they married. After six years they moved to London, where John thrived in business, becoming a successful coal-merchant, pawnbroker and moneylender. He traded from premises in Tyburn Road (today's Oxford Street). In a little over ten years, he had made enough money to enable him to sell his shop and take lodgings nearby. Catherine made her industrious husband's life miserable and once boasted to neighbours that she would think it no more sin to murder him than to kill a dog. She said that her husband was miserly and mean, which if it were true, was at odds with her own desire for luxury.

At the beginning of 1725, a young man named Thomas Billings called at the Hayes' lodgings. He was a tailor by trade and Catherine told her husband he was an old friend and John Hayes allowed Billings to stay with them. When John Hayes ventured out of London on business, his wife took Billings into her bed. While the husband was away, the lovers took advantage of his absence by throwing parties and being frivolous with money. When John Hayes returned, he gave his wife a beating. Billings remained in residence apparently blameless of any indiscretions in the eyes of his unsuspecting host. Not long after, another young 'friend' of Catherine's turned up on the doorstep. His name was Thomas Wood. Wood also shared her favours whenever the opportunity allowed. She offered him a share in her husband's estate, should she become a widow, which amounted to the then very large sum of £1,500, and persuaded him to help her kill him.

On 1 March 1725, when Wood called at the Hayes' lodgings, he found John and Catherine Hayes in high spirits with Thomas Billings, indulging in a drinking session. Wood joined in with the party and a challenge was issued by the boastful Mr Wood that he could consume more wine than Hayes and still remain sober. As Hayes drank his seventh bottle, he collapsed on the floor. A few minutes passed before he came round and staggered into the adjacent bedroom. Shortly afterwards, Billings went into the room and, finding Hayes face down on the bed, dealt him a violent blow with a coal hatchet, which fractured his skull. As Hayes stirred he was dealt two more blows which finished him off. It was now necessary to dispose of the body.

Notwithstanding the butchery that followed, the bedding was already drenched and the walls and ceiling of the bedchamber spattered with blood. Catherine apparently remained cool and calm. She suggested that in order to avoid identification, her husband's head should be cut off and disposed of separately. The head was placed over a bucket to catch the blood, while the neck was sawn through. The two men balked at the idea of Catherine's to boil the head to remove the flesh. While preparations were being made to dispose of the blood, which was poured down various sinks, Catherine put on a convincing performance calling out goodbye to her husband as if he was going on a journey, in the hope she would be heard by the neighbours, which of course, she was.

Wood and Billings took the severed head out of the house in a bucket concealed beneath Billings' coat, they walked on past Westminster to Horseferry wharf (where the present Horseferry Road meets Lambeth Bridge). There they went to the end of the dock and threw the head in the river and the bucket after it. At daybreak, nightwatchman Robinson saw the bucket and head floating near the shore, from where they were retrieved. Meanwhile, Billings and Wood made their way back to Catherine, expecting the head to have floated away on the next tide. They discussed how to dispose of the body. Catherine had procured a wooden box but it was not large enough for the corpse. They cut off the arms, then the legs at the knees but it still proved too big to fit in the box. They then hacked off the legs at the thighs and somehow managed to fit all the pieces into the box, which at nine o'clock that night they took out of the house wrapped in a blanket. They went north to Marylebone, where they took the remains out of the box and put them in a blanket and threw the package into a pond, where it sunk.

Meanwhile, the severed head had been handed over to parish

John Hayes' head displayed in the churchyard of St Margaret's, Westminster.
John D Murray collection

officers. It was washed to remove the blood and mud from the face and hair and the hair was combed. It was then attached to a pole and placed in the churchyard of St Margaret's, Westminster, for several days, in the hope that someone would recognise it. Eventually, someone did. During the next few days, when enquiries were made of Catherine as to the whereabouts of her husband, her inventive mind came up with the ridiculous story that he had killed a man and absconded. The body parts were found in the pond in Marylebone and as Catherine received more and more visitors enquiring after her husband, the net closed in. As it had been established that Billings and Wood were with Hayes the last time he was seen alive, when a warrant was issued for the arrest of the murderers, their names were included on it.

When Catherine asked if she could see the head that had been displayed in St Margaret's churchyard, Mr Justice Lambert went with her to the barber-surgeon, Mr Westbrook, who was looking after it. When Catherine was shown the head, she took the glass in which the head was preserved and called out:

It is my dear husband's head!

Catherine's performance knew no bounds. She shed tears as she embraced the container and, as the head was lifted out of the spirit, she kissed it rapturously and begged to be given a lock of its hair. As the barber-surgeon remarked that she had already had enough of her husband's blood, Catherine swooned away.

Wood was arrested and on hearing that the body had been found in the pond, confessed his part in the crime. Catherine obstinately refused to admit her guilt. She was an object of curiosity in NEWGATE, where she told varying accounts of events to the many visitors she received. Eventually, she admitted that she had wanted to get rid of her husband and had persuaded Billings and Wood to help her. At the trial she pleaded to be exempted from the penalty of petty treason on the grounds that she had not struck the fatal blow herself. However, her plea was disregarded and she was told the law must take its course. Thomas Billings and Thomas Wood were condemned to death by hanging and afterwards to be hung in chains. However, Wood was ailing fast in Newgate. He cheated the hangman and died of a fever, on 4 May, in the condemned cell. Although the ages of Wood and Billings were not recorded, they were believed to have both been teenagers.

On 9 May 1726, Thomas Billings was hanged at TYBURN and later his body was suspended in chains a little over a hundred yards from the gallows and not far from the pond where John Hayes' body had been disposed of. At Tyburn, when Catherine had finished

The burning of Catherine Hayes at TYBURN. Author's collection

her devotions, in pursuance of her sentence an iron chain was put round her body, with which she was fixed to a stake near the gallows. Faggots were then placed around her and the executioner lit the fire. On these occasions, when women were burned for petty treason, it was customary to strangle them, by means of a rope round the neck and pulled by the executioner, so they were dead before the flames reached the body. But Catherine was literally burned alive, as Richard Arnet let go of the rope sooner than usual, in consequence of the flames reaching his hands. The fire burned fiercely round her, and the spectators watched her pushing away the faggots, while she 'rent the air with her cries and lamentations'. Other faggots were instantly thrown on her; but she survived amidst the flames for a considerable time, and her body was not perfectly reduced to ashes until three hours later.

HEATH, NEVILLE GEORGE CLEVELY

Twenty-nine-year-old, 5ft 11in tall, handsome, charming, Neville Heath, on the surface the perfect escort for ladies, was in reality a confidence trickster with a long record of petty criminality, which included housebreaking, passing bad cheques, using a string of false identities and jewellery theft. During the war Heath served as an officer in the RAF and later the South African Air Force but was cashiered from both services for fraud and other offences. He had a fondness for passing himself off as high-ranking officers and laying claim to honours and medals he had not earned. More disturbingly, he also had perverted sexual tastes extracting gratification from cruel and sadistic acts, which came to a climax when he murdered two women in horrific circumstances.

After the war, Heath led a raffish life. He met a would-be actress and film extra, known as 'Ocelot Margie', at the *Panama Club*, Knightsbridge. Thirty-two-year-old Margery Gardner had left her husband and child in Sheffield and come to London to pursue an acting career. Her nickname resulted from the fake ocelot coat she often wore. Known to the police, Mrs Gardner mixed with pimps, thieves and black-marketeers and was known to be a masochist with sadistic inclinations. Heath and Mrs Gardner enjoyed at least one date at which the binding and beating being satisfactory to both parties resulted in this last fatal encounter on Thursday 20 June 1946. The following afternoon Margery Gardner's body was found in room No.4 at the *Pembridge Court Hotel*, Notting Hill Gate, which Heath had booked the previous week under the names of Lt Colonel and Mrs Heath. Mrs Gardner's naked body was lying on its back, her feet were tied together with a handkerchief and marks on her wrists suggested her hands had also been tied. Her face was extensively bruised and there were seventeen lash marks on various parts of her body, which had left distinctive diamond patterns on the flesh. Her nipples had almost been bitten off and a rough object had been savagely forced into her vagina causing severe bleeding. Home Office pathologist, Dr Keith Simpson, confirmed that the mutilation was inflicted while Mrs Gardner was alive. The actual cause of death was suffocation, which may have been the result of a gag or from the victim's face being forced into a pillow.

Meanwhile, Heath went to Worthing where he met with his fiancée, Yvonne Symonds, who had stayed overnight with him at the *Pembridge Court Hotel* the previous week, when he had proposed to her. In Worthing he again used his own name at the *Ocean Hotel*. He told Yvonne that a terrible murder had occurred in London, in the hotel room he had booked and that he had lent the room to a woman to entertain a friend named Jack. He also claimed that he had been invited by police to view the body the following morning. When newspaper reports contradicted this and mentioned wanting to interview Heath, he took to his heels. The police later discovered an RAF uniform and some medals in his room. Heath arrived in Bournemouth on Sunday 23 June, where he booked into room No.81 at the *Tollard Royal Hotel*. He sent a postcard to Inspector Barrett at Scotland yard in which he claimed to have lent his hotel room to Margery Gardener, having later '... found her in the condition of which you are aware... I have the instrument with which Mrs Gardner was beaten and am forwarding this to you today'. The 'instrument' never arrived.

Popular Scottish actress Molly Weir (1910-2004), who became famous after her appearances on the radio series *ITMA*, mentions in her autobiographical work, *Stepping into the Spotlight*, a lucky escape. During a break from recording, she visited a friend in Bournemouth. On Tuesday 2 July, before collecting her luggage for the return train home she had tea in *Bobby's Restaurant*, where Heath approached her. He enquired what she was doing that evening and when she told him she was going to London he persisted in his advances, eventually saying: 'Won't you change your mind...You could surely get an early train tomorrow morning.' Miss Weir left the restaurant and returned to London.

On the afternoon of Wednesday 3 July 'Brooke' met Doreen Marshall on the promenade. She was a pretty, twenty-year-old former Wren, who was staying at Bournemouth's *Norfolk Hotel* recuperating from a bad bout of influenza. He entertained her to afternoon tea and invited her to dinner at his hotel. After dinner witnesses stated at about 12.15am she asked for a taxi to be called for but Heath insisted on walking her back to her hotel. She was not seen alive again. Heath's attempt to establish an alibi by climbing into his room via scaffolding and a ladder failed. On 5 July, the manager of the *Norfolk Hotel* reported Miss Marshall missing. Heath, still claiming to be Group Captain Rupert Brooke, called into Bournemouth Police Station and confirmed when shown a photograph, that it was indeed the missing girl he had dined with. However, he was quickly recognised as Heath and arrested. A metal-tipped riding crop found among Heath's possessions matched the marks on Margery Gardner's body and there was also some bloodstained clothing. Doreen Marshall's body was found by a walker among rhododendron bushes at Branksome Dene Chine on 8 July. She had been attacked with even more bestial savagery than Heath's previous victim.

An imitation pearl found in Heath's pocket was identical to a broken string of imitation pearls found with Miss Marshall's body. Heath's trial began in the No. 1 Court at the OLD BAILEY on 24 September 1946 before Mr Justice Morris Heath was charged only with the murder of Mrs Margery Gardner, he pleaded not guilty. In an attempt to save him from the gallows, his defence claimed that a man would simply have to be mad to commit such crimes. However, medical experts disagreed and put him outside the scope of the McNAGHTEN RULES, declaring him definitely not insane. In his summing-up the judge said: 'A strong sexual instinct is not of itself insanity. Mere love of lust, mere recklessness, are not in themselves insanity. Inability to resist temptation is not in itself insanity. A perverted impulse could not be excused on the ground of insanity. Legal insanity could not be permitted to become an easy or vague explanation of some conduct which was shocking because it was also startling.' At the end of the three-day trial the jury's verdict was unanimous. They found Heath guilty after one hour's deliberation. Heath wrote to his parents: 'My only regret at leaving the world is that I have been damned unworthy of you both.' He did not appeal and was hanged on 16 October by Albert PIERREPOINT at PENTONVILLE.

HEDLEY, RONALD – see BINNEY MURDER, THE

HEFELD, PAUL – see TOTTENHAM OUTRAGE, THE

HELWYSS, SIR GERVAISE – see OVERBURY, SIR THOMAS

HENDERSON, MATTHEW

Executed in Oxford Street, 25 February 1746, near the scene of his crime, for the murder of Lady Dalrymple. Matthew Henderson, a Scot, had been in the employ of Sir Hugh Dalrymple since 1741, when he was fourteen years of age, working for the Dalrymples for three years, before being brought to the Dalrymples' London residence, where the murder took place two years later. A few days before the murder, Sir Hugh, who was about to depart for a month on business in the country, summoned Henderson to assist him to dress. While Henderson was about his duties Lady Dalrymple entered the chamber and Henderson accidentally trod on her toe. She said nothing to him but gave him such a hostile look that it made him feel very uneasy. After his master's departure Lady Dalrymple summoned Henderson and asked him why he had trod on her toe. Henderson assured his mistress that it was a mere accident but despite his profuse apologies Lady Dalrymple struck him on the ear and told him she would dismiss him from her service. Henderson said he would go without any fuss. Her ladyship called on Henderson to serve her later that day and did not refer to the incident again. In fact she treated him with great civility. However, Henderson felt so humiliated by Lady Dalrymple's treatment that he pondered on how he should avenge himself.

At length he resolved he would murder his mistress. A little after midnight, shortly after he had observed the watch passing by, Henderson procured a small meat cleaver from the kitchen, entered Lady Dalrymple's bed chamber and drew back the bed curtains. Her ladyship was asleep. He dealt her several blows with the cleaver, killing her as she slept. He then ransacked the room, stole two diamond rings and several other items of value. He then fled the scene. Henderson was quickly apprehended, tried at the OLD BAILEY and convicted of murder.

HILTON, JOHN

Wealthy diamond merchant, fifty-five-year-old Leo Grunhut was ambushed by two men armed with a sawn-off shotgun in Limes Avenue, Golders Green at 6.50pm on 28 February 1978. He was carrying almost £300,000 worth of precious stones and as he tried to flee was shot in the back. As Mr Grunhut fell to the floor he was shot again. The two assailants grabbed their booty and fled in a white Vauxhall Victor. A blood trail at the scene suggested that one of the robbers had also been injured. Severely wounded Mr Grunhut died of his injuries at Hampstead's Royal Free Hospital, three weeks later. For over twelve years the identity of the killers remained a mystery. Then in December 1990 sixty-one-year-old John Hilton, a known villain was captured on a concealed video camera during a jewel robbery in Piccadilly and subsequently arrested. Whilst on remand at Brixton Prison Hilton was interviewed at his own request by Flying Squad officers. He confessed to every crime he had committed including the murder of Leo Grunhut. In shooting Mr Grunhut he had accidentally shot his accomplice Ian Roberts in the thigh and he had died as a result of massive blood loss. Hilton buried Roberts in a shallow grave on a railway siding at Stone near Dartford, Kent. He took police to locate Roberts' remains on 26 February 1991.

On 9 September 1991, Hilton appeared at the OLD BAILEY before the Recorder of London, Judge Lawrence Verney. He pleaded guilty and told the jury: 'I want to come to terms with my conscience before I die. The history of armed robbery is littered with bodies. If Roberts had shot me in that incident then I have no doubt he would have acted afterwards in exactly the same way.' Hilton was sentenced to two life terms of imprisonment, with the recommendation that he serve at least thirty years.

HOCKER, THOMAS HENRY

At around 7.00pm on 23 February 1845, Police Constable John Baldock on patrol near the bridle path that ran through the fields between Primrose Hill and Belsize Park, was alerted by a baker Edward Hilton, to cries of 'Murder!' When he arrived at the scene (at today's junction of Belsize Park Gardens, England's Lane, Eton Avenue and Primrose Hill) accompanied by Sergeant Thomas Fletcher, in the dark they found the bloody and battered body of a well-dressed man. Whilst the sergeant went to get assistance, Constable Baldock stayed with the corpse.

A cloaked man, later identified as Thomas Hocker approached the constable and uttered the words: 'Hilloa, policeman, what have you got there?' He offered the constable brandy, which he refused, but Hocker persuaded him to take a shilling to get a glass of brandy later. At no time did he indicate that he knew the victim, although it would become clear that in fact he knew him very well. Shortly after, William Satterthwaite, a Hampstead shoemaker appeared, and Hocker left the scene. Dr Perry examined the body. His report stated:

Death is attributed to concussion of the brain, the consequence of the external violence. I should imagine the wounds were inflicted by a heavy instrument, such as a stick…

The man appeared to have been robbed, because the only item found on him was a letter written in blue ink addressed to J Cooper. The letter began 'Dear James' and in it the writer requested a meeting at their usual place; she also informed him that she was pregnant. It was signed Caroline. A coroner's inquest was held at the *Yorkshire Grey* in Hampstead, by which time the victim had been identified as James De La Rue. A verdict of wilful murder was recorded. Twenty-seven-year-old James De La Rue, a music teacher, lived in well appointed lodgings at 55 Whittlebury Street. The road no longer exists but in 1845 it led into Euston Square from Drummond Street, which straddles Hampstead Road. He earned his money

Thomas Hocker.
John D Murray collection

principally giving piano lessons. James De La Rue was buried in St John's Churchyard, Hampstead, on 28 February. Thomas Hocker, aged twenty-two, was a close friend of De La Rue's. He lived at 11 Victoria Place, situated near the western edge of Regent's Park, sharing a room with his brother, James. Although he considered his musical talents to be worthy of more, he scraped a living by giving the occasional violin lesson.

These friends were a pair of amorous aspiring gentlemen, dapper dressers, who had a penchant for collecting pornography in the form of prints. Using various aliases they had developed acquaintances with numerous women, mostly servant girls and those who, although not exactly prostitutes, had loose morals. They often indulged in orgies. Neither had any intention of cementing any of their relationships by marriage, hence the use of false names in their liaisons. During the police investigation that followed De La Rue's friendship with Hocker emerged. Following the funeral, Hocker's apparent indifference to his best friend's death, threw suspicion his way. Both Thomas and James Hocker were questioned and as matters unfolded James Hocker was able to give information about the letter found in De La Rue's greatcoat pocket. The letter, written in a supposedly girlish hand, had in fact been written by Thomas Hocker in one of his numerous false hands. The unusual blue ink was traced to his room, and this evidence, together with the discovery of De La Rue's watch and a pair of blood-soaked trousers, proved sufficient to convict him of his friend's murder.

Hocker was tried at the OLD BAILEY on 11 April, before Mr Justice Coleman, in a trial lasting less than ten hours. The jury found him guilty after just ten minutes deliberation. He protested his innocence to the end, blaming another he would not

Holloway Prison. The church spire on the distant horizon is St Michael's, Highgate.
Author's collection

name. He was hanged at NEWGATE before a crowd of 10,000, on 28 April 1845 by William CALCRAFT.

HOLLOWAY PRISON

Built as a House of Correction for the City of London and opened in 1852, Holloway was commonly referred to as Holloway Castle, because of its tower (loosely modelled on Warwick Castle) and battlements. After the closure of NEWGATE in 1902, Holloway became a prison for females only. During World War Two, the inmates were transferred to Aylesbury Prison, while Holloway was used to incarcerate those considered prejudicial to the war effort, including Sir Oswald and Lady Mosley, before reverting once again to a women's prison. In all there were five executions at Holloway. The first was a double execution, Amelia Sach and Annie Walters, in 1903 (THE ISLINGTON BABY-FARMING CASE); Edith Thompson in 1923; Styllou CHRISTOFI in 1954 and Ruth ELLIS in 1955.

HOPWOOD, EDWARD

Edward Hopwood was a married man who took as his mistress Florence Silles, better known as the actress Florence Dudley. Hopwood had passed himself off as a wealthy bachelor. In reality he was nothing of the kind and was wanted by police for passing bad cheques. Miss Dudley was appearing at the Tivoli Theatre. On the morning of 28 September 1912 when she learned the truth about her lover, horrified at the thought of bad publicity, she broke off the affair. That afternoon, pleading for forgiveness, Hopwood took a cab with Miss Dudley to Fenchurch Street Station. When she would not submit to his wishes he pulled a gun out and shot her dead. He then turned the gun on himself. He did not die and was nursed back to health. Hopwood was tried at the OLD BAILEY, found guilty of murder and hanged at PENTONVILLE on 29 January 1913.

HORSEMONGER LANE GAOL

Horsemonger Lane Gaol, built between 1791-9 in Southwark, was the name familiar to Londoners for what was officially Surrey County Goal, from that time until it closed in 1878. The most unusual feature of this gaol, a place of incarceration, mostly for petty criminals, who were housed in three of its four wings, the fourth housing debtors, was the scaffold erected on the roof of the gatehouse. This scaffold provided not only better security but also good views for the public who flocked to see executions held there. CATHERINE WILSON, the last woman to be publicly hanged in London, was executed here on 20 October 1862.

HOSEIN BROTHERS

Thirty-four-year-old Arthur and twenty-two-year-old Nizamodeen Hosein, Indian Moslems who had been born in Trinidad, bought Rooks Farm at Stocking Pelham, Hertfordshire in 1968. There the brothers hatched a plot to kidnap the wife of Australian newspaper tycoon Rupert Murdoch and collect a large ransom. Their preparations were severely flawed. They followed a Rolls Royce from the *News of the World's* headquarters to a mock-Georgian house in Wimbledon. They mistakenly believed the house to belong to the Murdochs. In fact it was the home of Alick McKay, deputy chairman of the newspaper. On Monday 29 December 1969, the Hosein brothers broke into the house and abducted Mrs Muriel McKay believing her to be Mrs Murdoch and later that evening Mr McKay received a ransom demand by telephone

Horsemonger Lane Gaol. Author's collection

for £1 million, within two days 'or we kill her'. A botched attempt to hand over the ransom money and secure the release of Mrs McKay resulted in the kidnappers being identified. Fingerprint evidence linked the brothers to the kidnap notes. No trace of Muriel McKay was found.

The Hosein brothers' trial began at the OLD BAILEY on 14 September 1970. It was an unpleasant affair full of drama and emotional outbursts, it being necessary for prison officers to restrain the brothers on several occasions. Their trial ended on 6 October after the jury took four hours to find them both guilty of kidnapping and murder. Both were sentenced to twenty-five years' imprisonment. Mrs McKay's body was never found.

HULTEN, KARL GUSTAV – see CLEFT CHIN MURDER, THE

HUME, BRIAN DONALD

In 1949, Donald Hume, a second-hand car dealer, murdered his business associate Stanley Setty (a forty-six-year-old Iraqi, whose real name was Sulman Seti), who was also a petty criminal, by stabbing him with a Nazi SS dagger at 620b Finchley Road. He cut up the body and put it into three parcels which he weighted with bricks. Hume had a private pilot's licence. He flew a light aircraft over the English Channel and dropped the parcels into the sea. One parcel washed up at Burnham-on-Crouch, Essex on 21 October and fingerprints from the hands in the package identified the victim as Setty, who had been reported missing from his home in Lancaster Gate since 4 October.

Scotland Yard's enquiries eventually led them to Hume, after they visited the United Services Flying Club at Elstree and found bloodstains in an Auster sports plane that had been hired by Hume on 5 October. He was charged with murder and on

18 January 1950 appeared at the OLD BAILEY, before Mr Justice Lewis. He claimed to know nothing about the murder, but said he had agreed to dispose of the parcels for three crooks he named as Mac, Greeny and 'The Boy'. The jury acquitted him on grounds of reasonable doubt. He was, however, sentenced as an accessory to the crime and jailed for twelve years. He served eight of them, receiving the maximum remission for good behaviour, being released from Dartmoor in the spring of 1958.

After his release, Hume admitted that he had invented the crooks and had simply based his descriptions of them on detectives who had interviewed him. His confession was printed in four issues of the *Sunday Pictorial*, which was reputed to have paid him £2,000 for the story. Under English law he could not be tried again for the same crime, and with the proceeds made from his confession he went to Switzerland, where he spent most of the money on high living. He returned to the United Kingdom to commit two armed robberies, on 2 August 1958, when he held up the Midland Bank at Brentford in Middlesex, getting away with over £1,000, and on 12 November at another Midland Bank on the Great West Road. This time he got away with just a handful of notes, having shot and seriously wounded the manager. He returned to Switzerland, where he murdered again, shooting fifty-year-old taxi driver Arthur Maagr during an aborted bank robbery in Zurich in January 1959. He was soon captured and tried. Found guilty of murder, there being no death penalty in Switzerland, Hume was sentenced to life imprisonment with hard labour. In August 1976, the Swiss authorities judged him insane and returned him to Britain, where he was incarcerated in Broadmoor. In 1988, at the age of sixty-seven and considered low risk, he was moved to a hospital in West London.

I

IRELAND, COLIN

Serial killer Colin Ireland terrorised London's gay community for twelve weeks in 1993. During what was a series of horrific murders Ireland decided to fulfil his warped ambition to become famous as a serial killer.

Ireland's first victim was forty-five-year-old theatre director, Peter Walker, who was found strangled and tied to his four poster bed at his home in Vicarage Crescent, Battersea. Ireland rang the *Sun* newspaper on 9 March and tipped them off about the murder, saying he was worried about his victim's dogs. He next killed on 28 May, when he picked up thirty-seven-year-old librarian, Christopher Dunn in *The Coleherne*, at Earls Court. Ireland picked his third victim up at the same pub on 4 June. American sales director Perry Bradley, aged thirty-five, was found naked, bound and strangled at his Kensington flat. Four days later Ireland struck again, killing thirty-three-year-old housing supervisor Andrew Collier. The fifth and final victim of Ireland's killing spree was forty-three-year-old, Maltese-born chef Emmanuel Spiteri, who was killed on Saturday 12 June. His body was found at his flat after Ireland phoned the police on 15 June. CCTV film taken on 12 June showed Mr Spiteri with a heavily built man at Charing Cross Station. A wanted poster was created but the picture police were able to produce from the indistinct image brought little response.

Then on 21 July Colin Ireland walked into a Southend-on-Sea solicitor's office and said he needed a lawyer. Ireland was accompanied to Kensington Police Station where he admitted being the man caught on CCTV but denied any involvement in the murders. However, a single fingerprint at the home of his fourth victim linked him to the killings and he was arrested.

At the OLD BAILEY Ireland pleaded guilty to all five counts of murder and on 20 December 1993 in sentencing him to life imprisonment, Mr Justice Sachs recommended that he should never be released, he told Ireland:

> *You are an exceptionally frightening and dangerous man. In cold blood and with great deliberation you have killed five of your fellow men. You killed them in grotesque and cruel circumstances… To take one life is an outrage; to take five is carnage.*

ISLINGTON BABY-FARMING CASE, THE

Baby-farming was a peculiarity of late Victorian England: unwanted babies and children, whether illegitimate or simply a burden to their parents, were farmed out to women who acted as foster-mothers. These women were paid to 'adopt' the children or to look after them for a specific period, before they were moved to permanent homes. Large financial rewards could be obtained by taking these unwanted children and the result was that some women obtained money to place a child in a good home and, having found none, 'took care' of their charges simply by killing them. Rivers, canals, reservoirs and even rubbish tips were common dumping grounds for these unfortunate innocents. Two such baby-farmers were Amelia Sach and Annie Walters.

Mrs Amelia Sach, aged twenty-six, lived at Claymore House, Hertford Road, East Finchley, which she had converted to serve as a private lying-in hospital. There she operated a successful business as an *accoucheuse*. She claimed to be a certified midwife and nurse and attended to her female patients herself. In difficult cases she arranged for a doctor to be present. She had a ready supply of unwanted babies to baby-farm. Her accomplice in crime was fifty-one-year-old Annie Walters, who described herself as a 'short stay foster parent'. Exactly how many babies were killed by these evil women

11 Danbury Street, Islington, an address closely linked with the notorious Islington Baby-Farming Case.
Paul T Langley Welch

will never be known. Annie Walters often changed address, probably so her activities were not subjected to too close a scrutiny. While lodging at 11 Danbury Street, Islington with a police constable named Sale and his wife, her many accounts of how babies were given new homes made him suspicious. Her fanciful stories did not ring true with PC Sale. He and a colleague Detective Constable Wright decided to watch her. On 18 November 1902 Annie Walters had in her possession a baby boy, believed to be the child of Ada Galley, a single young woman and a patient at Claymore House. Walters was followed to South Kensington railway station by DC Wright, who arrested her after the child was found to be dead. It had been dead for between eight and twelve hours. Chlorodyne, a painkiller containing morphia, chloroform and prussic acid, mixed with a baby's milk in sufficient quantity would soon cause death. Walters said to police: 'I never murdered the dear. I only gave it two drops in its bottle, the same as I take myself.' A whole catalogue of grim events unfolded and Amelia Sach was also arrested. Both were charged with murder. Their trial commenced before Mr Justice Darling at the OLD BAILEY on 15 January 1903. Found guilty of murder, they were sentenced to death. Mrs Sach's plea for clemency on the grounds that it was most unusual to be hanged as an accessory was turned down and the two women were executed together at HOLLOWAY Prison by the BILLINGTON brothers on 3 February 1903. Amelia Sach and Annie Walters were the first of only five women to be executed at Holloway (no men were executed there).

J

JACK THE RIPPER

'The Whitechapel Murderer' was the original title accorded to the unknown 'Jack the Ripper'. In reality, although his murders occurred within one square mile, they strayed outside Whitechapel proper to Spitalfields. Five murders are known to have been committed by the Ripper, some commentators credit him with six murders, and the general public of the day believed that a seventh Whitechapel murder was the work of the Ripper. The authorities claimed just the five, committed over a three-month period in 1888. All the victims were prostitutes: Mary Ann (Polly) Nichols, aged forty-two, killed in Bucks Row, 31 August; Annie Chapman (known as Dark Annie), aged forty-seven, killed in the back yard of 29 Hanbury Street, 8 September; Elizabeth Stride (a Swede, known as Long Liz), aged forty-four, killed in Berners Street, 30 September; Catherine Eddowes, aged forty-three, killed in Mitre Square, 30 September and Mary Jane Kelly, aged twenty-five, killed in her flat at 13 Miller's Court, Dorset Street, on 9 November. The brutality of these murders has been well documented in an enormous number of books written about this unsolved case.

JACK THE STRIPPER – see HAMMERSMITH NUDES MURDERS

JACOBY, HENRY JULIUS

In the Spring of 1922, eighteen-year-old Henry Jacoby took the position of pantry boy at the *Spencer Hotel*, in the heart of the West End. Before he had been there a month, young Henry decided to avail himself of some of the wealthy residents' property. With robbery in mind, on the night of Monday 13 March 1922, he put his plans into action. The *Spencer Hotel*, a private hotel (now the *Mostyn Hotel*), was situated in Portman

Jack the Ripper. The 'two in one night' murders of Elizabeth Stride and Catherine Eddowes.
The Illustrated Police News

Street. It was a comfortable place, dignified and quiet, the kind of hotel where retired people of good standing could spend the remaining years of their lives, being well taken care of, in pleasant surroundings. One of the residents was sixty-year-old Lady White, the well-off widow of Sir Edward White, a former Chairman of London County Council. That evening, Lady White had been playing bridge in the drawing room. She had been at the hotel since the previous November. The forty or so other guests liked her and as Lady White received the domestic attention she required, the *Spencer Hotel* evidently suited her. She retired to her room at about eleven o'clock.

At five past eight on the morning of the 14 March, chambermaid Sarah Ann Pocock went into Lady White's room, Room No. 14, as part of her usual routine. The room was in semi-darkness, as the curtains were drawn, when she opened them she saw that Lady White was covered in blood and had serious head injuries. Police Divisional Surgeon, Dr Percy Bertram Spurgeon, was called to the hotel and found Lady White still breathing. She had an extensive fracture of the skull. The bone had been splintered and brain matter and blood clots were protruding. There was a laceration about eight inches long across the scalp and the edges were gaping. He concluded that the injuries were caused by more than one blow with a blunt instrument and that Lady White must have been rendered unconscious by the first blow. There was also an injury to Lady White's left hand. There were no signs of a struggle and no traces of forced entry. Lady White died during the early hours of the following morning. She never regained consciousness.

On the night of the murder, eighteen-year-old pantry boy, Henry Jacoby, told the porter he had heard some men whispering outside his basement room. However, nothing untoward was found and the porter returned to his duties, and young Henry to his bed.

The inquest was opened at Marylebone Coroner's Court, by Mr H R Oswald, on 16 March. Meanwhile, police enquiries were continuing. Young Henry's all too eager enthusiasm to help, and his theories as to how the murder might have been committed, along with his tale of hearing men whispering outside his room, threw suspicion his way. When his room was searched, two blood-stained handkerchiefs were found. Henry caved in and told the police what had happened. Robbery was the motive. He entered the room and before he had the chance to steal anything, Lady White woke up. He saw her in the beam of his torch, panicked and hit her with the hammer he had taken from a toolbox, which he had later returned after cleaning it.

The trial opened on 28 April at the OLD BAILEY. The jury consulted for some time in private, then the foreman said they were all agreed that Jacoby went into the room without intending to murder, but for the purpose of robbery. They wanted to know whether, bearing this in mind, they could bring a manslaughter verdict. Mr Justice McCardie said, that if Jacoby went into the room for the purpose of stealing, then the next question was, did he strike Lady White intending either to kill or inflict grievous bodily harm? Yet inasmuch as the victim had died from the injuries inflicted by Jacoby, he would be guilty in law of murder. They brought in a guilty verdict. There was to be no reprieve and Henry Jacoby was hanged at Pentonville on 7 June 1922. In the Condemned Cell, Jacoby wrote several letters, one of which concluded:

H. J. 382 – please excuse this curious signature, as this is what I shall be buried under.

JENKINS, CHARLES HENRY – see ANTIQUIS MURDER, THE

JENKINS, THOMAS – see BINNEY MURDER, THE

JOHNSON AND HOUSDEN

Butcher William Johnson moved from his native Northampton to open a shop at Newport Market, which was not the success he had hoped for. He made several other business speculations before going to Gibraltar and, having made a little money there, he returned to England and promptly spent it. He then took to highway robbery. Apprehended at one such robbery he was convicted and pardoned. He had an accomplice in crime, Jane Housden, who had been convicted of coining and also pardoned. In 1714, Jane found herself charged with the same offence and incarcerated in NEWGATE. At her trial at the OLD BAILEY, just as she was being brought down to the bar, Johnson called to see her. On being told by Mr Spurling, the head turnkey, that he could not speak to her until the trial was over, Johnston drew a pistol and shot Spurling dead on the spot, all the time being encouraged by Jane Housden, in the presence of the Court. The judges were of the opinion that it was unnecessary to continue with the trial for Housden's coining and ordered both parties to be immediately tried for murder of which charge both were duly convicted and sentenced to death. They were hanged on 19 September 1714. Johnson's body was hanged in chains at Holloway, between Islington and Highgate.

William Johnson shoots NEWGATE'S head turnkey Spurling in the Sessions House, OLD BAILEY. Author's collection

JONES, ELIZABETH MARINA – see CLEFT CHIN MURDER, THE

JONES AND WELCH

Richard Coleman, a brewery clerk, was executed on Kennington Common on 12 April 1749 for a murder he did not commit and had no connection with. The victim, Sarah Green, was attacked and sexually abused by three men in Parsonage Walk near Newington churchyard, on the night of 23 July 1749, after they had been drinking at an inn called *Sot's Hole* and later the *King's Head*. She died several days later of appalling injuries at St Thomas's Hospital. Thomas Jones, James Welch and John Nichols were the culprits. Two years after the murder James Butts was in company with a man walking to Newington Butts, when conversation turned to those innocent persons who had been hanged. The man, James Welch said:

> *Among whom was Coleman. Nichols, Jones and I were the persons who committed the murder for which he was hanged.*

The matter played heavily on Mr Butt's mind and sometime later, believing himself to be terminally ill, he imparted this conversation to his father. Enquiries were made and Jones, Welch and Nichols were arrested. (Nichols turned King's evidence and the full particulars of the crime were revealed. At the time of the murder Jones and Welch called Nichols Coleman, which led to the wrongful conviction of Richard Coleman.) Jones and Welch were convicted of murder at Kingston Assizes and hanged on Kennington Common on 6 September 1751.

Kennington Common.
Author's collection

JONSON, BEN

One of England's finest dramatists was also a convicted murderer. Red-headed Ben Jonson (1572-1637), the posthumous son of a clergyman was educated at Westminster School and for a brief period worked in his stepfather's trade as a bricklayer. He joined the army and served in Flanders, returning to England in 1592. In 1594 he married Anne Lewis and about 1597 joined a theatrical company owned by Philip Henslowe as actor and playwright. In September 1598, Jonson's play *Every Man in his Humour* was being successfully performed at the Curtain Theatre in Shoreditch. On 22 September Jonson fought a duel in the fields near the theatre with an important actor in the Admiral's Company, Gabriel Spencer. Spencer possessed a vicious and ungovernable temper and less than two years before had quarrelled with a goldsmith's son in Shoreditch. When the boy picked up a candlestick and threatened to throw it at Spencer, Spencer lunged at him with his sword still sheathed in its scabbard, which pierced his head just above the right eye. The boy died three days later. Exactly what the quarrel was between Jonson and Spencer is not known, as the report of the coroner's inquest is missing. Jonson was injured in the arm by Spencer's rapier but he managed to run in under Spencer's guard and pierce his side, which killed the actor instantly.

Jonson was imprisoned in NEWGATE charged with murder. He appeared before the next sessions on 6 October in the open air court held in the street called OLD BAILEY that ran by the prison (in years gone by trials had been held in Newgate itself but the fear of the judges and officials catching gaol fever resulted in trials being held in the open air). The jury having considered Jonson's case decided that:

the aforesaid Benjamin Johnson [sic] *feloniously and willfully* [sic] *slew and killed the aforesaid Gabriel Spencer at Shoreditch aforesaid.*

Ben Jonson (1572-1637). Author's collection

Jonson promptly pleaded BENEFIT OF CLERGY as soon as the verdict had been handed down; the bishops' representative present in court gave him a psalter. Jonson was allowed to choose his own passage for what was commonly referred to as the 'neck verse'. In accordance with ancient tradition the judge asked if he had read it like a clerk, '*Legit ut clericus?*'; the reply came from the bishop's representative, '*Legit.*' With those words the shadow of the hangman's noose at TYBURN had been lifted. To ensure that he could not plead benefit of clergy a second time he was immediately branded with a letter M on the base of the left thumb and after paying the jailer's fees Jonson was allowed to leave prison.

K

KELSEY, TOM

Born in Leather Lane, Holborn, Tom Kelsey in early childhood went to live in Wales where his mother had inherited a small estate. Aged fourteen, he returned to London to seek his fortune and fell in with bad company, mostly thieves and within a short time Tom was as bold and dextrous as the best of them. He became involved in some daring robberies but before he had reached the age of sixteen had been condemned to be hanged for stealing a large quantity of silver and £40 from a grocer in the Strand. He got off on account of his youth and at the intervention of his aged father, who upon hearing of his son's sentence, came up to London and procured a full pardon on the day before the appointed execution by enlisting the help of some powerful friends. Tom was apprenticed to a weaver in the hope he would mend his ways but he simply took to tutoring other young would-be thieves, one of his more promising pupils soon being hanged. Tom robbed the Earl of Feversham's lodgings and got away with £200 worth of silver plate. He also robbed Lady Grace Pierpont and disposed of his ill-gotten gains to a Jew in Amsterdam. He then robbed the Jew and sold the booty to another Jew in Rotterdam, after which he returned to England. Not long afterwards, he was caught breaking into a house in Cheapside. He was sent to NEWGATE where he was given no hope of ever being released. He resolved to do all mischief he could there. Tom Kelsey stabbed one of the turnkeys, a Mr Goodman, in the belly. He instantly died and his murderer was convicted at the OLD BAILEY. Tom Kelsey was hanged on Friday 13 June 1690 on an especially erected gibbet, close to the prison in Newgate Street. 'Being no more than twenty years of age. As a terror to the other prisoners who were then in confinement, his body was suffered to hang on the gibbet the space of three hours.'

KETCH, JACK (hangman)

Jack Ketch (or John Catch) was London's executioner from at least as early as 1678 until 1686, when he was removed from office shortly after he had bungled the beheading of the Duke of Monmouth. He had also bungled the beheading of Lord William Russell in 1683. He executed about 200 of Monmouth's rebels in 1685. Thereafter, all London hangmen were popularly known as Jack Ketch.

KLOSOWSKI, SEVERIN – see CHAPMAN, GEORGE

KRAY TWINS, THE

The Kray twins, Ronald and Reginald, were born on 24 October 1933. During the 1950s and 1960s the twins were at the forefront of organised crime in the East End and parts of the West End. They organised their empire from their

Jack Ketch. Author's collection

mother's house at 178 Vallance Road, Bethnal Green, and surrounded themselves with hardened criminals who became known as the 'Firm'. Although they were involved in hijacking, arson and armed robbery, the Krays owned successful nightclubs and several well-known personalities from show business and politics were associated with them. The police were well aware of the Krays' criminal activities, but their reputation for dealing harshly with anyone who crossed them was such that witnesses were reluctant to come forward, particularly as by then Ronnie had developed serious mental health problems and was prone to paranoia, manic rages and extreme violence.

By 1964, national newspapers were mentioning, although not by name, a gangster family who were openly ruling London. Try as they might the police could not pin anything on the twins themselves. George Cornell, a south London gangster was associated with an equally notorious firm of villains, the Richardson gang. Ronnie, who had not entirely come to terms with his homosexuality, was deeply offended by Cornell when he called him a 'fat poof' at one of their West End haunts. Ronnie seethed for almost two years about this slight. Then, on 9 March 1966, shortly after George Cornell entered *The Blind Beggar* in Whitechapel Road, within the Krays' own 'manor', Ronnie decided to act. The twins, who were drinking nearby at the *Lion*, in Tapp Street, were informed of Cornell's audacity. At about 8.30pm Ronnie walked in to the bar and shot Cornell through the head. Police were unable to find any witnesses to the killing, even though they believed that as many as thirty people probably saw what happened. His own appetite sated by the killing, Ronnie said to Reggie: 'I have done my one. Now you do yours.'

A long term member of the 'Firm' was Jack McVitie. Nicknamed 'Jack the Hat', because of the pork-pie hat he wore, McVitie had crossed the twins by not fulfilling a contract killing they had paid him to carry out. One night in November 1966, McVitie was invited to a 'party' at a flat in No.1 Evering Road, Stoke Newington. The twins were waiting for him. Reggie tried to shoot McVitie but the gun jammed. As Jack the Hat tried to escape through a window, he was dragged back and while Ronnie held him Reggie stabbed him through the eye, elsewhere in the face and in the stomach. Afterwards, the body was wrapped in a bedspread, put in a car and disposed of. Exactly where has never been discovered.

The Kray twins were responsible for at least one more murder: Frank Mitchell, known as the 'Mad Axeman', who they had sprung from Broadmoor on 12 December 1966 was killed after he became a liability. Detective Superintendent Leonard 'Nipper' Read had been assembling evidence against the Krays' for some time. He heard rumours that they had killed Cornell and McVitie and believed he could bring them to justice if he could get the right people to testify against them. In the end he managed it and decided the time had come to act.

At 6.00am on 7 May, Nipper Read lead a team that swooped on the Kray brothers and the Firm. All three brothers and twenty-five members of the 'Firm' were arrested. The Krays' trial began in Number One Court at the OLD BAILEY before Mr Justice Melford Stevenson, on 8 January 1969. It lasted thirty-nine days. Ronnie was found guilty of murdering Cornell and Reggie convicted of being an accessory. Both twins were convicted of the murder of McVitie. They were sentenced to life imprisonment with a recommendation that they serve thirty years. The twins' elder brother, Charlie, who they had persuaded to dispose of McVitie's body, was given a ten-year sentence as an accessory to murder. Ronnie Kray died of a massive heart attack in Broadmoor Hospital on 17 March 1995. In August 2000, Reggie, having been diagnosed with terminal cancer, was given only weeks to live and released from prison on the orders of Home Secretary Jack Straw. He died on 1 October 2000. Despite being separated and behind bars, the twins continued to hold influence in underworld activities up until their deaths.

L

LAMBETH POISONER, THE – see CREAM, DR THOMAS NEILL

LAMSON, DR GEORGE HENRY

Twenty-nine-year-old Dr George Lamson was not content with the share of his late parents-in-law's fortune that his wife had brought. He coveted his eighteen-year-old brother-in-law's share also. Percy Malcolm John, a cripple, was a boarding pupil at Blenheim House School, at 1 and 2 St George's Road, Wimbledon. On 31 December 1881 Lamson visited Percy and in company with the headmaster, Mr Bedbrook and some fellow pupils partook of some ready cut slices of Dundee cake, supplied by Dr

Lamson. The Doctor also gave Percy a capsule, which he had ostentatiously filled with sugar, evidently a ruse to draw attention away from Percy's slice of cake, laced with aconitine. The Doctor then left for Paris. Within hours Percy was taken ill and died later that night. The police suspected foul play. Percy had certainly been poisoned. When it was discovered that Lamson had bought a quantity of the little-known vegetable poison aconitine from a manufacturing chemist on 24 November, on his return from Paris on 8 December he was brought in for questioning and subsequently charged with Percy's murder. Tried at the OLD BAILEY and found guilty, Dr Lamson was hanged at WANDSWORTH on 28 April 1882. He confessed to the prison chaplain that he had injected Percy's slice of cake with the poison.

LEPIDUS, JACOB – see TOTTENHAM OUTRAGE, THE

LIPSKI, ISRAEL

Israel Lipski, a twenty-two-year-old Jewish immigrant, working as an umbrella manufacturer, lodged in the attic of a three-storey house at 16 Batty Street, Stepney. Among the fourteen other residents was eighteen-year-old Miriam Angel who occupied a second floor room. On 28 June 1887, Miriam was found on the bed by a relative with yellow foam coming from her mouth. She was dead. Beneath the bed was Israel Lipski also with foam coming out of his mouth. A doctor suspected corrosive poisoning and a container of nitric acid was found, which confirmed this. Lipski was still alive and his claim that he and Miriam had been attacked by two labourers was not believed. Police suspected that Lipski had tried to rape Miriam, and having failed had forced her to drink the acid and then attempted to commit suicide. Considerable unrest among the immigrant community surrounded this case. After his trial and conviction at the OLD BAILEY the authorities were unsure whether Lipski should be reprieved. However, it became clear that justice had been served when Lipski admitted that robbery, not rape had been his motive, shortly before he was hanged at NEWGATE on 22 August 1887.

Miriam Angel lies dead on the bed as police attend to Israel Lipski. Author's collection

LITVINENKO, ALEXANDER (victim)
Born on 30 August 1962, Alexander Litvinenko was a Lieutenant Colonel in the Federal Security Service of the Russian Federation. He later became a dissident and

writer, who after his arrest by the Russian authorities and subsequent release fled to Britain where he was granted political asylum. On 1 November 2006, Litvinenko was taken ill and was hospitalised. His illness was later attributed to poisoning with radionuclide polonium 210. He died on 23 November 2006 and was buried on Thursday December 7 in a lead-lined casket placed within a reinforced concrete vault in Highgate Cemetery. Throughout his illness, resulting in a slow and uncomfortable death, Alexander Litvinenko was given worldwide press coverage, with suggestions that the Russian government were behind his murder.

LONDON NAIL BOMBER, THE – see COPELAND, DAVID

LOWTHER AND KEELE

Twenty-three-year-old Will Lowther, born in Whitehaven, Cumbria, had spent ten years at sea, latterly as master on a collier given to him by his father, which traded between Newcastle and London. He was seduced by the seedier elements of London's docks and took to robbing ships as they lay at anchor. He also indulged in petty thieving elsewhere in the capital, whenever the opportunity arose and struck up a friendship with another thief, Dick Keele, with whom he was apprehended in the act of stealing and incarcerated in Clerkenwell Bridewell, where they caused a riot, during which Edward Perry, a servant to Mr Boreman, the keeper, was killed. Moved to NEWGATE, Lowther and Keele were found guilty of murder at the OLD BAILEY and hanged on Clerkenwell Green on 23 December 1713.

LUCAN, THE SEVENTH EARL OF

Richard John Bingham, seventh Earl of Lucan, was born on 18 December 1934, and succeeded his father to the earldom in 1964. On the night of Thursday 7 November 1974, the thirty-nine-year-old peer, known as 'Lucky' to his friends, disappeared following an incident at his former Belgravia residence. Lord Lucan had separated from his wife Veronica in January 1973. While she remained at the house in Lower Belgrave Street, with their three children and nanny, he moved into a basement flat nearby at 72a Elizabeth Street. A little after nine o'clock on the evening of 7 November 1974, Lady Lucan stumbled into *The Plumbers' Arms* a few doors away from her home at 46 Lower Belgrave Street. She had blood streaming from a gaping wound to the head, and she blurted out to the alarmed customers and staff:

> *Help me, help me. I've just escaped from a murderer... My children
> ... my children ... He's in the house. He has murdered the nanny.*

By the time the police broke open the door of No. 46, Lady Lucan had been taken by ambulance to St George's Hospital, Hyde Park Corner. In the basement breakfast room they found the battered body of the children's nanny, twenty-nine-year-old Sandra Rivett, stuffed in a US mail sack. A bent, bloodstained bludgeon, made of lead piping with an Elastoplast grip, nine inches long and weighing two and a quarter pounds, was laying on the half landing of the basement stairway. When Miss Rivett's body was examined by pathologist, Professor Keith Simpson, he found six splits in the head, severe bruising on both shoulders, caused by the bludgeon and other bruising which may have been defence wounds. The Lucans' eldest daughter, Lady Frances, aged ten, made a statement, part of which read:

At 9.05 the news was on TV and Daddy and Mummy both walked into the room. Mummy had blood over her face and was crying. Mummy told me to go upstairs. Daddy didn't say anything to me and I said nothing to either of them. I don't know how much blood was on her face. I didn't hear any conversation between Mummy and Daddy. I didn't see any blood on Daddy's clothes. I wondered what had happened but I didn't ask.

46 Lower Belgrave Street. The Author

At 9.50pm Lord Lucan telephoned his mother, the Dowager Countess of Lucan and told her that while passing the house he saw a stranger grappling with Veronica and had let himself into the house and fought him off, only to have Veronica think that he had attacked her. After asking his mother to pick up the children, he drove to friends in Sussex and told them the same story. He also wrote letters to friends telling them what had happened and declared his intention of 'lying doggo' for a while. On Friday 8 November, Lord Lucan's car was found abandoned in Newhaven. In the boot was an empty US mail sack and a bludgeon made from the same lead piping as the one used to kill Sandra Rivett. Despite numerous alleged sightings, all around the world, the missing peer's whereabouts remain a mystery.

LUPO, MICHAEL DE MARCO

On 15 May 1986, handsome, thirty-three-year-old Italian, gay serial killer Michael Lupo, known as the 'Silken Strangler', was identified by a narrowly escaped victim and arrested in *Heaven*, a gay nightclub situated beneath the arches of Charing Cross Station. Described as London's leading sadistic rent boy, willing to flog men or women for high prices, he had taken his bent for sadism an extreme further and committed four murders, strangling his victims with a silken ligature and inflicting appalling bite injuries. On 5 April 1986, he killed thirty-six-year-old, railwayman James Burns in a derelict house in Warwick Road. On April 3, he killed unemployed Anthony Connolly. His body was discovered in a hut near a railway line in Brixton. He also killed IRA suspect Damian McClusky and an unknown vagrant who he strangled on Hungerford Bridge. Four men who had narrowly escaped death came forward and identified Lupo as their attacker. Michael Lupo had arrived in England twelve years earlier, after he realised he was gay. He estimated that during his time in London he had had sex with more than 3,000 men. Although he never explained what had driven him to kill, many believe the fact that he was doomed to die of AIDS had resolved him to take revenge on the gay community.

Michael Lupo's trial began at the OLD BAILEY on Friday 10 July 1987. He pleaded guilty to four murders and four attempted murders. When Sir James Miskin, the Recorder of London sentenced Lupo to life imprisonment, he told him: 'For a man whose life has been such that he suffers from AIDS, whether your fault or not, it would be absurd to make a minimum recommendation on your sentence. In your case, life means life.'

M

McCARTY, PATRICK

A Marshalsea writ having been issued against Patrick McCarty, a court officer, William Talbot was instructed to execute the warrant. He met McCarty near Drury Lane and accompanied him into the *King's Head*, at the corner of Prince's Street. Apparently without any harsh words being passed between the two men, McCarty pulled out a knife and stabbed William Talbot through the heart and immediately ran off. He was captured by a soldier in Vere Street, Clare Market and taken before magistrate Sir John Fielding, who committed him to NEWGATE. He was imprisoned in Newgate and tried at the next OLD BAILEY Sessions, where he was found guilty of this wanton murder. Patrick McCarty was hanged at the bottom of Bow Street, Covent Garden on 24 October 1760.

Good fortune did not smile upon McCarty, for had his execution not been scheduled for 24 October but merely a day later, he would have been reprieved under the general amnesty and pardon to criminals that followed the death in the early hours of the next morning of King George II, which according to ancient custom, his successor decreed.

McNAGHTEN, DANIEL

Daniel McNaghten (variously spelled McNaughten or McNaughton), described by his landlady as sullen and reserved, was a well off wood-turner from Glasgow, lodging at 7 Poplar Row, Newington. McNaghten spent a week skulking around the Whitehall area in 1843 then shot William Drummond, secretary to the Prime Minister, Sir Robert Peel, dead, in the *Salopian Coffee House*, Parliament Street, believing him to be the Prime Minister himself. It emerged at his trial that McNaghten had suffered for many years from delusions that the 'Jesuits' or the 'Tories' were conspiring to murder him and when he was in this deluded condition believed that anyone might be a persecutor. Concerns were raised about the BELLINGHAM case and the court was concerned not to repeat such a scandal by hanging a madman. The prosecution were so convinced by the evidence of McNaghten's severe condition that the judges stopped the trial and committed him to the Bethlehem Hospital (commonly known as Bedlam). Queen Victoria was concerned that madmen might be seen as licensed to take pot

Daniel McNaghten. Author's collection

shots at her Royal Person and demanded that the sentence be redefined as 'Guilty but Insane'. This resulted in the formulation of the McNAGHTEN RULES.

McNAGHTEN RULES, THE

The McNaghten Rules were introduced in 1843 after the tragic case of Daniel McNAGHTEN, a madman, who shot the Prime Minister, Sir Robert Peel's, secretary, William Drummond. Whereas for several decades insanity had been viewed by the courts that a madman was not guilty if it had been established that his crime was a direct result of his madness, the McNaghten Rules were a retrograde step in viewing the insane, harping back to the principles established in the early eighteenth century, that a madman was guilty of any crime he committed if he knew it to be wrong. These rules have been widely used in British courts

The trial of Daniel M'Naghten.
Author's collection

as the accepted definition of insanity in law. The rules were modified by the Homicide Act of 1957, to allow the concept of diminished responsibility and for a person to be convicted of manslaughter instead of murder, if abnormality of the mind was established at the time of the crime, sufficient to substantially impair responsibility for the act.

MACKAY, DONALD

In 1989, Donald Mackay murdered twenty-six-year-old prostitute Ann Petherick, who was last seen alive on 2 January. Following a visit to Mackay's Archway flat for sex on 17 February, by another prostitute, Rosemarie Saunders, police were called in. Mackay had tied Miss Saunders up and abused her in such a bestial fashion that she brought charges against him. In relation to that incident Mackay was eventually convicted of 'threats to kill, assault with intent to commit buggery, indecent assault and assault occasioning actual bodily harm'. When police went to Mackay's flat on 19 February they found Ann Petherick's decomposing body in a bin bag. No exact cause of death could be established due to the amount of decay. Mackay had killed before. In 1984 he was found guilty of manslaughter after killing a man with a sword. Found guilty of murder at the OLD BAILEY in December 1989, he was sentenced to life with a minimum tariff of twenty years. In January 2007, an appeal to have his sentence cut was dismissed. He was told that the twenty-year tariff does not mean that he will automatically be released in 2009. Only if he can convince the Parole Board he is no longer a danger to the public, will he be released on a perpetual 'life licence', which would see him returned to prison for the slightest offence.

MACKLIN, CHARLES

The Irish-born actor Charles Macklin (whose real name was McLaughlin), was descended from Terence McLaughlin, a landowner of County Down. In 1716 he joined a company of strolling players. Four years later he appeared in Bath and was engaged by Christopher Rich for the Lincoln's Inn Theatre. He was known as the Wild Irishman, noted for his joviality and excellent boxing skills. In 1732 he was engaged at Drury Lane, where he played secondary comic parts. Before he rose to greater heights, this hot-blooded and intemperate actor in May 1735, quarrelled with his fellow actor Thomas Hallam over a wig, in the scene-room at Drury Lane, where the actors used to warm themselves and this resulted in Hallam's death. Macklin was fortunate not to have been hanged for murder. Frances Asprey Congreve describes the event:

> Mr Macklin had not long been settled as an actor at Drury-Lane, when an incident occurred which had nearly been attended with fatal consequences to him, and which certainly impressed an unfavourable opinion of him in the minds of the public during the rest of his days. On the 10th of May, 1735, a new farce was to be performed, called Trick for Trick, written by Mr. Fabian, in which Mr. Macklin and Mr. Hallam both performed. In attiring for their respective characters, the latter gentleman had got possession of a wig belonging to the house, and which Mr. Macklin having performed in the preceding evening, he demanded the restoration of; with the demand, Hallam did not readily comply, and much foul language was exchanged by both parties. At length, Macklin, irritated at Hallam's non-compliance, and inflamed by the scurrility which passed between them, drove at him with a stick which he had in his hand, without any aim it is supposed, but unhappily with too fatal effect, as it entered the right eye of his opponent, penetrated the brain, and caused his death the next day.

Further notes from F A Congreve's account state that following the tragic event:

> Mr. Macklin immediately absconded, and did not take his trial until the 12th of December, when he surrendered himself at the Old Bailey, where he was found guilty of manslaughter. It appeared by the evidence to be the result of a hasty fit of passion, unpremeditated and repented as soon as done. On this occasion, Mr. Rich, Mr. Fleetwood, Mr. Quin, Mr. Ryan, Mr. Thomson, Mr. Mills, and several others, appeared as candidates for his character, and testified him to be a man of quiet and peaceable disposition. It was not, however, until the 31st January, 1736, that he returned to his station at the theatre, by the performance of Ramillie, in Fielding's Miser.

At his trial at the OLD BAILEY, many of the most renowned actors of the day showed their support for their fellow player, effectively committing perjury as they lied about his good character. He got off lightly, with a manslaughter verdict and was sentenced to be burned in the hand. Macklin's career went from strength to strength and he became a major player, working into extreme old age. He died on 11 July 1797, aged 97.

MALCOLM, SARAH

Twenty-two-year-old Sarah Malcolm was born in County Durham into a good family. Her father having spent the family money, Sarah moved to London, where she worked for a time at the *Black Horse* in Boswell Court near Temple Bar, a public house frequented by criminals and she fell into bad company. She then secured the position of laundress at some chambers in the Temple. There, at Tanfield Court, where amongst others Sarah worked for, lived Mrs Lydia Duncomb, variously described as being somewhere between sixty and eighty years old, a wealthy lady who was looked after by two servants, Elizabeth Harrison aged sixty and Ann Price aged seventeen. Sarah decided to rob the old lady and in the process of stripping the chambers of everything of value she could lay her hands on, she murdered Mrs Duncomb and her servants. Mrs Duncomb and the older servant were strangled. The servant girl's throat was slit. A silver tankard was found in Sarah's possession, its handle was smeared with blood. She was committed to NEWGATE, where a considerable number of gold and silver coins were found secreted in her clothing. At her trial at the OLD BAILEY on Friday 23 February, she tried to blame others for the murders, the jury did not believe her. She was hanged by John Hooper at Temple Gate near Fetter Lane on Wednesday 7 March 1733 on Newgate's portable scaffold. Parish records show that Sarah Malcolm was buried in St Sepulchre's churchyard on 10 March.

Sarah Malcolm as depicted by William Hogarth. Author's collection

MALTBY, CECIL

Mrs Alice Hilda Middleton was the wife of a merchant seaman, who was on a long voyage to the Far East. Mrs Middleton took lodgings while her husband was at sea and in the early summer of 1922 she went to lodge with Cecil Maltby, a forty-seven-year-old tailor, who lived above his shop at 24 Park Road, a street that runs from Lord's cricket ground to the top of Baker Street. Although Maltby had inherited his father's successful business, he had become a heavy drinker and allowed business to decline to the point of bankruptcy. Separated from his wife and children,

The execution of Sarah Malcolm. Author's collection

following Mrs Middleton's arrival he clearly gained some relief from his alcoholic despair, neglecting his business affairs even further to spend a great deal of time attending race meetings with her. Mrs Middleton was not seen alive again after August. When her husband returned from his sea voyage in December 1922 he reported her missing.

Police made enquiries, which led them to Maltby. He did not allow them entry into his living quarters but told them Mrs Middleton had left him on 15 August. The place smelled abominably, and all his utility services had been cut off. The police decided to watch the premises as neighbours informed them that Maltby had effectively barricaded himself in and would not allow anyone access, nor had he left the premises for months. Increasing complaints about the worsening sanitary conditions resulted in a health order being issued on 10 January 1923, which allowed the authorities to break in. The police entered the premises from both the front and rear of the shop. On reaching the first floor living quarters they heard a single shot. Maltby was found lying dead in a bedroom shot through the mouth. The entire place was in a disgustingly filthy state. Worse still, in the kitchen, was a bath that had been boarded over and used as a dining table. Inside the bath, wrapped in a sheet, were found the decomposing remains of Mrs Middleton. Attached to the sheet was a note:

> *In Memory of darling Pat, who committed suicide on 24 August 1922, 8.30 am.*

Maltby had left several letters implying that on 24 August he had struggled with Mrs Middleton who was threatening to shoot herself and during the struggle to take the gun from her it went off. However, a post-mortem examination of Alice Middleton's remains revealed that she had three bullet wounds in her back, and the bullets had struck her body while she was in either a sitting or lying position. At the inquest on the body of Mrs Middleton the jury returned a verdict of murder and *felo de se*, stating that Cecil Maltby was in a sound state of health and mind and took his own life to avoid the consequences of his act.

MANNINGS, THE

Maria de Roux was born in Switzerland. She came to England to work as a lady's maid and shortly had an affair with fifty-year-old Irishman Patrick O'Conner, a London docks exciseman and money lender, who had built up a considerable fortune. After she met twenty-eight-year-old Frederick Manning, a guard on the Great Western Railway, who was the same age as herself, she married him in May 1847, although she kept in touch with O'Conner. After Manning was dismissed on suspicion of being involved in two robberies on trains, their financial difficulties began. Having moved to 3 Minver Place, Bermondsey, the Mannings invited O'Conner to dine with them on 8 August 1849. They murdered him and buried his body beneath a large flagstone in the kitchen. They then went to his lodgings and stole money and some share certificates. Not long after police had visited them to find out if they knew anything about O'Conner's whereabouts, the couple absconded in different directions. He to Jersey, she to Edinburgh. When police returned to Minver Place again they made a search and discovered O'Conner's body buried in quicklime. He had been shot through the head and hit with a blunt instrument. The couple had not covered their tracks very well and were quickly apprehended and taken to HORSEMONGER LANE GAOL. At their trial at the OLD BAILEY it was revealed that Maria Manning had shot O'Conner and her

The discovery of Patrick O'Conner's body in the Mannings' kitchen at 3 Minver Place, Bermondsey.
Author's collection

husband had finished him off with a crowbar. The Mannings were hanged at Horsemonger Lane Gaol on 13 November 1849 before a crowd of 50,000. The black bombazine dress Maria Manning wore at her execution created such an unfavourable impression that sales of the material were severely reduced for a considerable time afterwards.

MARCHANT, WILLIAM JOHN

Eighteen-year-old William Marchant worked as footman to magistrate Henry Edgell, at 21 Cadogan Place, Chelsea. On Friday 17 May 1839, under-housemaid Elizabeth Paynton was found with her throat cut in the drawing room, a razor lay by her side. When it was discovered Marchant had absconded suspicion immediately fell on him. On Sunday 19 May, Marchant gave himself up to a police officer in Hounslow. Although he appeared to be terrified at what he had done and on the journey back to London fancied he heard the murdered woman at his back, he never gave any explanation why he had killed Elizabeth Paynton. Marchant was tried at the Central Criminal Court, OLD BAILEY on Friday 21 June and pleaded guilty to the indictment of murder. He was hanged outside NEWGATE on 8 July 1839.

MARSHALL, CLARENCE JOHN

On Sunday 27 October 1903, the East End was stunned at the news of the terrible tragedy at 89, Griggs Road, Walthamstow. Clarence Marshall had once been a chef in fairly good circumstances, working in America and Canada for several years, returning to London in 1899. He married in 1900 and opened a confectionery shop in Woolwich, which failed. He then took a job at the Woolwich Arsenal. In July 1902, having given up his job, he and his wife Amelia moved to Griggs Road, Walthamstow, where their daughter, Elsie, was born in December that year. Marshall took out a pedlar's certificate in April 1903, since when he had been scraping a living by selling laces and such like in the street. However, he had been so hard up that he and his family were living chiefly on handouts from the Wesleyan church he attended.

At a quarter to seven on Sunday morning a neighbour heard a thud and then a scream, and the scurrying of footsteps in the passage. Mrs Marshall could be heard shrieking in agony, as she pitifully called out: 'Oh, Almighty God – my baby, my baby.' A gurgling sound and a thud followed and then there was silence. A

Main Picture: Mr Friend and other neighbours break into the bedroom and make a horrific discovery. Top right: Mrs Marshall, dressed only in her nightdress, lay huddled against the wall. The Illustrated Police News

few moments later there was a cry of: 'Fire!' As neighbours broke down the door, they tripped over Mrs Marshall's lifeless body in the smoke-filled passageway. Her throat was slashed and there were three stab wounds to her chest. On the hearthrug in the front room lay the baby, her head severed all but for a shred of skin. On the bed lay Marshall. He had murdered the baby, then his wife, lit several fires using paraffin, in an attempt to burn down the house, then cut his own throat. By his side lay a long, broad-bladed knife. There was an open bible in the room, with several passages heavily underlined. All around the room were illuminated texts. They were on the walls, on the mantelpiece and even on the door. Above the bed was hung the motto *God is Love*.

At the inquest, one witness told of a letter, which he picked up and began to read, but it was lost in the flames. He remembered seeing the words: 'No food.' At the time of this carnage two ducks were roasting on a spit over the fire. A list of articles found on the premises was read out. It included three ducks, two cooked, one uncooked, a quantity of bacon, tea, sugar, milk, biscuits, potatoes and butter. The jury returned a verdict, 'That Amelia Marshall and her daughter, Elsie, were wilfully murdered by Clarence John Marshall, who afterwards committed suicide, and that at the time Marshall was suffering from a fit of insanity.'

MARSHALL HALL, SIR EDWARD (barrister)

Born in Brighton, the son of an attorney, Sir Edward Marshall Hall, KC (1858-1927), known as the Great Defender, had a formidable reputation as an orator. He was admitted to the bar in 1888 and served as a Unionist MP for Southport (1900-06) and as a Conservative for Toxteth (1910-16). Some said of him had he chosen to enter that profession he had the makings of a great actor. His courtroom antics turned him into a popular hero and he was one of the best-known legal figures in England. He built his reputation defending in many notorious murder cases, some of his clients being acquitted even though the evidence against them was seemingly incontrovertible. Some of his most notable cases were: defending Robert Wood (CAMDEN TOWN MURDER, THE) 1907; Edward Lawrence, 1909; the SEDDONS, 1912; GEORGE JOSEPH SMITH (The Brides in the Bath Murderer), 1915; Ronald Light (the Green Bicycle Murder) 1919; Harold Greenwood, 1920 and Marie-Marguerite Fahmy (FAHMY CASE), 1923. Marshall Hall's marriage shortly after he graduated from

Sir Edward Marshall Hall.
Author's collection

Cambridge to Ethel Moon was a disaster. She was unfaithful to him on their honeymoon in Paris. The couple soon parted and Ethel died young. He never married again and found consolation in his work. He died aged sixty-nine in 1927. His career has been the subject of several films and radio and TV programmes.

MARWOOD, RONALD HENRY

On 14 December 1958, in the early days of the 'Teddy Boy' era, Ronald Marwood, a twenty-five-year-old scaffolder, was celebrating his first wedding anniversary. He lived with his twenty-year-old wife Rosalie, in Huntingdon Street, Islington. Trouble flared up between two rival gangs, the Angel Mob and the Finsbury Park Lot, outside Eugene Gray's Dancing Academy at 133 Seven Sisters Road near that part of Holloway known as Nag's Head. Amongst other weapons, knives bottles and knuckledusters were used. When matters got out of hand, the police intervened. While 6ft 5in, twenty-three-year-old police constable Raymond Henry Summers was arresting his best friend, Marwood was said to have pulled a 10-inch knife out and stabbed him in the back. The policeman died of his injuries.

Eleven youths were charged with brawling but Marwood, who denied any involvement was released. However, he

Evening Standard. Author's collection

attracted attention to himself when he disappeared. The killing of a policeman was a very serious matter indeed and Marwood's unexplained absence from home threw suspicion his way. He hid out with some friends in Chalk Farm. The police issued a picture on 3 January 1959 and he gave himself up on 27 January, when he walked into a police station and allegedly admitted: 'I did stab the copper that night.' This claim was later denied by Marwood who insisted the police 'put down things' he did not say. At his trial which took place at the OLD BAILEY in March 1959, Marwood said he heard police constable Summers telling the brawlers to break it up and he struck out at the officer intending to push him away. He also said he did not know he had a knife in his hand. It transpired that on the night of the murder during his anniversary celebrations Marwood visited various pubs where he consumed ten pints of brown ale. The defence claimed there was no evidence connecting the accused man with the fatal blow but if in the excitement of the fight he did stab the constable, whilst his brain was clouded with drink, then the verdict should be one of manslaughter. On 19 March, Ronald Marwood was convicted of the capital murder of a policeman and became the first person to be sentenced to death under the section of the Homicide Act of 1957 that protected police officers and warders. He was hanged at PENTONVILLE on Friday 8 May 1959. There is a widely held belief in pockets of North London communities that Marwood was in fact entirely innocent of the killing of PC Summers – the alleged real killer being one of Marwood's close associates, who later achieved national fame and indeed celebrity status more than two decades after Marwood was hanged.

MARWOOD, WILLIAM (executioner)

William Marwood (1820-83), a cobbler by trade, was appointed hangman in 1874. Marwood did not like to be referred to as a hangman but as executioner. He looked down on his predecessors, taking a more scientific approach to hanging the condemned. He would point out to anyone who used the word hangman when referring to himself that Calcraft, his predecessor throttled the condemned, whereas he executed them. This claim was not without foundation as he took great lengths to ensure that the condemned met a swift and painless end. Being aware that previously, even after the introduction of 'the drop', many were strangled by the rope, sometimes surviving and writhing in agony for a considerable time before they died, Marwood experimented with a series of lengths of drop designed to break the convict's neck, or at the very least dislocate the vertebrae in the neck resulting in loss of sensation. The prisoner's weight had also to be taken

William Marwood was appointed executioner at Newgate in 1874 on the retirement of his predecessor, William Calcraft. He served as the nation's official executioner until he retired in 1883, and found the key to successful hanging was the 'long drop'.
Author's collection

into account. If a drop was too short then strangulation was often the result, whereas if a drop was too long then this could result in decapitation. His calculations proved successful for the most part. The correct length of drop would ensure that the prisoner's neck was broken, usually resulting in instantaneous death. The drop had been developed more than a century before Marwood's appointment but had seldom been used to its full potential, to ensure a swift and painless death. In part this was because many law-makers were of the opinion that a slow, painful and excruciating death on the scaffold was a far greater deterrent. Until Marwood's time, when he introduced the long drop, the breaking of a neck during execution was usually more by accident than design. Marwood also invented a new form of noose that involved fixing a metal eye through one end of the rope and drawing the other through it, which replaced the slip knot used previously. Marwood was proud of his calling and on being questioned whether his process was satisfactory, he replied that he heard 'no complaints'.

MASON, ALEXANDER CAMPBELL

Alexander Campbell 'Scottie' Mason, was a deserter from the Canadian armed forces. On the evening of 9 May 1923, Scottie aged twenty-two was allegedly seen struggling with taxi driver Jacob Dickey in Baytree Road, Brixton. Three shots were fired and the gunman escaped over the fence into the back gardens of Acre Lane. By the side of the dying taxi driver a distinctive gold-topped walking stick incorporating a pencil case had been left. It was later identified as the property of a petty-thief called James Vivian, who lived with his girlfriend, prostitute Hetty Colquhoun in Pimlico. Vivian acknowledged the stick as his but said he had lent it to his friend Scottie Mason. Mason confirmed this and told police a story that was initially confirmed by Vivian and his girlfriend. He said he and Vivian had planned to rob a house in Brixton and had organised for a bent taxi driver to pick them up. When a different taxi turned up and a young man got out shots had been fired and he and Vivian had fled. Vivian later changed his story claiming a stomach upset had prevented him joining Mason. Mason was tried at the OLD BAILEY in July 1923 with Vivian as chief prosecution witness. Although the jury found him guilty of murder and sentence of death was duly pronounced, the Home Secretary reprieved him, as he would not hang a man on such accomplice's lies. His sentence was commuted to life imprisonment. He was released in 1937. Scottie Mason died an honourable death serving in the Merchant Navy during World War Two.

MASSET, LOUISE (OR LOUISA) JOSEPHINE

In 1899, Louise Masset, the daughter of a Frenchman and an English woman, lodged with her sister at 29 Bethune Road, Stoke Newington. Aged thirty-six and unmarried, she was an attractive looking woman who earned her living either as a piano teacher or as a governess. She had a four-year-old son, Manfred Louis, the result of an affair she had in France but the father's identity was never revealed, although according to the child's foster mother, Miss Gentle, he regularly sent money to support the boy. Manfred was lodged separately with Helen Gentle, in Clyde Road, Tottenham. Louise began an affair with a nineteen-year-old French student Eudore Lucas but after he found out about little Manfred his ardour waned and Louise decided to get rid of what she clearly regarded as an unwanted encumbrance, in order to retain Eudore's affections.

She informed Miss Gentle that his father was going to take over Manfred's upbringing in France and collected him on the morning of 27 October, along with a parcel containing his clothes. Louise Masset was last seen with her son at London Bridge station. Later that same day his battered and naked body was found wrapped in a black shawl in the ladies' lavatory on Platform No. 3 at Dalston Junction station. Nearby was a bloodstained stone that had been used to kill him. After reading a report about the dead child in a newspaper, Miss Gentle came forward and identified him. When questioned by police Louise Masset told them that she had handed her son over to two ladies at London Bridge, a Mrs Browning and her associate who were opening a new orphanage in Chelsea. She said she had handed over the boy and £12 to the two women, but could not produce a receipt, nor could the women be traced. She had then caught a train to Brighton, where she spent the weekend in the company of her lover. The weight of evidence was stacked against her. A paper parcel containing Manfred's clothes was found in the waiting room at Brighton station and the black shawl in which the boy's body had been found was identified as having been bought by Louise Masset at a shop in Stoke Newington. Even more damning was the stone that had been used to kill little Manfred. It fitted a hole in the rockery at 29 Bethune Road.

The public were outraged by this uncaring mother's cruel act, compounded by the fact that having killed her son she had gone immediately to the arms of her lover. They could not find a grain of sympathy for her and there was no outcry when she was hanged at NEWGATE on 9 January 1900. Louise Masset had the dubious honour of being the first person to be hanged in Britain in the twentieth century. Her executioner was James BILLINGTON.

MEEK, ROBERT GEORGE (JOE)

Legendary homosexual record producer Joe Meek was born in 1929 in Newent, Gloucestershire. After his stint of national service as a radar technician he was briefly a television engineer before becoming a recording engineer at IBC Studios, then going to work for the independent record producer Landsdowne, where he engineered some of Lonnie Donegan's early hits. He began to write music and decided to branch out on his own. Meek is acknowledged as one of the world's first and most imaginative independent record producers. He built his own studio in a rented flat above Shenton's travel goods and handbag shop at 304 Holloway Road, where he wrote and produced possibly his most notable work, *Telstar* (1962) for The Tornadoes, which has the distinction of being the first No.1 record by a British group in the USA. He was obsessed with the late Buddy Holly and the occult. Meek had bouts of paranoia, which may have been fuelled by his drug taking. During a period fraught with self-doubt and financial uncertainty for Meek he committed murder. On the morning of 3 February 1967, the eighth anniversary of Buddy Holly's death, Meek killed his landlady Mrs Violet Shenton with a shotgun before turning the gun on himself.

MERCIER, FRANCIS

Francis Mercier, otherwise known as Louis De Butte, a Frenchman, resided in London and was retained as an interpreter to his fellow countryman Jacques Mondroyte, a jeweller and watchmaker of Paris, who treated him as a friend. Monsieur Mondroyte journeyed to London in order to find a

A present-day view of 304 Holloway Road. The plaque above the shop sign was unveiled in March 2007, it reads:

> *JOE MEEK*
> *RECORD PRODUCER*
> *THE TELSTAR MAN*
> *1929-1967*
> *PIONEER OF SOUND*
> *RECORDING TECHNOLOGY*
> *LIVED WORKED AND*
> *DIED HERE*

The Author

market for the different articles he manufactured and the stock he had brought with him consisted of curios and costly articles. It seems that Mercier had for some time planned to kill his employer and enrich himself with his valuable property. To that end he had a weapon especially fashioned of a singular construction: it resembled an Indian tomahawk.

On his arrival in London, Monsieur Mondroyte took lodgings in Prince's Street. One autumn evening in 1777, he invited Mercier to his lodgings. They played cards, sang French songs and drank wine. As soon as all the other inhabitants of the house had retired, Monsieur Mondroyte by now addled by a copious quantity of wine proved easy prey to his assailant. Mercier attacked him with the weapon he had concealed in his greatcoat, striking him on the head several times until he was dead. He then put the body in one of the trunks in which the owner had brought his merchandise. Mercier then proceeded to plunder the apartment. He returned next day and asked if Mr Mercier had left on his journey yet. He pretended that he had proposed a trip to the country. The proprietors assumed that he had left before they had risen. Mercier continued to call for several days to ask if his friend had returned and having aroused suspicion that all might not be well with their lodger, a ladder was procured to gain entry into his locked chamber. His putrefying body was found crammed in the trunk.

A warrant was issued for Mercier's arrest. In his lodgings were found sixteen gold watches, many diamond rings, some gold trinkets of great value and seventy-five guineas. Mercier confessed to the murder. He was convicted at the OLD BAILEY on 6 December and hanged on 8 December 1777 in Prince's Street, opposite Swallow Street, Westminster, as close as practicable to where the murder was committed.

METROPOLITAN POLICE ACT 1829

In 1812, 1818 and 1822 Parliamentary committees investigated the question of maintaining law and order and considered the matter of crime and policing. However, it was not until 1828 when Sir Robert Peel took charge of matters that it paved the way for the setting up of an organised police force throughout London. The Metropolitan Police Act 1829 established London's Metropolitan Police Service and Sir Charles Rowan and Richard Mayne were appointed Justices of the Peace in charge of the force. Constables soon became known as 'Peelers' and more commonly 'Bobbies' in honour of Sir Robert Peel.

In 1839, the Corporation of London agreed to reform its own police force along modern lines in order that it should not be amalgamated with the Metropolitan Police Force. The City of London Police is a direct successor of the Watch, which has its origins in the thirteenth century. The City of London Police is distinguished from all other British police forces, which have silver-coloured badges, by their distinctive gold badges. Officers are also distinguished from other forces by their red and white chequered sleeve and cap bands (the colours of the City of London).

METYARDS, THE

Sarah Metyard and Sarah Morgan Metyard, her daughter, were milliners, in Bruton Street, Hanover Square. In 1758, the Metyards had five parish apprentice girls in their service, from different workhouses, among whom were Anne Naylor and her sister. Anne was a sickly girl and unable to carry out her tasks as quickly as the other girls. This caused the Metyards to ill-treat her and after a while she absconded. Being brought back she was locked in an upper room and allowed only a little bread and water each day. Anne tried to escape again but was brought back by the daughter and forced onto the bed and while the mother held her down the daughter beat her with a broom handle. She was then tied up with a cord and fastened to the door handle in such a way that she could neither sit or lie down. She was left in that position for three days, but was permitted to go to bed at night. The other girls were called to work in an adjoining room in order that they might be deterred from disobedience. Having been given neither food nor water for three days and two nights Anne was weak and unable to walk. On the fourth day her speech failed and within hours she died. Anne was still tied to the door. The other girls were greatly alarmed and called out: 'Miss Sally! Miss Sally! Nanny does not move.' The daughter came upstairs and said: If she does not move, I will make her move.' She then proceeded to beat the dead girl on the head with the heel of her shoe. Mother and daughter tried to administer some hartshorn drops. They ordered the other girls downstairs and took the body to the garret. Afterwards they told the girls that Nanny had been in a fit but was perfectly recovered. As a further act of subterfuge they took plates of food upstairs to Nanny for the next few days. Four days after the murder they locked the body in a box and left the door to the room open. They told one of the girls to go and fetch Nanny for her dinner and to tell her if she behaved well in future she would be allowed to join the other girls. As Nanny was not to be found a search of the house was organised at the end of which the Metyards said Nanny had run away.

When Anne's little sister said she didn't think she had run away as many of her possessions were still in her room, the Metyards killed her and disposed of her body. As for Anne's body, that remained in the locked box in the garret. The stench became so overpowering that the Metyards realised the body must be disposed of. On Christmas Day 1764, they cut it into pieces. The head and trunk were tied in one piece of cloth, the limbs in another, with the exception of one hand which had a missing finger, amputated some time previously. After the girls had gone to bed Mrs Metyard put the hand into the fire. The two bundles were disposed of by a grate leading to the common sewer at Chick Lane. At about midnight some body parts were discovered by a watchman who fetched a constable. Mr Umfreville, the coroner, concluded that the body parts must have been taken from a churchyard for the use of some surgeon.

For four years the murders remained undiscovered. As the daughter grew to maturity she took to arguing with her mother who was also mistreating her. After one particularly savage beating, she threatened to kill herself and to give information against her mother as a murderer. Eventually the overseers of Tottenham parish got to hear about the murders of the Naylor sisters and mother and daughter were committed to the GATEHOUSE. They were later transferred to NEWGATE, tried at the OLD BAILEY and hanged at TYBURN on Monday 19 July 1768. The mother was in a state of high anxiety when she was put in the cart and remained laying down throughout the entire journey to Tyburn; and was completely insensible as she was hanged. The daughter wept throughout the journey to the scaffold. After hanging for an hour the Metyards' bodies were taken by hearse to Surgeons' Hall and exposed to the curious eyes of the public, before being dissected.

MILSOM AND FOWLER

On the morning of 14 February, 1896 seventy-nine-year-old retired engineer Henry Smith, was found by his gardener, Charles Webber, bound, gagged and brutally murdered, in the kitchen of his imposing house, Muswell Lodge, situated in

Tetherdown, Muswell Hill. He had been tied up with strips of cloth, cut with two penknives left nearby, the safe had been refiled and there were signs of forced entry through the kitchen window. Significantly, as would later be shown, a broken toy lantern left in the kitchen sink, was to prove crucial in the detection of the culprits. The lantern had multi-coloured bull's-eye glasses, and was similar to the type used by railway guards. There were several distinctive marks on the lantern indicating that it had been repaired. The murder victim, although attended by a servant during the day, chose to live alone. He had been a widower for twenty-four years and despite his advanced years, was a strong and remarkably fit man. Very security conscious he took various precautions regarding the protection of his home, which included a spring gun,

Henry Smith, of Muswell Lodge, Tetherdown, Muswell Hill, seen here at Muswell Lodge in 1883. Author's collection

Henry Fowler attacks Albert Milsom in the dock at the Old Bailey. The Daily Graphic

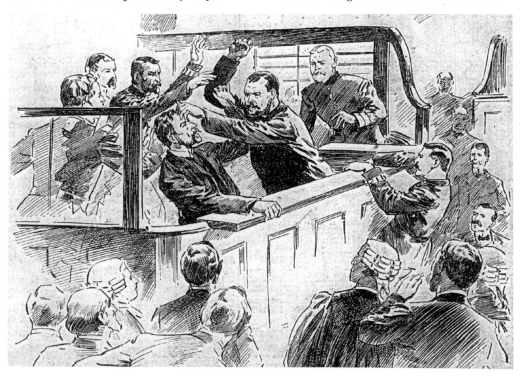

activated by trip wires in the garden. Unfortunately, the criminals had not activated the gun and all signs pointed to a burglary that had gone disastrously wrong.

The police worked on the premise that they were looking for two men and the behaviour of two known felons immediately following the crime left the police with few doubts that they were the suspects they were looking for. Thirty-two-year-old Albert Milsom, although not by nature a violent man, had already been convicted of a long list of crimes, mostly burglary. He lived with his wife Emily and their two children at his mother-in-law's house, along with fifteen-year-old Henry Miller, Emily's brother, at 133 Southman Street, Kensal Town. Milsom had been for sometime associated with another Kensal Town resident, Henry Fowler. Thirty-one-year-old Fowler had a long record and was known to be violent. Fowler had been released from prison on parole on 16 January. Fowler's renewed association with Milsom had been noticed by the local police and their disappearance drew further attention to themselves. Once Henry Miller had identified the toy lantern as his own, pointing out the repairs he had undertaken himself, the police knew they had their men. Milsom and Fowler managed to evade their pursuers until Saturday 10 April, having travelled to various parts of the country as part of a travelling show. They were captured in Bath and brought back to London and tried at the OLD BAILEY on 19 May before Mr Justice Hawkins. The evidence was heavily stacked against them. This case is notable for the violent outburst that came as the jury returned with their guilty verdict. Fowler flung himself across the dock at his accomplice and tried to strangle him, very nearly succeeding in saving executioner James Berry the job of hanging him. Milsom and Fowler were hanged at NEWGATE on Wednesday 10 June with Whitechapel murderer William SEAMAN between them. This was the last triple execution at Newgate.

MORGAN, THOMAS

Fifty-six-year-old Thomas Morgan was the proprietor of a coffee house at 17 Amhurst Road, Hackney. He had living quarters above his business premises, where he lived with his wife of four years, Emma, aged forty-eight and her son from a previous marriage Arthur George Jennings, aged fourteen years and eleven months. As well as the Morgans' domestic servants, there were also two lodgers living there.

On Monday 23 May 1893, Maud Austin, who worked as a domestic servant for the Morgans, arrived back from her day off at about 10pm. She said goodnight to her employers and went to bed with her fellow servant. A little over three hours later, Maud was awakened in the early hours of Tuesday morning, by the ringing of the bell in their room. On going downstairs she heard her master say: 'Oh' several times. The door to Mr and Mrs Morgan's room was locked but she noticed Arthur Jennings' door was ajar and on looking inside saw his lifeless body lying on the bed covered in blood. The lodgers appeared on the scene but declined to become involved, so Maud rushed out into the street and brought back Police Sergeant Albert Cornish, who on observing Arthur Jennings' body went to the Morgans' bedroom door and forced it open. Mrs Morgan was lying dead on the bed. Sergeant Cornish noticed a gunshot wound in her left cheek. Thomas Morgan was lying on his back next to his wife, groaning and in considerable pain. It was later discovered that Morgan had shot himself penetrating his bowels in several places. He died of his injuries in the German Hospital.

On Saturday 12 May 1893, the three victims of the tragedy were buried in three separate strangers' graves in Ilford Cemetery. The inquest on the bodies of Mr and Mrs Morgan and Arthur Jennings was held at Hackney Coroner's Court on Thursday 1 June

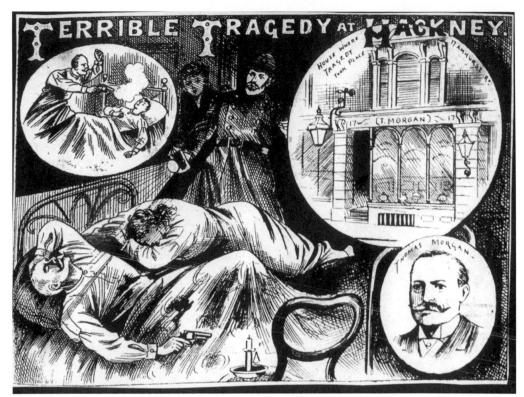

1893. Deputy coroner Alfred Hodgkinson stated that he thought the evidence would establish the fact that the boy died first, then the woman, and that it was after her death that the man received the ultimate fatal injuries. Thomas Morgan's sister said that her brother had enjoyed good health up to 17 July 1892, when he was seized with paralysis and the condition had affected his brain. The jury returned a verdict of wilful murder against Thomas Morgan in the cases of Mrs Morgan and her son, and they found that he afterwards committed suicide while mentally deranged.

[Main picture] *Sergeant Cornish shines his torch on the body of Emma Morgan and the recumbent Thomas Morgan, while Maud Austin looks on.* [Top left] *Thomas Morgan shoots his stepson Arthur Jennings.* [Top right] *Thomas Morgan's coffee house and the family home.* [Bottom right] *The murderer and suicide victim, Thomas Morgan.*

The Illustrated Police News

MORRISON, STINIE

Stinie Morrison, alias Morris Stein, was a Ukranian Jew convicted in 1911 of the murder of another Russian Jew, East End property owner forty-eight-year-old Leon Beron, this case being known as the Clapham Common Murder.

On Sunday 1 January 1911, PC Joseph Mumford came across Beron's body at 8.10am, on Clapham Common, near a path north-west of the bandstand. A post-mortem examination at Battersea Mortuary revealed that death was as a result of a blow on the head with a horseshoe-shaped blunt instrument. There were other superficial

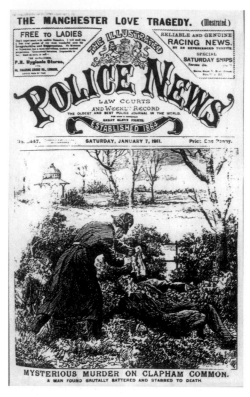

THE MANCHESTER LOVE TRAGEDY. (Illustrated)

FREE to LADIES

RELIABLE AND GENUINE
RACING NEWS.
BY AN EXPERIENCED TIPSTER

SPECIAL
SATURDAY SNIPS.

THE ILLUSTRATED

POLICE NEWS

LAW COURTS
AND WEEKLY RECORD
THE OLDEST AND BEST POLICE JOURNAL IN THE WORLD.
GREAT GLOVE FIGHTS.
ESTABLISHED 1864

No. 447.   SATURDAY, JANUARY 7, 1911.   Price One Penny.

MYSTERIOUS MURDER ON CLAPHAM COMMON.
A MAN FOUND BRUTALLY BATTERED AND STABBED TO DEATH.

Police Constable Joseph Mumford discovers the body of Leon Beron on Clapham Common, on Sunday 1 January 1911.
The Illustrated Police News

scratches to the face and three stab wounds to the chest. Coming at a time when foreign anarchist activities were rife throughout London, two crudely carved cuts resembling the letter S, one on each cheek, were later thought to be for the Russian word *spic*, which meant a double agent. Beron had been seen the previous evening in the company of handsome thirty-year-old Stinie Morrison. Circumstantial evidence led police to arrest Morrison who upon being charged said: 'All I can say is that it's a lie.'

Stinie Morrison's nine-day trial began in the No. 1 Court at the OLD BAILEY on 6 March 1911. Although the judge in his summing-up directed the jury to acquit on the grounds there was no direct evidence against Morrison, the fact that during the trial they had learned that he was a habitual criminal, a liar and a libertine did not go in his favour. They found Morrison guilty in just thirty-five minutes. In passing sentence of death Mr Justice Darling having delivered the words: 'May God have mercy on your soul,' Morrison replied: 'I decline such mercy. I do not believe there is a God in Heaven either.' Morrison's execution was fixed for 20 April. However, Home Secretary Winston Churchill commuted the sentence to life imprisonment on 13 April in view of the considerable disquiet about the verdict. Stinie Morrison died at Parkhurst Prison on 24 January 1921, having starved himself. He protested his innocence to the last.

MÜLLER, FRANZ

On Saturday 9 July 1864, seventy-year-old Thomas Briggs, chief clerk at the bankers Messrs Robarts & Co of Lombard Street boarded a train on the North London Railway which left Fenchurch Street station for Chalk Farm at 9.50pm. He was on his way home to 5 Clapton Square, near to the Hackney or Hackney Wick (Victoria Park) stations. He travelled in a first class carriage, Carriage No.69. The train arrived at Hackney at 10.11pm. Two bank clerks got into empty carriage No.69 and found blood on the seats and on the window. The guard was summoned and he found a hat, a walking stick and a small black leather bag. He took these away and the carriage was locked. About the same time Mr Briggs was found barely alive lying in the 6ft way between the Up and Down lines near Victoria Park, by two railway workers. Help was summoned from the nearby *Mitford Castle* public house to where Mr Briggs was carried and received medical attention. He had several severe wounds to the head apparently inflicted by a blunt instrument to ferocious effect. He died of his injuries twenty-seven hours later.

It was established that Mr Briggs had been wearing gold-rimmed spectacles and a gold watch and chain. They were missing. The facts of the murder and the object, robbery, were thus conclusively proved. Of the items found in the railway carriage, the stick and bags were his but not the hat. It was established that the hat had been bought at Walker's, a hatters in Crawford Street, Marylebone, while within a few days Mr Briggs's gold chain was traced to a jeweller's at 55 Cheapside. The jeweller, Mr Death had given another in exchange for another to a man thought to be a foreigner. In little more than a week after the murder, following newspaper reports a cabman came forward and made a statement which drew suspicion to a German, Franz Müller, who had been the cabman's lodger. A photograph of Müller was shown to Mr Death. He identified Müller as the man who had exchanged Mr Briggs's chain. The cabman swore that he had bought the very hat found in the carriage for Müller. It was a distinctive hat of a new short design (a short top-hat instead of the usual stovepipe).

Franz Müller. Author's collection

Franz Müller, aged twenty-five, was from Saxe-Weimar. In his native country he had been apprenticed as a gunsmith and he had arrived in England in 1862 hoping to find work. Unable to get a job as a gunsmith he found employment as a tailor in Threadneedle Street. At the time of the murder Müller was lodging at 16 Park Terrace, which was part of the Old Ford Road, Victoria Park. There was no mystery about his departure: he had gone to Canada by the *Victoria* sailing ship, starting from London docks and bound for New York. Two detectives accompanied by the jeweller and cabman, went to Liverpool and took the first steamer, the *City of Manchester*, across the Atlantic. It arrived in New York before Müller's sailing ship. When the *Victoria* docked Müller was identified and arrested. Mr Briggs's watch was found in his luggage and Müller was wearing Mr Briggs's hat which he had had cut down.

Müller was brought back to England and his trial followed at the next Sessions at the Central Criminal Court, within the OLD BAILEY, beginning on 27 October 1864 and lasting for three days. He was found guilty of murder and hanged outside NEWGATE by William CALCRAFT on 14 November 1864. This case is notable for being Britain's first railway murder.

MURPHY, FREDERICK

In 1937, Frederick Murphy lived in Islington at 57a Colebrooke Row and worked for Harding's, a furnishing company at 22 The Green, Islington. On 14 May he informed his employers that he had discovered the body of a woman in the cellar of their warehouse. When the police arrived to investigate, Murphy had already left the scene.

The dead woman was identified as a well known prostitute, Rosina Field. She habitually took a room at 13 Duncan Terrace and had last done so on 11 May.

When Frederick Murphy turned up at Poplar police station the next day he had bloodstains on his clothes. Declaring himself completely innocent and wishing to clear himself he made a long statement. He told the police he had been on a pub crawl at the time Field was killed and listed various pubs he had visited. This statement was later contradicted after witnesses said they had seen Murphy enter the warehouse with Rosina Field, at the time he claimed to have been drinking elsewhere. This was not the only time that Murphy had been linked to a murdered prostitute. He had been accused of murder previously when he had been seen in the company of Katherine Peck, known as 'Carbolic Kate', shortly before she had been found in Aldgate with her throat cut. On that occasion Murphy had been fortunate as the main witness for the prosecution disappeared. This time however, he was not so lucky. He was found guilty of the murder of Rosina Field and hanged at PENTONVILLE on 17 August 1926.

N

NEWGATE GAOL

Prisoners were held at Newgate from Norman times until 1902. There were four gaols all called Newgate built on the site of today's Central Criminal Court, in the street known as OLD BAILEY. The first, built *c.*1130, lasted until 1423. The

Newgate Gaol, Old Bailey c.1850.
Author's collection

second, referred to as Whittington's Newgate, lasted from 1423 until 1666. The third, from 1666 to 1770 and finally the last Newgate was built between 1770-74 and served as a place of incarceration and, from 9 December 1783 until 6 May 1902, a place of execution. The grim corridor that connected Newgate to the adjoining Sessions House, officially known as Birdcage Walk but more commonly referred to as Dead Man's Walk, was where executed prisoners were buried beneath the flagstones. The initial letters of those buried there were carved into the wall, marking the spot beneath which they lay. Shortly after the last execution the prison closed and the scaffold was removed to PENTONVILLE. The remains of the ninety-seven executed prisoners recorded to have been buried in Dead Man's Walk, were lifted and reburied in the City of London Cemetery. Some of the dressed stone of this final Newgate was incorporated into the building of today's Central Criminal Court, Old Bailey.

NILSEN, DENNIS

During the first week in February 1983, Dyno-Rod, a drain cleaning company, was called to Cranley Gardens, Muswell Hill to attend to blocked drains. When an inspection cover adjacent to No. 23 was lifted, pieces of rotting flesh were clogging the pipes. 23 Cranley Gardens was owned by an Indian woman who lived in New Delhi. The house was divided into flats and bedsits, managed by estate agents in Golders Green. The top floor flat had been occupied since 1981 by thirty-seven-year-old Dennis Nilsen, a mild mannered civil servant, who had formerly served in the Army as a cook and on his discharge had briefly joined the police force. Once it had been established that the body parts were human the police paid Nilsen a visit. When asked if he knew anything about the human body parts he enthusiastically poured out a horror story of how he had killed three men in his flat, dismembered them and boiled their heads in a pan on the kitchen stove. He had flushed pieces of flesh down the lavatory, which over a period of time had resulted in the drains becoming blocked. Body parts were found in black dustbin bags and three severed heads were found in a wardrobe. Nilsen admitted that at his previous home at 195 Melrose Avenue, Cricklewood, where he lived in the ground floor flat from 1976 to 1981, he had committed another twelve murders, the first being on the last day of 1978. Nilsen often picked up men for casual sex. It transpired that in fifteen cases he could not bear the thought of being left alone, so he had 'killed for company', strangling his victims, often leaving them seated in the chair, presumably until the stench of decomposition urged him to dispose of their bodies. Most of Nilsen's victims were drifters. Some of his victims were identified as Malcolm Barlow, Martyn Duffey, John Howlett, Kenneth Ockenden, Steve Sinclair and Billy Sutherland. Nilsen's trial began in the No. 1 Court at the OLD BAILEY on 24 October 1983. At its conclusion on Thursday 3 November the jury took twenty-four hours to find him guilty. He was sentenced to life imprisonment with a recommendation that he serve at least twenty-five years. On Thursday 9 November 2006, the London *Evening Standard* was able to reveal the name of Nilsen's first victim, as a result of a letter they had received from his prison cell. Nilsen disclosed he had picked up fourteen-year-old Stephen Holmes in a Cricklewood pub in December 1978 and fearing he might leave him alone again had killed him.

O

O'CONNELL, MARTIN – see
BALCOMBE STREET SIEGE, THE

OLD BAILEY, THE

The Central Criminal Court in England is commonly known as the Old Bailey, after the street in which it stands (a bailey being part of a castle), the name probably being derived from the ballium of the city wall between New and Lud gates. The first court was built in the Old Bailey at a cost of £6,000 in 1539. Previously, trials had taken place in NEWGATE Gaol itself. A new Hall of Justice opened in 1774 and the present building was constructed on the entire site of Newgate Gaol, which had stood there in various forms since *c.*1130. Designed by E W Mountford, it was officially opened on 27 February 1907 by King Edward Vll. An extension was added between 1968-72, designed by architects Donald McMorran and George Whitby.

*The Old Bailey seen here c.*1908. Author's collection

The layout of the New Sessions House, Old Bailey. Author's collection

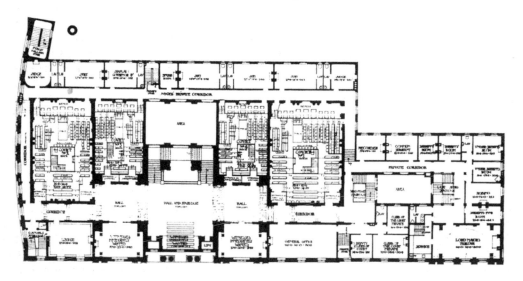

ONEBY, MAJOR JOHN

Major John Oneby was a distinguished officer from the Duke of Marlborough's campaigns. Noted as a swaggerer and a bully, he had gained a reputation as a duellist, and had twice killed rivals in Bruges and Jamaica. Following the signing of the treaties of the Peace of Utrecht in April and July 1713, the Major was placed on half pay. To supplement his reduced income he turned to gambling, at which he became a professional.

The quick-tempered Major was said to have been seldom without dice or cards in his pocket. His regular gambling partners knew only too well that it was unwise to pick a quarrel with him. One night in 1727, Major Oneby fell out over a bet with a Mr Gower in the *Castle Tavern*, Drury Lane. He threw a decanter at Gower, who returned the compliment by throwing a glass back at him. Swords were drawn but after the intercession of their fellow gamblers were put up again. Mr Gower was keen to make peace with Oneby but the Major was not of the same frame of mind and swore to 'have his blood', a threat that was clearly heard by all present. When the party broke up, Major Oneby called Mr Gower into a private room and shut the door. Swords could be heard clashing and a waiter broke open the door. As the assembled company rushed in, the Major, with his sword in his right hand, was holding Mr Gower up with his left. Gower's sword was laying on the floor and a bloodstain, ever increasing in size, marked his waistcoat. When someone called out:

You have killed him!

the Major replied:

No, I might have done it if I would, but I have only frightened him.

The wound in Mr Gower's abdomen proved to be more serious than the Major believed and he died the next day, which resulted in Major Oneby's incarceration in NEWGATE. At his trial at the OLD BAILEY a month later, the jury could not agree on the measure of his guilt. This resulted in a special verdict requiring further consultation with the judge and eleven other judges debating the issue. The Major was remanded in Newgate until his case could be heard. The Major was confident that a verdict of manslaughter would be brought but when over two years later his case was finally heard, eleven of the judges decided against him, he was found guilty of murder and sentenced to death. Two days before he was due to be executed, his servant Philip discovered Major Oneby in his cell bleeding profusely from a deep gash to the wrist. He died before a surgeon could attend him.

OVERBURY, SIR THOMAS (victim)

Sir Thomas Overbury (1581-1613), poet and statesman, was the victim of the greatest scandal of James I's court. He was the son of a Gloucestershire landowner and was educated at Queen's College, Oxford and the Middle Temple. He served as Secretary of State under the Earl of Shrewsbury, who sent him travelling to the Low Countries. Tall, good looking and extremely vain, Overbury possessed a literary talent. His influence increased after he became a friend of Robert Carr, a page to the Earl of Dunbar, whom he met in 1601. They came to London together, and Carr attracted the eye of the King who made him his favourite and created him firstly Viscount Rochester and after Overbury's death, Earl of Somerset. Carr's homosexual relationship with

James I is well documented. Some commentators suggest that a homosexual triangle existed between Overbury, Carr and the King. Overbury retained some influence over the far less astute Lord Rochester, who turned to him as friend and confidante and it was said by many at court that 'Rochester ruled James and Overbury ruled Rochester'. In 1611 Lord Rochester fell in love with the young Countess of Essex, Frances Howard. Her marriage was unconsummated and she wished to obtain a divorce and marry Rochester. Overbury took a dislike to her and was concerned that his influence might be usurped by the powerful Howard family. Overbury enraged the lovers with his opposition to their union and, with the help of the Earl of Northampton, Overbury was imprisoned in the Tower on the dubious charge of refusing to go as an ambassador to Russia, as this was contrary to the King's wishes. Frances Howard, it was said by some, dabbled in black magic. Using her influence, through the agency of the Lieutenant of the Tower, Sir Gervaise Helwyss, who saw to it that one of her servants, Richard Weston, was employed as Overbury's personal gaoler; he with the assistance of a physician's widow named Anne Turner, and a city apothecary, James Franklin, poisoned Overbury in a slow and ghastly manner, with copper vitriol. Sir Thomas Overbury died in September 1613. Two years passed before the truth came to light. Meanwhile, the lovers had married and Rochester had been created Earl of Southampton. A dying young man who had worked in the Tower spilled the beans and confessed to his part in the poisoning and implicated the others involved. Sir Gervaise Helwyss, Anne Turner, Richard Weston and James Franklin were convicted of murder in November 1615 and hanged but not

Sir Thomas Overbury (1581-1613).
Author's collection

Robert Carr and Frances Howard, later the Earl and Countess of Somerset.
Author's collection

before they had implicated Lord and Lady Somerset. The Somersets were tried before the House of Lords, found guilty and condemned to death. However, the King pardoned them and they were confined in the Tower until 1621.

P

PALEOTTI, THE MARQUIS DE

The Marquis De Paleotti was an Italian nobleman born at Bologna, who came over to England following the Peace of Utrecht, after serving in the Imperial army. He led an extravagant lifestyle and spent a good deal of his time at the gaming tables, running up debts for considerable sums. After spending his own money, he was constantly bailed out of trouble by his wealthy widowed sister, the Duchess of Shrewsbury. She grew tired of his constant requests for money and eventually refused to support his gambling. The Marquis habitually sent his servant out to borrow money for him but as his debts increased the task of procuring funds for his master was an onerous one and one day the servant declined to go, at which point the Marquis drew his sword and killed him. The Marquis was immediately arrested and committed to NEWGATE. On being tried at the next Sessions, his sister having little interest or few acquaintances in England, no efforts were made to save the Marquis from the gallows. He was hanged at TYBURN on 17 March 1718.

PEARCEY, MARY ELEANOR

Mrs Pearcey, as this particular murderess preferred to be known, was in fact not married, nor was her surname Pearcey. Her real name was Mary Eleanor Wheeler, but after she went to live with a man in Camden Town at the age of sixteen, named Pearcey, she assumed his name and the title of his wife. Pearcey left her but she retained his surname until the day she died. By the beginning of 1890, twenty-four-year-old Eleanor Pearcey was emotionally unstable, depressed and lonely. She had few relatives, just an elderly mother and an older sister. She was a kept woman, her ground floor apartment consisting of three rooms in a house at 2 Priory Street (now Ivor Street), situated on the border of Kentish Town with Camden Town, being paid for by her admirer, Charles Chrichton of Gravesend in Kent, who visited her once a week. Another admirer, a furniture remover called Frank Hogg, she was particularly fond of and would place a light in her window to let him know when she was free. Hogg was not as emotionally attached to Mrs Pearcey as she was to him. He used to see other women. One of them, a thirty-one-year-old spinster named Phoebe, who was known to Eleanor Pearcey, became pregnant. This hapless lothario was virtually forced into marriage by Phoebe's family and in due course Phoebe Hogg was delivered of a baby girl, also called Phoebe.

The marriage was not a happy one and Frank used to pour out his woes to Eleanor Pearcey, who became jealous of his wife, which developed into deep hatred. The Hoggs lived in rooms at 141 Prince of Wales Road, Kentish Town. On Thursday 23 October, Mrs Hogg received a note from Mrs Pearcey inviting her to tea, an invitation that was declined due to prior commitments. When another note arrived the next day Mrs Hogg accepted. She left her home at about 3.30pm, pushing little Phoebe in her bassinet. Mrs Pearcey's neighbours heard 'banging and hammering', some said they heard screams, coming from the Pearcey household at about 4pm. Phoebe Hogg had been killed in Mrs Pearcey's kitchen with a poker and more than one knife. She had clearly put up a struggle as both her arms were bruised and, as was later discovered, so were Mrs Pearcey's. Mrs Hogg's throat had been so savagely cut that her neck had been all but severed. That evening Mrs Pearcey put Mrs Hogg's body into the bassinet on top of the baby and covered it with an antimacassar. Little Phoebe had either already been suffocated or was smothered by the weight of her mother's body. Mrs Pearcey pushed the bassinet for six miles. Her first port of call was Crossfield Road near Swiss Cottage. There she unloaded Mrs Hogg, leaving her body in a partly-built house. She took a long walk up the Finchley Road to Cock and Hoop Field, where she dumped the baby's body and continued to push the empty bassinet until it collapsed outside 34 Hamilton Terrace, near Maida Vale, where she left it.

The bodies were discovered over the following two days. It was not long before the finger of suspicion was wagging at Mrs Pearcey. When the police visited her at Priory Street she ascribed the bloodstains in the kitchen to killing mice and calmly sat at the piano humming a tune. Eleanor Pearcey was charged with the murders of Mrs Phoebe Hogg and her baby. She was tried at the OLD BAILEY on 1 December. The trial lasted for four days. Found guilty, she was resentful that Frank Hogg had offered her no support. She couldn't grasp that in killing his baby daughter, his feelings for her had changed. She was hanged at NEWGATE on 23 December 1890, by executioner James BERRY. As she was being led to the scaffold, Mrs Pearcey said to the chaplain, Mr Duffield: 'The sentence is just, but the evidence was false.'

PECH, MICHAEL

Michael Pech murdered his ex-girlfriend Clare Bernal at Harvey Nichols store in Knightsbridge, where she worked, on 13 September 2005 by shooting her four times. He then killed himself. Miss Bernal had told Pech that she wanted nothing more to do with him and had reported his repeated stalking of her to the police. On Thursday 18 January 2007, Westminster coroner, Dr Paul Knapman said the killing of Clare Bernal by her ex-boyfriend 'could have been reasonably foreseen'. Dr Knapman said that Clare Bernal, aged twenty-two, was unlawfully killed when she was shot dead by Michael Pech, who then killed himself. In giving his ruling, Dr Knapman said that the Metropolitan Police had made a number of mistakes in handling the case.

PENTONVILLE PRISON

When it opened in 1842, in Caledonian Road, about a mile to the north of King's Cross Station, Pentonville was known as a model prison and built to an American pattern. It originally held prisoners in readiness for transportation to Australia In 1902, shortly before the entire site was cleared to build the present Central Criminal Court in the OLD BAILEY, the gallows from NEWGATE were moved to Pentonville. Thereafter, men were hanged at Pentonville for crimes committed north of the River Thames. WANDSWORTH was the place of execution for crimes committed in South London and Surrey.

PERUSI, GUISEPPE

Sixty-two-year-old Peter Arne was well known and highly respected as a stage, television and film actor. His films included three in the popular Pink Panther series and among many others, *Victor Victoria*, *Straw Dogs* and *Chitty Chitty Bang Bang*. Courteous and well-groomed, Arne led an almost secret life as a homosexual. He lived in an apartment

Pentonville Prison c.*1850.* Author's collection

at 54 Hans Place, Knightsbridge. At 8.30am on 2 August 1983, Eva BRAVO the childminder of one of Arne's neighbours, found bloodstains in the hallway of the building. The police were called and forced open the door of the ground floor apartment and were immediately confronted by Peter Arne's body lying face down on the floor. Blood was spattered everywhere. Investigations revealed that Arne had first been attacked in the living room with a log from the fireplace. Only slightly wounded, he had rushed to the hallway where his assailant had struck him again. He had opened his doorway and gone into the communal hallway, where he had been felled with the log, then dragged back into his own apartment, hit with a wooden stool and finally his throat had been cut, but by this time Arne was already dead.

Investigations revealed that Arne had befriended an Italian man who was living rough in Hyde Park. On the day of his death, 1 August, Arne had been to a costume fitting at the BBC. An eye-witness came forward and said he had seen a bearded man sitting on the steps of No. 54 shortly before Arne arrived back from the BBC. An Identikit picture was created and it corresponded with descriptions of Arne's Italian friend. On 4 August Thames police fished a man's body from the River Thames near Wandsworth Bridge. The body was completely naked. One of the officers immediately recognised a likeness between the corpse and the man wanted in connection with the Peter Arne murder enquiry. The body was identified as Guiseppe Perusi, a thirty-two-year-old schoolteacher from Milan, who had come to London several weeks before and had been sleeping rough. A pile of clothes was found at Putney on the north bank of the river with Perusi's passport. Bloodstains corresponded with Arne's blood group and Perusi's fingerprints were found on a honey pot in Arne's kitchen. The coroner concluded that Arne had been unlawfully killed by Perusi, who then committed suicide while the balance of his mind was disturbed.

PETTY TREASON

A verdict of petty treason, considered more serious than murder, was established when any person out of malice took away the life of someone to whom he or she owed special obedience. For instance, a wife murdering her husband, or a servant killing his or her master, or an ecclesiastic his superior. However, a wife's accomplices in the murder of a husband would not be guilty of petty treason.

PHIPOE, MARIA THERESA

Maria Theresa Phipoe, also known to some by the name of Mary Benson, was powerfully built and of masculine behaviour and disposition. In 1795, she attempted to kill John Cortois after having tied him up and under threats of violence procured a promissory note for £2,000 from him. He managed to escape as she tried to stab him, sustaining severe cuts to his hands and fingers as he fended her off. For this crime, due to a point of law being raised, having been found guilty of assault on 23 May 1795, Phipoe was committed to twelve months in NEWGATE. Within months of her release she murdered Mary Cox by stabbing her five times in the throat and in several other parts of the body at her home in Garden Street, in the parish of St George's-in-the-East. She had sold the woman a gold watch and other articles for which she had been paid eleven pounds, after which a frenzied knife attack began. Mary Cox lived long enough to tell her tale to the surgeon and beadles. Found guilty of murder at the OLD BAILEY, Maria Theresa Phipoe was hanged outside Newgate on Monday 11 December 1797 and afterwards her body was publicly exhibited before she was anatomised.

PIERREPOINTS, THE (twentieth-century family of hangmen)

The Pierrepoint family from Clayton near Bradford in Yorkshire's West Riding, provided three of Britain's chief executioners during the twentieth century. Henry Albert Pierrepoint (1878-1922) was appointed to the list of executioners in 1901 and carried out 105 executions over a nine-year period. He persuaded his brother Thomas to become an executioner. After Henry's removal from the Home Office list of executioners, his position as Chief Executioner was taken over by John ELLIS. Thomas William Pierrepoint (1870-1954) who worked as executioner for thirty-seven years until his mid-seventies, executed about 300 criminals, sometimes assisted by his nephew, Albert, who succeeded him as Chief Executioner. Albert Pierrepoint (1905-92), son of Henry was the most prolific and longest serving executioner, occupying the office from 1932 and becoming Chief Executioner in 1941 until he resigned in 1956 over a disagreement with the Home Office about his fees. Such was his standing that the government tried to persuade him to continue in the post. The exact number of criminals executed by Albert Pierrepoint has never been precisely verified but including the Nazis he dispatched in the aftermath of World War Two and the executions he undertook in Ireland, a figure of more than 450 has been estimated, including seventeen women. When Albert was not occupied with 'Government work' he initially ran a grocery business with his wife Anne, who he married in 1953. Later, he became a publican, running a public house situated between Oldham and Manchester and named *Help the Poor Struggler*, a name which was often the butt of journalistic puns. The Pierrepoints later moved to another pub, the *Rose and Crown*, Hoole, near Preston. His autobiography *Executioner Pierrepoint*, was published in 1974.

PIMLICO POISONING CASE, THE

This extraordinary mid-Victorian case attracted enormous press attention, notably for the curious relationship that existed between those involved, Edwin Bartlett, his wife Adelaide and Methodist minister George Dyson. Adelaide Blanche de la Tremouille was born in Orleans, France in 1856, and was said to be the natural daughter of a high-born Englishman. During and following the sensational Pimlico Poisoning case, newspaper reports speculated about her parentage, as Queen Victoria and Prince Albert had been to France on a state visit in 1855, during the period that Adelaide had been conceived, prompting suggestions that her father was a gentleman from the Royal household. Very little is known about her early life, not even the identity of her mother. The surname she took was that of her guardian, Count de la Tremouille. Illegitimacy among the French upper classes did not have the same stigma as it did in England, neither being considered particularly uncommon or indeed, scandalous.

When she was eighteen, Adelaide came to England for the Christmas holidays to stay with the family of a school friend. She spoke English fluently, wore her hair fashionably short, which served to highlight her wide eyes and sensual mouth. Her manner and personality were described by many as vivacious. Edwin Bartlett, a handsome thirty-year-old, with fair hair, blue eyes and a moustache, was a successful businessman with a chain of six grocery shops in South London, known as Baxter and Bartlett. Adelaide and her school friend were invited to tea at Bartlett's parents' home. Edwin was immediately attracted to Adelaide and within half an hour had proposed to her, a proposal she accepted. A marriage was arranged by Adelaide's guardian, with financial help being offered to her prospective husband to assist him in business, as part of the marriage settlement. The next time the couple met was on 6 April 1875, when a secret marriage took place at Croydon Parish Church. Shortly afterwards, Edwin introduced his new bride to his parents, who were not only surprised by the marriage but startled at his announcement that he looked upon Adelaide more as a daughter than as a wife. He also informed them that Adelaide would be leaving for Belgium to complete her education. By the time Adelaide returned to Edwin at Christmas 1876, as a result of the hefty dowry he had received, Edwin's business empire had grown to include nine shops and a large warehouse in Southwark. The couple set up home above Baxter and Bartlett's shop in Herne Hill, which Edwin had had sumptuously decorated in the latest style. He also purchased a piano for Adelaide and a large double bed, which, although they shared, Edwin adopted the unusual philosophy: 'A man should be allowed two wives; one for companionship, and one for use.' However, as far as is known Edwin did not procure a wife for use and Adelaide later claimed that she had only had sexual intercourse on one occasion with her husband.

Edwin kept several St Bernard dogs in kennels at Herne Hill. Adelaide took an interest in their welfare, and gleaned knowledge from the small library of veterinary books she built up. Edwin's younger brother, Frederick, often used to visit his sister-in-law. Much closer to Adelaide in age, they got on well together. When Edwin's mother was taken seriously ill, he neglected his wife, who fell into the arms of his brother, the ever attentive Frederick. Shortly afterwards, Mrs Bartlett died and Edwin's father came to live with them at Herne Hill. The affair between sister and brother-in-law was soon discovered and in its wake Frederick left for America. Edwin forgave his wife and their odd relationship continued in the same manner as previously. Mr Bartlett senior referred to his daughter-in-law as a continental hussy, disliking her from then onwards. Edwin and Adelaide decided to move to accommodation above the shop at Lordship

Lane, Dulwich. As there was insufficient room for Mr Bartlett, he found accommodation elsewhere. Edwin experienced over a year of extremely painful dental problems, in which a number of rotten molars were extracted and some good teeth sawn down to the root in order to fit a dental plate, all this being carried out without anaesthetic.

In January 1881, Edwin suffered a nervous breakdown. To recuperate, a holiday followed, his first. They travelled by steamship to Aberdeen, then took a hundred mile journey by pony and trap to Balmoral. The holiday agreed with him and before returning home by another sea trip, Edwin's libido had been sufficiently stimulated to enable him to indulge in one bout of sexual intercourse with his wife, which resulted in an uncomfortable pregnancy. In October 1881, the child was stillborn. In 1883 the Bartletts moved to Phipps Road, Merton, where Adelaide devoted much of her time to walking the St Bernards. Shortly after their arrival they met twenty-seven-year-old Methodist minister, George Dyson. He was the same age as Adelaide. Edwin encouraged his wife to resume her studies and arranged for George Dyson to tutor her in history, geography, mathematics and Latin. Dyson arrived at the Bartletts' house every morning at 11.00am. He stayed throughout the day and dined with them on three evenings each week. Edwin was not at all concerned by the intimate relationship that was growing between his wife and Dyson, in fact he encouraged it. He even went as far as to write to thank Dyson for sending Adelaide a love letter and allowed the couple to kiss in his presence. Dyson also wrote Adelaide several love poems, one of which read:

> Who is it that hath burst the door,
> Unclosed the heart that shut before,
> And set her queen-like on the throne,
> And made its homage all her own –
> My Birdie.

In August 1885, the Bartletts took a holiday at Dover, Dyson joined them at Edwin's request. On 3 September 1885, Edwin Bartlett made a new will, leaving everything to Adelaide, without the usual stipulation, common in those days, that she should not re-marry. He named George Dyson as executor. The following month, the Bartletts moved to central London and took rooms in the house of Mr and Mrs Dogget, at 85 Claverton Street, Pimlico. Dyson continued with his visits and for greater convenience obtained a ministry in Putney. Edwin paid for his season ticket from there to Pimlico. Dyson arrived every morning at 9.30am and he stayed until the evening. The unrestrained canoodling continued and Dyson and Adelaide openly kissed and cuddled, even in front of the maid.

By November 1896, Edwin's health had begun to deteriorate, his teeth were rotting again, and he complained of insomnia. He had taken to sleeping in an iron cot beside Adelaide's bed because he was suffering from muscle spasms in his legs. Light hurt his eyes and he complained of a strong metallic taste in his mouth. He suffered from bouts of vomiting and diarrhoea. On the morning of 10 December, Dr Alfred Leach was called in to examine Edwin and diagnosed gastritis. He then noticed a distinctive blue line round his patient's gums, a clear symptom of mercury poisoning. Edwin gave him an explanation. He told the doctor that a few days before, he was not feeling well. He had taken at random one of a sample of pills supplied to his shop. Dr Leach concluded that the pill had contained mercury and that it had reacted with Edwin's rotten teeth, producing acute mercury poisoning. Edwin was given a purgative and told to rest. However, Edwin's father was not satisfied and called in a specialist, Dr John Gardner Dudley, who concluded that apart from depression, the only thing that was wrong with Edwin was indigestion. Later, Edwin started passing roundworms, a condition usually associated with dogs. Edwin was told to rest over Christmas and on 26 December Dr Leach returned to administer anti-worm medication. Adelaide asked Dyson to purchase some chloroform, which he did. Edwin's teeth were now troubling him so much that on 31 December he had a molar extracted. At 4.00am the following morning, New Year's Day, Adelaide woke their landlord and told him that her husband had died in his sleep. Mr Dyson later remarked that the room smelled of ether and a wine glass on the mantelpiece also smelled of ether. There was also a half empty glass of brandy, with which Adelaide said she had tried to revive her husband.

Dr Leach was sent for and he said that Edwin had been dead for two or three hours. A post-mortem examination was carried out on 2 January, where it was found that Edwin Bartlett's stomach was grossly inflamed and contained one-sixteenth of an ounce of liquid chloroform, more than enough to have killed him. Although chloroform taken orally is a strong poison, it would be impossible to drink because it inflames and burns the internal organs and would cause excruciating pain. Puzzlingly, although his stomach smelled strongly of chloroform, neither Bartlett's mouth, throat nor his digestive passages were in any way burnt or in the least bit inflamed. This fact has remained to this day inexplicable. How so much chloroform could be ingested without causing severe damage elsewhere in the body remains a complete mystery. There were some traces of lead acetate in his jaw, which could possibly be construed as being the result of long term poisoning or may have been related to the victim's severe dental problems.

An inquest was held in February. After two adjournments, on 18 February the coroner brought in a verdict of wilful murder against Adelaide Bartlett and George Dyson. The pair were brought up for trial before Mr Justice Wills on 12 April 1886 at

The trial of Mrs Adelaide Bartlett, pictured top left. Methodist minister George Dyson is pictured top right. Author's collection

the OLD BAILEY. The charges against Dyson were dropped at the outset of the trial, the judge declaring that there was insufficient evidence against him. However, in some quarters it was believed that this decision was taken to enable him to give evidence against Adelaide, which as a defendant he could not. Attorney General, Sir Charles Russell, led the prosecution. Much was made of a sex manual found in the Bartletts' apartment, a somewhat scandalous publication in those days; as was the discovery of six condoms in Edwin Bartlett's trouser pocket. Sir Charles claimed that Adelaide had given her husband chloroform in a disguised form, such as in brandy or that he had drunk it himself. Adelaide admitted administering small quantities of chloroform sprinkled on a handkerchief, to help her husband sleep during his illness and also to stifle his sexual advances, chloroform that had been procured for her by George Dyson at chemists in Putney and Wandsworth. However, Adelaide's claim that she had administered chloroform to stifle Edwin's sex drive, was refuted as nonsense by Dr Patrick Toseland, who said that unless she gave her husband sufficient to actually knock him out, if sniffed in very light doses, it could in fact increase sexual sensation.

Expert witnesses agreed that both ways of administering chloroform as suggested by the prosecution were impossible, as there was no burning or scarring anywhere in the body other than the stomach. Mr Justice Wills, in referring to the liquid chloroform found in Bartlett's body, said to the jury: 'If you take the evidence on either hand alone, you would say the thing could not be done. Yet it has been done, and one of the two impossible theories must be right.' There being insufficient evidence to show how such a large quantity of the poison was administered the jury had no alternative but to acquit Adelaide Bartlett. The foreman of the jury said: '... and although we think there are circumstances of grave suspicion attaching to the prisoner, we do not think there is sufficient evidence to show how, or by whom, the chloroform was administered.' The case was a bone of contention to the medical establishment. Queen Victoria's own surgeon, Sir James Paget, who attended the trial declared: 'Now that it is all over, in the interests of science, Mrs Bartlett should tell us how she did it.' Having been acquitted, Adelaide Bartlett, who had been secretly corresponding with her brother-in-law, Frederick, changed her name. Frederick came to England and took her back to America with him. George Dyson did not feature in her life any more.

POISON UMBRELLA MURDER

Forty-nine-year-old exiled Bulgarian playwright and novelist Georgieu (Georgi) Markov, a staunch anti-Communist, defected to the West in 1969 and arrived in London in 1971. He obtained a post with the BBC World Service. His weekly broadcasts, although not exactly overtly anti-Communist, were tinged with satirical references to the Bulgarian hierarchy. On the afternoon of 7 September 1978, Markov was on his way to Bush House on foot, having left his Simca car parked on the South Bank. His journey took him across Waterloo Bridge. As was revealed much later, on the orders of Bulgarian President Todor Zhivkhov, Markov was assassinated. As he walked across the bridge past a crowded bus stop he felt a stinging sensation in his leg. He turned round and a man with a thick foreign accent apologised to him. The man was brandishing an umbrella. When he arrived at Bush House Markov discovered an angry red spot on the back of his right thigh. During the next few hours, he became extremely ill and his condition rapidly deteriorated. Doctors at St James's Hospital, Balham, where Markov had been admitted, were puzzled by his symptoms and concluded that he was suffering from a form of septicaemia. He died at 9.45am on 11 September.

During a post-mortem examination a pinhead-size spherical object, just 1.5mm in diameter was found embedded in the wound on Mr Markov's leg. When analysed, traces of a little known poison derived from the castor bean and known as Ricin, 500 times as toxic by weight as either cyanide or arsenic, was detected. The tiny capsule had been fired into Georgi Markov's thigh from a gun cleverly adapted to be shot from an innocuous looking umbrella.

PRICE, JOHN

John Price was born in Soho in about 1677. His father, a soldier, was killed in Tangier in 1684. As a boy Price was apprenticed to a rag merchant but after two years ran away and eventually served in the navy in various men-of-war for the next eighteen years. Shortly after his discharge from the navy in 1714, through the contacts of his wife, Betty, employed at NEWGATE in the capacity of a run-around (procuring goods and services for those prisoners who could afford to pay) he secured the position of hangman of London and the County of Middlesex, worth at that time about £40 a year. This was increased by gratuities and other perks.

Price rejoiced in the usual official soubriquet of 'Jack Ketch'. However, despite this relatively large income, Price was a heavy drinker and he spent his money faster than it came in and soon ran up debts. One day in 1715, John Price was passing through Holborn, carrying the clothes of three criminals he had just hanged, when he was arrested for a debt of 7s 6d. He managed to avoid imprisonment by handing over to the bailiffs all the ready money he had on his person and the three suits of clothes, which settled the debt. However, he was arrested a short time later for two further debts. As

An eighteenth century engraving of the Session House, Old Bailey, where John Price was found guilty of murder during the Old Bailey Sessions of 23 - 26 April 1718. Trials were held in the open air to prevent disease spreading from the pestilence ridden criminals to the judge, lawyers and court officials. Author's collection

he did not have the means to pay the debts this time he was committed to the Marshalsea Prison for debt and his position passed to William Marvell, a former blacksmith. This was unfortunate for Price as the post of common hangman was shortly due to prove more lucrative following the 1715 rebellion. Price remained in the Marshalsea Prison until 1718, where he enjoyed the privilege known as the liberty of the Marshalsea, which enabled him to leave the confines of the prison during the day but he was required to return at night. However, he and another prisoner decided to break this parole and abscond.

Not long afterwards, on Sunday 13 March 1718, a great many citizens were making merry and stalls were set up in the fields just outside Moorgate. That evening Price was walking across Bunhill Fields in a state of intoxication when he came across Elizabeth White, an old woman who sold cakes and gingerbread in the streets, who had set up her stall there. Intending to both rob and rape her he set about the woman, who resisted the attack, which angered him. He beat her savagely and two passers-by who came to investigate the noise found him 'busy about her' with her 'coats up to her belly and streams of blood issuing out of her eyes and mouth'. They apprehended Price and left the victim alone and senseless, while they took him to the watch-house in Old Street, where a constable detained him. When the old lady was attended to she was found to have a badly bruised scalp one eye knocked out of its socket, by Price's cudgel, some teeth knocked out, a bruised throat, a broken arm and a lacerated womb. Price was held overnight but later released. When Elizabeth White died four days later Price was arrested on a charge of murder as he was taking a prisoner to be executed at TYBURN

The arrest of John Price, hangman.
Author's collection

or so the popular story goes.

He was incarcerated in Newgate Gaol to await trial, which took place at the Old Bailey Sessions of 23-26 April. He pleaded not guilty and claimed that as he crossed Bunhill Fields on the night in question, he 'found something lying in his way'. He kicked it and found that it was a woman. He said he lifted her up but found that she was unable to stand and it was while he was doing this that he was apprehended. The jury did not believe him and he was found guilty of murder and sentenced to death. He was to be hanged on a temporary scaffold near the place of the murder, and afterwards his body was to be gibbeted. During the time he awaited his execution in the condemned cell, Price attended chapel at Newgate, more often than not in a drunken state, he being allowed to drink spirits, which he did to excess. The Revd Paul Lorrain found that in drink Price was 'Insensible of his misery... and unapprehensive of his future state'. In *The Original Weekly Journal* of 7-14 June 1718, it was reported: '*A little girl who used to carry victuals to John Price the hangman in Newgate, has declared that a few days before his execution, he had carnal knowledge of her body in the said* [gaol].' John Price was hanged at Bunhill Fields on Saturday 31 May 1718. Before he was hanged by an executioner named Banks, who had succeeded William Marvell, Price finally confessed his guilt. He told the spectators that they should take warning from his untimely end. After the execution that same day his body was hung in chains at Stonebridge near Holloway.

PRINCE, RICHARD ARCHER

This is the tale of a practical joke that went seriously wrong, of baseless jealousy arising from another actor's cruel hoax. The principal players in this tragic tale are fifty-year-old William Terriss (William Charles James Lewin), actor and murder victim; Richard Archer Prince, a supernumerary, stagehand and murderer; and William L Abingdon, actor and perpetrator of the joke that turned sour.

William Terriss was affectionately known by the British public as 'Breezy Bill and No.1, Adelphi Terriss' (Adelphi Terrace being one of London's most fashionable streets, and the Adelphi Theatre, where Terriss mainly worked). He was good-natured, handsome, athletic and an accomplished swimmer and rescued several people from drowning resulting in him being presented with the medal of the Royal Humane Society.

Richard Archer Prince was born in Dundee. At his trial, his age was given as thirty-two, but his mother maintained that he was her eldest son, born in 1858. This would have made him thirty-nine. In any event, he looked considerably older than his years. Richard Archer (he adopted the name of Prince later, because he thought that name was more becoming of a future great actor), was short of stature, with a slight cast in his right eye and a heavy, dark, droopy moustache, which he waxed at both ends. He dressed eccentrically, and often wore the attire associated with a stage villain. Many of his acquaintances simply regarded him as a harmless eccentric. Others, who perhaps saw deeper into his psyche rightly nick named him 'Mad Archer'. He had a wretched, poverty-stricken childhood, and nurtured a burning ambition to become a great actor. Apprenticed to a Dundee shipbuilder, sometime later he secured a walk-on part, swelling the ranks of a visiting company at the Theatre Royal. This was the beginning of his undistinguished theatrical career. Prince's sister, Maggie, moved south to London, where she became a lady of easy virtue. One of her regular gentleman friends was the actor William L Abingdon.

Billy Abingdon as he was known by his intimates, had joined the Adelphi company in 1887 and had been largely in the employment of that company ever since. Prince found his way to London in 1881. He sought out his sister, who it is believed sweet-talked Abingdon, to secure her brother some employment. *The Silver Falls* opened in December 1888 with Terriss as leading man. Prince was in the cast as a supernumerary. After the run ended Terriss left the Adelphi for five years. He went on a tour of America and Prince found himself out of work. However it was as 'R.A. Prince, late Adelphi Theatre' that he presented himself to potential employers. He established a connection with the provincial manager J F Elliston, a reputable manager who was based in Bolton, Lancashire and remained with Elliston's company for several seasons until the end of the 1894-95 tour. After this, unable to find work he returned to Dundee where he obtained a job at an ironworks. He began writing abusive and threatening letters to numerous theatrical figures accusing them of 'blackmailing' him. He uses this expression many times and presumably meant 'blackballing'.

THE LATE WILLIAM TERRISS

HOUSE WHERE PRISONER LIVED

MR. TERRISS'S HOME. BEDFORD PARK.

The murder scene. The Illustrated Police News

Towards the end of 1895, Prince returned to London, where he secured an engagement as a supernumerary in Seymour Hick's *One of the Best*, opening on 21 December. Terriss was leading man. During this engagement a cruel practical joke was formulated. Abingdon was appearing in a principal role in the play. He and a couple of his cronies, found Prince's inflated opinion of himself quite hilarious. They encouraged his caprices, adding fuel to spark the fire of hatred, already smouldering and soon to burn ferociously in Prince's twisted brain. They convinced Prince that in their opinion he had true greatness and he only needed the right opportunity to stake his claim. *One of the Best* closed and Prince's services were not required in the following play. He sent several begging letters to various actors, including Terriss, who sent him money. By the summer of 1896 Prince's situation was becoming desperate. Unable to find work, he ventured north to his home town, Dundee, where he obtained work at the Wallace Foundry, which he left after he managed to secure a theatrical engagement. Prince's general behaviour and his inability to remember lines resulted in his dismissal when the company reached South Shields. Prince's last engagement followed. He was engaged for 25/- a week by Ralph Croydon. Before the end of the first day of rehearsals he had been dismissed.

Prince made his way back to London by sea. It was reported that of the many and various jobs which Prince took between theatrical engagements, that he had served as a ship's steward and also as a valet. Short of money, he may have used his contacts to secure his passage. He found lodgings in Eaton Court, Buckingham Palace Road – a room at 3/- a week, knocked down by his sympathetic landlady, Mrs Charlotte Darby, from 4/-. Shortly afterwards, Prince went to the business premises of Mr George Lauberg, a cutler in Brompton Road, where he purchased a knife for 9d. Prince also paid a visit to the stage door of the Adelphi Theatre on 9 November and asked the stage-doorkeeper, Henry Spratt, if a note could be sent to Mr Terriss. The note was taken to Terriss's dressing room and a reply returned to Prince. This took the form of a reference to the Actors' Benevolent Fund. It was later given in evidence. It read:

I have known the bearer, R. A. Prince, as a hard-working actor.

Prince made frequent requests to the Actors' Benevolent Fund. His begging letters were produced at his trial. On the morning of 16 December, Prince left his lodgings, after being refused hot water by Mrs Darby. He was behind with his rent and she had had enough. He paid a final visit to the Actors' Benevolent Fund, but was told that his application for assistance had been rejected. Prince went to see the agent C St John Denton, in Maiden Lane, seeking work. His visit proved fruitless. He walked into the Strand and by an unlucky chance, came face to face with his sister, Maggie. He asked her for money. She replied: 'I would rather see you dead in the gutter than give you a farthing.' This final rejection was too much for him. He walked back to Maiden Lane and positioned himself opposite the private entrance.

During this period Terriss had every reason to be pleased with himself. His company was to appear in a Command Performance on Christmas Eve, before the Queen, at Windsor Castle. The word was out, he was to be knighted. On 16 December Terriss was discussing moving from his West London home Bedford Park, in Turnham Green to a larger house in Maida Vale, with John Graves. They played poker with Fred Terry at the Green Room Club and afterwards went to Jessie Millward's (Terriss's leading lady and mistress) flat in Prince's Street, Hanover Square. She provided them with a light meal and left them playing chess. Terriss and his companion were dropped off at the end of Maiden Lane and walked the short distance to the private entrance (which allowed quick access to the four principal dressing rooms). It was a little after seven o'clock that, as Terriss was bending to put the key in the lock, a figure emerged from across the narrow lane and hurriedly stabbed him twice in the upper back. Terriss turned to confront his assailant and, in doing so received a third blow to the chest, which pierced his heart. Then, when Terriss cried out: 'My God! I am stabbed,' Graves took hold of Prince and held him until Police Constable Bragg arrived and took Prince into custody at Bow Street. Medical help was quick to arrive from nearby Charing Cross Hospital. Terriss died a few moments before eight o'clock. The funeral took place five days later at Brompton Cemetery, being preceded by a service at the Chapel Royal of the Savoy. Terriss was laid to rest on the East Terrace, sharing a vault with his mother and his baby grandson who had been buried there two weeks previously. *The Times* reported that some 50,000 people lined the streets to watch the funeral procession and pay their respects to their lost favourite of the London stage. Nothing was mentioned to the police about the affair and Abingdon was not called to give evidence at the trial. However, Prince's sister Maggie conveniently disappeared, sometime between the murder and the trial.

The trial took place on 13 January 1898, less than a month after the murder and lasted one day. It was an extremely disturbing affair. Prince was tried at the OLD BAILEY before Mr Justice Channell. The jury retired at 6.35pm, and having considered the evidence returned after just half an hour. They found Prince guilty of wilful murder, but taking the medical evidence into account, not responsible for his actions. He was ordered to be retained as a criminal lunatic at Holloway until Her Majesty's pleasure be known. Richard Archer Prince was not kept at the institution in Holloway for long, he was transferred to Broadmoor, where he remained until his death in 1937. Billy Abingdon, having moved to America died by his own hand. He was found at his apartment at 235 West 76th Street, New York, having slit his throat, on 19 May 1918.

Broadmoor, seen here in 1867. Author's collection

R

RAILWAY MURDERER, THE – see DUFFY AND MULCAHY

RATCLIFFE HIGHWAY MURDERS, THE

The Ratcliffe Highway Murders rank amongst the most brutal of all London murders. They occurred on 7 and 19 December 1811 in what is today simply known as The Highway, described by Thomas De Quincey (1785-1859) as:

> *A public thoroughfare in the most chaotic quarter of eastern, or nautical London; and at this time, when no adequate police service existed except the detective police of Bow Street, admirable for its own peculiar purposes, but utterly commensurate to the general service of the capital, it was a most dangerous quarter.*

The first victims were the Marrs and an apprentice boy. Mr Marr, a young man who kept a lace and hosiery shop at No.29, sent his servant girl out to buy some oysters. When she returned she found Mr Marr's body and those of his wife, baby and thirteen-year-old apprentice boy, all violently slaughtered, their heads smashed in and their throats cut.

A nineteenth century engraving showing the body of John Williams having been paraded through the streets, arriving at the crossroads at the junction of Cannon Street Road and Cable Street, near St George's Turnpike. Williams was buried there with a stake through his heart and his body covered with quicklime. The grave, deliberately dug too small, can be seen in the right foreground. Author's collection

On 19 December, a man named Williamson, landlord of the *King's Arms*, 81 New Gravel Lane (now Garnet Street), his wife and an elderly maidservant were similarly murdered. A sailor's maul, or hammer, and a ripping chisel were discovered at the murder scene. Identified as belonging to a labourer named John Williams, he was apprehended at the *Pear Tree Tavern* in Cinnamon Street and remanded in Coldbath Fields Prison (situated where Mount Pleasant Sorting Office stands today), pending further investigation. On 28 December, Williams was found hanging from a beam in his cell. Some said he had cheated justice, others took a different view and it was suggested that John Williams was not guilty of the killings and that he did not commit suicide but was himself murdered, to prevent him telling the truth. On 31 December, Williams' remains were taken to St George's watch-house, in preparation for his internment. The body was placed on a cart on an inclined platform, so as to afford the public a better view and the maul and ripping chisel placed on either side above his head. Escorted by the High Constable of Middlesex and hundreds of constables, officials and parish officers, the procession, watched by thousands of onlookers, many of whom carried torches, took a circuitous route passing the scene of the crimes until the cart stopped at St George's Turnpike at what is now the crossroads of Cable Street with Cannon Street Road, which was where Williams was buried in a grave over which the main water pipe ran. During the hours of darkness between twelve and one o'clock the body was taken from the platform and lowered into the grave and then a stake was driven through it, piercing the heart before the grave was filled in, a common practice at that time for suicides.

RICHARDSON, ELIZABETH

Former prostitute Elizabeth Richardson was taken under the protection of Mr Pimlot an attorney-at-law, in Symond's Inn, Chancery Lane. One night in November 1768, after he had quite innocently been out late engaged on business, filled with misplaced jealousy, she stabbed him in the heart in the presence of the watchman, Mr Wilson. When she saw the blood spurting from her lover's breast she said:

What have I done! Oh Mr Wilson, it was I that did this shocking deed; instantly send for a surgeon, send for a surgeon! I have murdered my dear Pimlot.

Elizabeth Richardson was found guilty of wilful murder at the OLD BAILEY, hanged at TYBURN on 21 December 1768 and afterwards dissected at Surgeons' Hall.

ROBERTS, HARRY MAURICE – see BRAYBROOK STREET MASSACRE, THE

ROBINSON, JOHN

At a little after 1.50pm on Friday 6 May 1927, a man described by luggage attendant Mr Glass as being of military bearing, arrived by taxi-cab and deposited a large black trunk in the left luggage office at Charing Cross Railway Station. The letters F and A were painted on either end of the trunk and a label read 'F AUSTIN to ST LENARDS [sic]', actually St Leonards-on-Sea and, as later discovered, pertaining to the quite innocent previous owner.

On Monday 9 May, attention was drawn to the trunk when an unpleasant smell was noticed. The next morning the police were summoned. When opened and emptied at Bow Street Police Station it was discovered that the trunk contained five brown paper parcels tied up with string, a pair of woman's shoes and a black handbag. The parcels contained five portions of a woman. Her limbs had been severed at each shoulder and hip joint and wrapped in items of female clothing and a towel, before being wrapped and tied up with string. A duster had been wound around the victim's head, which was still attached to the torso. The remains were moved to Horseferry Road Mortuary and on Wednesday 11 May a post-mortem examination was carried out by Dr Rose and Dr Henry Bright Weir. Home Office pathologist Sir Bernard SPILSBURY also examined the remains. There were several bruises on the woman's forehead, stomach, back and limbs. These, Spilsbury concluded, had been inflicted before she died and he suggested that she had been beaten unconscious and that the cause of death was asphyxia. He further concluded that the woman had been dead for perhaps a week, that she had been short and stout and was aged about thirty-five.

Horseferry Road Magistrates' Court and Mortuary. The Author

Two of the items of clothing bore a laundry mark and a name-tag on a pair of slate coloured knickers bore the name 'P Holt'. Investigations led to a former cook once employed by a Mrs Holt of Chelsea. Her name was Mrs Minnie Alice Bonati, the estranged wife of an Italian waiter. Bianco Bonati told the police that Minnie had left him to go with a roadworker, Frederick Rolls, on 21 September 1923 and they had lived at various addresses until the relationship came to an end in July 1926. The police were quick to satisfy themselves that neither Mr Rolls nor Mr Bonati were in any way connected with the murder and mutilation of Mrs Bonati.

Enquiries about the trunk and the taxi in which its depositor had left led police to 86 Rochester Row, Westminster. One of the occupants of a two-roomed, second-floor office that overlooked the street, was one John Robinson, who traded as an estate agent under the business name 'Edwards and Co., Business Transfer Agents'. Mr Robinson had not been seen for several days. Apart from a cracked window pane and a broken fender in the fireplace, nothing seemed amiss, and the police could find no traces of blood.

When police visited Robinson's lodgings in Camberwell Gate, they discovered he'd left without leaving a forwarding address and discovered a telegram addressed to 'Robinson, Greyhound Hotel Hammersmith', had been returned marked addressee unknown. As was later discovered, the telegram had been returned to sender by a new maid at the *Greyhound*, unaware that the Robinson mentioned in the telegram actually worked there. However, this was not John Robinson himself, but *Mrs* Robinson.

Thirty-six-year-old John Robinson was born in Leigh, Lancashire. He left school at the age of twelve and began his working life as an errand-boy for the Co-op. He also worked as a clerk, a tram-conductor, bartender and butcher's assistant. He had four children by his first wife, whom he married in 1911. He later bigamously married a Tasmanian girl from whom he was estranged. She worked at the *Greyhound Hotel*,

Hammersmith. She cooperated with the police and when Robinson contacted her, at his request, she agreed to meet him. On Thursday 19 May, they met at a public house, the *Elephant and Castle*, Walworth. She was escorted by Chief Inspector George Cornish of Scotland Yard. Robinson denied any knowledge of either buying the trunk or of Mrs Bonati. At the identity parade, of the three witnesses who attended, the station porter, the taxi-driver and Mr Ward, the dealer who had sold the trunk, not one of them recognised him. The police had no alternative but to release him.

The bloodstained, dirty duster, in which the murder victim's head had been wound was washed to see if it revealed any further clues. A small tab on the hem of the duster revealed the name 'GREYHOUND'. A further painstaking search of Robinson's office suite revealed a bloodstained match, which had been caught in the wickerwork of a waste-paper basket. A small clue, yes, but the bloodstained match, combined with the duster proved sufficient to break Robinson's confidence and, having been brought back to Scotland Yard from his lodgings in De Laune Street, Kennington, on Monday 23 May, he decided to make a statement.

He said that Minnie Bonati had propositioned him at Victoria railway station at about 4.15pm on the afternoon of Wednesday 4 May. At his office suite, she asked him for money and when he told her he hadn't any, she was abusive and threatened violence. There was a struggle in which he broke a window pane as he stumbled backwards and his head hit it. She fell, knocking herself insensible as she struck her head on a chair. Fearful of the racket they had made and well aware of the close proximity of the police station, in a panic, Robinson said he decided to leave the office building. On his return to the office the following morning he found Mrs Bonati was lying face-down on the carpet dead. At no time did Robinson ever admit to killing her but he did not deny that he had cut up her body and placed the remains in the trunk.

Robinson's trial was held at the OLD BAILEY and began on Monday 11 July 1927, before Mr Justice Rigby Swift. The defence was unable to convince the jury that Minnie Bonati was the victim of an unfortunate accident. In his own evidence Robinson admitted virtually everything that was put to him, excepting an intention to kill. Sir Bernard Spilsbury's contention that the bruises on Mrs Bonati had been caused by direct blows and pressure and that she had been asphyxiated after a violent assault, seemed to hold more water with both the judge and the jury. On Wednesday 13 July the jury returned a verdict of 'guilty'. John Robinson was hanged at PENTONVILLE on 12 August 1927 and buried within its precincts.

ROLT, TERENCE PETER – see ANTIQUIS MURDER, THE

S

SACH, MRS AMELIA – see ISLINGTON BABY-FARMING CASE, THE

SAVAGE, RICHARD
In December 1727, Richard Savage (1697-1743) English poet and satirist and intimate friend of Dr Samuel Johnson, found himself on trial for his life, charged with murder, following a quarrel in a West End coffee house. Savage was the illegitimate son of the Countess of Macclesfield, the result of a love affair with Captain Richard Savage, afterwards Earl Rivers.

On the evening of Monday 20 November 1727, Savage was in the company of two friends, William Merchant and James Gregory. All three men were the worse for drink when they entered Robinson's Coffee House, near Charing Cross. They forced their way into a room where a private party was just splitting up and began to quarrel with the departing guests. Merchant entered first and kicked over a table, whereupon angry words were exchanged and Savage and Gregory drew their swords. Savage was subject to fits of blind rage, particularly when drunk and on this occasion it seems he lost his head altogether. Mr Nuttal asked them to put them up, but they refused to do so. In the ensuing fight, Savage came up against James Sinclair, made several thrusts at his opponent and ran him through the belly. Sinclair fell, calling out as he did so:

I am a dead man, and was stabbed cowardly.

Someone put out the candles and in the darkness one of the maids received a cut to the head while trying to prevent Savage and Merchant fleeing the building. They did manage to escape but were quickly apprehended in a dark court nearby. Gregory was held in the coffee house, where he was arrested. James Sinclair died the next morning but not before identifying Savage as his assailant. The deceased was attended by a clergyman and Sinclair told him he had been stabbed before he had time to draw his sword. Savage later said he had drawn his sword in self-defence. Savage, Merchant and Gregory were taken by soldiers and lodged in the roundhouse, and in the morning were carried before a magistrate who committed them to the GATEHOUSE, but following the death of James Sinclair, they were sent to NEWGATE. Arraigned before Sir Francis Page, notorious for his severity and commonly known as the 'hanging judge', their trial took place on Thursday 7 December, in the OLD BAILEY and lasted eight hours. In his summing-up, the judge instructed the jury that if the prisoners had acted without

Newgate Gaol, where Richard Savage, James Gregory and William Merchant were imprisoned. Author's collection

provocation, they were all three guilty of murder. He rejected the plea of hot blood and dismissed the character witnesses' evidence as irrelevant. In his summing-up, Sir Francis Page said:

Gentlemen of the jury, you are to consider that Mr. Savage is a very great man, a much greater man than you or I, gentlemen of the jury; that he wears very fine clothes, much finer clothes than you or I, gentlemen of the jury; that he has abundance of money in his pocket, much more money than you or I, gentlemen of the jury; but, gentlemen of the jury, is it not a very hard case, gentlemen of the jury, that Mr. Savage should therefore kill you or me, gentlemen of the jury?

The jury found Savage and Gregory guilty of murder, and Merchant, who had been unarmed, guilty of manslaughter. When Savage and Gregory were brought into court for sentencing, Savage, on being given an opportunity to address the court made a plea for clemency: Savage's plea did nothing to soften the sentence as both he and Gregory were sentenced to die. In Newgate, as Savage awaited his execution, loaded with chains weighing fifty pounds, he wrote to his friend, the actor Robert Wilks, asking him to seek help for him from Mrs Oldfield. (Anne Oldfield 1683-1730, the celebrated actress, who had rendered financial help to Savage, partly because of her admiration for him and partly because he had been left nothing in his father's will, whereas Savage's father, Earl Rivers, an admirer, had left her £500.)

Mrs Oldfield, who had many admirers at Court and in the higher echelons of society meant that many doors were open to her. She secured an interview with Sir Robert Walpole, First Lord of the Treasury. She spoke of Savage's many attributes, his talent, his unfair trial, the lack of premeditation and at the end of the interview, Sir Robert promised to do his best. Mrs Oldfield secured the help of Lady Hertford, patroness of literature, who used her influence also. Savage was released with a free pardon, after he had already ordered a suit of clothes for the scaffold. The pardon for both Savage and Gregory was ordered on 6 January

Burning on the hand in the Sessions House, Old Bailey. Author's collection

1728 and both were released on bail on 20 January. The pardon passed the seals on 1 February, thereafter Savage and Gregory could not plead His Majesty's pardon in court until the last day of the following sessions during the first week in March, when their bail was discharged. William Merchant, although convicted of manslaughter, claimed BENEFIT OF CLERGY and got off with a branding in the thumb.

SEAMAN, WILLIAM

William Seaman was responsible for a double killing known as 'The Turner Street Murders'. The victims were Mr John Goodman Levy, aged seventy-seven and his housekeeper Mrs Anna Sarah Gale, aged thirty-five. Mr Levy had retired just a few weeks previously having been in business as an umbrella manufacturer, trading as M J Myers. It was generally believed that Mr Levy had made a considerable fortune as a fence, which subsequent events seemed to confirm. This case was instrumental in bringing detective sergeant F P Wensley to the notice of his superiors. He later became the first Assistant Commissioner to be promoted from the ranks.

Early on the afternoon of Saturday 4 April 1896, the East End was plunged into a state of wild excitement by the harrowing details which came to hand of one of the most brutal double murders, accompanied by attempted burglary, that had been seen in Whitechapel since the JACK THE RIPPER murders of 1888. The scene of the outrage was 31 Turner Street, Commercial Road East. The first suspicion of foul play was aroused a little before one o'clock on Saturday when Mrs Martha Lawton, a cousin of Mr Levy, who lived in the same street at No. 35, went to the house to keep a luncheon appointment but there was no reply. The next-door neighbour, a tailor, named William Schafer, came out to see what was the matter. He went to his backyard to see if he could ascertain anything and was astonished to see a strange man in a brown cloth cap inside the house. The constables on duty in the vicinity, having being summoned gained entry to No. 31 and proceeded to search the premises. Half concealed behind the lavatory door at the back of the ground floor, they discovered the body of Mr Levy, lying in a pool of blood. His throat had been cut from ear to ear with some sharp instrument, while the back of his skull had been battered in with what appeared from the terrible nature of the wounds to be a hammer. In the back second floor bedroom the housekeeper Mrs Gale lay on the floor, also in a pool of blood. Her head had been almost completely severed from her body, and her skull unmercifully beaten with a blunt instrument.

In the front room of the second floor the police officers noticed that a hole had recently been made in the ceiling giving access to the roof. There was a loud cry from the street below that there was a man on the roof. Just as one constable had got his body half-way through the hole into the void to the roof, he caught sight of a man standing in the gutter which ran round the roof. Moments later, the man had mounted the coping, hauled himself over by his hands, and dropped into the street below, a distance of between forty and fifty feet. As he fell, his body struck the back of a little girl, Leah Hyams, who was standing with her mother close under the wall at the Varden Street entrance to the house. Several gold watches, some rings, and other jewellery, as well as a quantity of money were found in two parcels he was carrying. He had sustained serious injuries. The injured man was taken to the London Hospital as was little Leah Hyams, where she received attention for injuries to her back and for fright. She was discharged from the hospital later that day. The man was identified as William Seaman.

On Saturday 2 May 1896 *The Times* reported:

Yesterday morning, William Seaman, 46, described as a lighterman of Claud-street, Millwall, was brought from the London Hospital and charged at the Thames Police-court with the wilful murders of Sarah Annie Gale and John Goodman Levy, of 31, Turner-street, Whitechapel on the 4th ult. The prisoner was lifted into the Court seated on an armchair and was evidently suffering considerable pain. Seaman, who was undefended, was on Thursday night interviewed by Mr. Bedford, solicitor, but declined that gentleman's services.

Constable G Bryan, 176H, said in his evidence given at Thames Police Court that, on 11 April while he was in charge of the prisoner at the London Hospital, Seaman said to him: 'I suppose old Levy is dead by this time and buried? Constable Bryan told Seaman that he didn't know. Seaman went on: 'I am glad I have done for him. I have been a good many times for the money, amounting to £70, and the old man always made some excuse. I made up my mind to do for him. I am not afraid of being hanged.' The next day, on waking up, Seaman said: 'I have been a frequent visitor to the house in Turner Street, where the job was done; and if the old Jew had only paid me the £70, the job would not have happened...'

Dr Lewis Smith, house surgeon at the London Hospital, said that when Mrs Bowater, Seaman's landlady, was called to identify him he said to her: 'I am guilty. I did it for revenge. He swindled me years ago. I did it for revenge.'

The outcome of Seaman's trial at the OLD BAILEY was almost a foregone conclusion. Found guilty of wilful murder, he was sentenced to death. Seaman was hanged at NEWGATE on 10 June 1896 by James BILLINGTON along with Albert

The Royal London Hospital, where William Seaman was taken to recover from the injuries sustained when he jumped from the roof of 31 Turner Street. The Author

The triple gallows at Newgate on which William Seaman was hanged between Albert Milsom and Henry Fowler on 10 June 1896. Author's collection

MILSOM and Henry FOWLER, two petty thieves turned murderers, who had fallen out during their trial, Fowler having almost strangled Milsom in the dock. At their execution, Seaman was placed between Milsom and Fowler. Seaman's last words are reputed to be: 'This is the first time I've ever been a bloody peacemaker.'

An unusual mishap occurred during the execution. Four warders were in close attendance on the scaffold. One of them obscured Billington's view of his assistant, Warbrick. Warbrick was still pinioning the feet of one of the prisoners when Billington operated the lever that opened the trap door. The three criminals plummeted to their deaths as Warbrick was catapulted into the pit. Fortunately, the latter heard the bolt beneath him being withdrawn and instinctively grabbed the legs of the man in front of him. He ended up swinging below the feet of the three dead men. The execution of Seaman, Milsom and Fowler was the last triple execution that took place at Newgate.

SEATON, JAMES

On November 30 2005, the battered and almost decapitated body of thirty-nine-year-old Jacqueline Queen was found by a dog walker in a park in East Finchley. Her Scots lover, forty-six-year-old gravedigger and unemployed bricklayer James Seaton, of Gainsborough House, Thorpedale Road, Finsbury Park, admitted killing her but claimed he was suffering from mental illness. He battered her to death with a claw hammer and sawed through her neck with a knife after she had spurned him for a lesbian lover. Prosecutor Brian Altman said at Seaton's trial at Snaresbrook Crown Court in October 2006: 'He refused to believe it when Miss Queen said she was a lesbian. The defendant refused to believe that she no longer wanted him.' Seaton was found guilty of murder and sentenced to life imprisonment on Friday 13 October 2006. After the trial was over investigating officer Detective Inspector John Nicholson said outside the court: 'I am pleased the jury recognised that James Seaton was neither provoked into his actions nor was suffering from such abnormality of the mind that he could claim the defence of diminished responsibility.'

SEDDONS, THE

Lancashire-born Frederick Henry Seddon was employed as District Superintendent of Canvassers for North London with the London and Manchester Industrial Assurance Company, a position he had occupied since 1901. A freemason and one time chapel-goer and preacher, this hard-working, thrifty man had a shrewd eye for business and took pride in meticulously attending to even the simplest of transactions. He was not particularly likeable as his general manner and an air of superiority tended to alienate him. By 1909, in addition to his insurance work, Seddon owned a second-hand clothes business, which he ran in his wife's name at 276 Seven Sisters Road, Finsbury Park and he and his family lived above the shop. Seddon invested his additional income in mortgaged property and regularly sold it on at a profit. After one successful business deal he bought a fourteen-roomed house at 63 Tollington Park, situated north of his shop between

Frederick Seddon. Author's collection

Stroud Green Road and Hornsey Road. He and his family moved in, along with Seddon's elderly father in November 1909. Seddon decided to rent out the top floor and the basement office he rented to his employers, who finding him scrupulously honest, allowed him to bank their money in his own account and paid him 5s a week rent.

On 12 August 1910, Miss Eliza Barrow became Seddon's tenant. She was a forty-nine-year-old spinster of independent means with private property amounting to about £4,000, which included the *Buck's Head*, Camden Town. Miss Barrow had taken on the responsibility of looking after two orphaned children, an adolescent girl named Hilda Grant, who was away at boarding school and her little brother Ernie, aged eight. They had lived with Miss Barrow in a succession of lodgings, ending up with her cousins, the Vonderahes, at 31 Evershot Road but they did not get on, so Miss Barrow moved around the corner to Tollington Park. Seddon said that Miss Barrow had become increasingly worried about her investments since 1909 when she believed Lloyd George's budget and 'soak the rich' policies might reduce her to penury. Miss Barrow eventually signed over all her property to Seddon in exchange for an annuity and subsequently increased this by signing over her India Stock also, which she was apparently highly delighted with. London sweltered in a heatwave in late August and early September 1911.

On 1 September, Miss Barrow was taken ill with what Dr Sworn diagnosed as epidemic diarrhoea and added that her mental state appeared to be as bad as her physical health. Her condition gradually deteriorated. She refused hospitalisation insisting that Mrs Seddon could nurse her just as well. On 4 September, Mrs Margaret Seddon said Miss Barrow instructed her to go and get some flypapers. The smell of her offensive

Miss Eliza Barrow. Author's collection

motions was attracting swarms of flies. The stench became so bad that it was necessary to hang sheets soaked in carbolic in all the rooms in an attempt to fumigate the air. Miss Barrow began to worry about what would happen to little Ernie and Hilda if she were to die. She asked Seddon to draw up a will for her. He did so and the will was witnessed by his married sister, Emily Longley and Mrs Seddon. The will made Frederick H Seddon sole executor, 'to hold all my personal belongings, furniture, clothing and jewellery in trust' until Ernest and Hilda Grant came of age. Miss Barrow died at about 6.15am on Thursday 14 September. Dr Sworn made out the death certificate giving the cause of death as 'epidemic diarrhoea'. Seddon arranged the funeral. William Nodes, undertaker, commented as follows at the Seddons' trial:

63 Tollington Park. Paul T Langley Welch

...having regard to the state that the body was in and the diarrhoea that had taken place, the warmth of the weather, and the fact that there was no lead lining to the coffin, it seemed quite reasonable that the body should be buried on Saturday...I explained to him what kind of funeral it would be for the price; it was a £4 funeral really...it would mean internment in a public grave...it is used for more than one person.

Seddon pointed out to Mr Nodes that Miss Barrow was not a relation and in consideration for the business he had brought him, accepted 12s 6d commission. The funeral took place on the afternoon of Saturday 16 September. Miss Barrow was buried in East Finchley in a public grave. When the Vonderahes learned of their cousin's death they wanted to know why they had not been informed and expressed astonishment that she had not been buried in the family vault in Highgate Cemetery. Seddon produced a copy of a letter he had sent them to Evershot Street but the Vonderahes had changed address. They also wanted to know what had happened to her money and were not satisfied with Seddon's answers. They caused such a fuss that the police, unbeknown to the Seddons, arranged to have Miss Barrow's remains exhumed on 15 November. Examined by Dr Bernard SPILSBURY and Dr William WILLCOX, arsenic was found in the hair and various organs. Further detailed tests took place, resulting in forty-year-old Frederick Seddon's arrest for murder on 4 December.

Various financial transactions involving £5 notes endorsed by Margaret Seddon using false names, were investigated. Thirty-three fivers, through their serial numbers, were traced to Miss Barrow. Thirty-eight-year-old Mrs Margaret Seddon was arrested on 15 January 1912. The trial of the Seddons opened at the OLD BAILEY on 4 March 1912 before Mr Justice Bucknill. Arsenic found in flypapers used in the Seddon household and in Miss Barrow's room formed the basis of the prosecution's case. Although the formidable Edward MARSHALL HALL put up a convincing defence, the trial resulted in Mrs Seddon's acquittal and her husband's conviction for wilful murder. Fred Seddon's lack of affability went strongly against him. The jury simply did not like him. His flippant response to cross-examination did not endear him. Before sentence of death was pronounced, Seddon gave a long and powerful speech, quoting facts and figures, and gave a full protestation of his innocence. He concluded by raising his hands as if he was taking a freemason's oath. The judge, too, was a freemason. He was moved to tears. An appeal was heard on 1 April and dismissed the following day. Despite a petition containing over 250,000 signatures protesting his innocence, Seddon was hanged at PENTONVILLE on 18 April 1912 by John ELLIS. Considerable doubt has been expressed about Seddon's guilt by some criminologists and true crime authors, many suggesting in all probability that if it was indeed murder, Mrs Seddon was the guilty party.

SHARPE, THOMAS

A violent murder took place on 4 October 1814, at Millfield Farm, a cottage situated

Millfield Farm (today known as Millfield Cottage), Millfield Lane, Highgate, where Elizabeth Buchanan (aka Elizabeth Dobbin) was murdered. The Author

in Millfield Lane, then a narrow thoroughfare, pretty much as it is today, which runs along part of the eastern edge of Hampstead Heath, adjacent to Highgate Ponds. The body of Elizabeth Buchanan (also known as Mrs Dobbins), a washerwoman, was found in the kitchen. She lived with her common-law husband, named Dobbins, who worked as a turncock for the Hampstead Water Company. Mrs Dobbins had been savagely beaten about the head with a poker, which had been left nearby covered with blood and bent with the force of the blows. At about the same time the body was discovered, a vagrant named Thomas Sharpe, had been apprehended as he retreated furtively towards Highgate Hill carrying two bundles of washing, stolen from Millfield Farm and he had been seen in the vicinity by several witnesses. The implausible story he told about buying the bundles from gypsies was not believed. At his trial, Lord Ellenborough, having passed the death sentence, concluded with the words: '...and may the Lord have mercy on your soul.' Sharpe replied: 'May the curse of God attend you day and night, both in this world and the next.'

SHOREY, MICHAEL

Michael Shorey, born in Barbados, became known as the Bodies in the Car Killer. On the morning of Monday 23 July 1990, passers-by noticed two young women, apparently asleep in the front passenger seat and the back seat of a parked car, a gold Toyota Corolla, in Spears Road, Holloway. Concern was raised when workers at the various factories in the street noticed that neither appeared to be breathing. The police were called. Both women were dead. The car belonged to one of the victims, Patricia Morrison aged twenty-eight, who with the other victim Elaine Forsyth aged thirty-one, shared a flat in Grenville Road, situated off Hornsey Road, Holloway. They also worked together at an estate agents. Post-mortem examinations of the bodies showed that death must have occurred about thirty-six hours previously, on Saturday 21 July, and that both victims had been strangled. Pathologist Dr Vensa Djorovic said Patricia had been approached from the front and strangled with a handbag strap, which was still around her neck when her body was discovered. Elaine had been attacked from behind and strangled with a curtain tie-back cord, found in their flat. Neither had been sexually assaulted. Both women were badly bruised, suggesting they had attempted to fight off their attacker. Scotland Yard's Detective Superintendent Geoff Parratt, who headed the inquiry, concluded that the killer had put the bodies into the car and driven it to Spears Road. An examination of the women's flat showed that they had been killed there. There were bloodstains on the walls and a carpet had been removed from the hall. Neighbours reported hearing sounds of screaming and fighting coming from the flat on Saturday evening but believed it to be a domestic row between the two girls. They had also heard bumping sounds, which was probably the killer taking the bodies down the stairs. Various reports came in of the car being seen being driven along Junction Road, Upper Holloway during the rush hour on Monday morning in a slow and erratic manner. A detailed description of the driver was given. He was a young black man with long, permed hair. Police were approached by a former boyfriend of Elaine Forsyth, thirty-four-year-old accounts clerk, Michael Shorey. He fitted the description perfectly. He denied harming the two women. His former record of violence suggested things might be otherwise but after being questioned he was released. Shorey had given the missing length of carpet, wrapped in plastic to a friend to look after. When he heard about the murders, the friend contacted police. The carpet had blood and saliva from both murder victims. Shorey was arrested and charged with double murder. Michael Shorey's trial began at the OLD BAILEY on 11 June 1991. Although some of the evidence was circumstantial, a pair of trainers worn by Shorey clinched the prosecution's case when it was revealed they had traces of blood on them from both the murdered women. Found guilty of murder, Michael Shorey was jailed for life on 3 July 1991.

SIDNEY STREET, THE SIEGE OF

During the closing years of the nineteenth century until the commencement of the First World War, various Russian and Eastern European socialist agitators abused the hospitality that Britain extended to refugees and foreign visitors. These anarchists, in order to fund their revolutionary struggles, committed burglary, robbery and murder. Such outrages although not exactly commonplace were beginning to unsettle law-abiding citizens and the TOTTENHAM OUTRAGE in January 1909 had shocked the nation. Tragedy preceded the incident that was to become known as the Siege of Sidney Street.

Friday 16 December 1910, a gang of anarchists met in a flat rented by Latvian Fritz Svaars, in Grove Street, Whitechapel, to put the finishing touches to plans for a robbery later that night. The leader of the gang was another Latvian, George Gardstein, and others present included gunrunner Karl Hoffmann, Peter Piatkow, known as 'Peter the Painter', Yourka Duboff, Joseph Federoff, John Rosen, Max Smoller, and Joseph Sokoloff.

The anarchists' target was the premises of H S Harris, situated at 119 Houndsditch. Henry Harris was a jeweller. His premises contained stock reputedly worth £20,000. The plan was to empty the shop of its entire contents. Entry was to be gained by a hole broken through the back wall from a cul-de-sac known as Exchange Buildings. Work began in an outside lavatory. With many people in the area observing the Jewish Sabbath the gang expected to be undisturbed. Frank Weil, who on coming home to the flat above his fancy-goods business next door to the jeweller's, at about 10pm was alerted by his sister to peculiar noises. The persistent banging, scraping and hammering had been going on for some time. Mr Weil went straight to Bishopsgate to look for a policeman. When he came back with PC Walter Piper, the constable, suspecting a burglary was in progress, didn't blow his whistle but went to fetch help. PCs Walter Choate and Ernest Woodhams joined him and they caught the anarchists in the act. The anarchists decided to shoot their way out and in the ensuing mayhem as more police arrived, Sergeants Robert Bentley and Charles Tucker and Constable Walter Choate were shot dead. The entire gang escaped, although George Gardstein was badly wounded, being hit in the back by a stray bullet. They managed to get back to Grove Street and called a doctor to attend to Gardstein's injuries. Dr John Scanlon said that he needed immediate hospitalisation but they refused to allow this and the doctor was allowed to leave. He immediately alerted the police and when they arrived at about midnight, all they found was Gardstein's body and a room full of weapons.

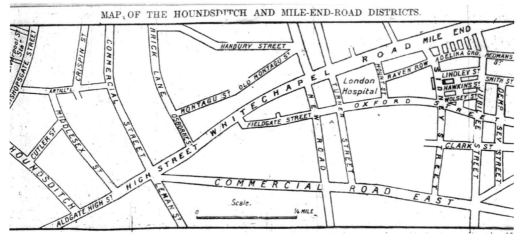

MAP OF THE HOUNDSDITCH AND MILE-END-ROAD DISTRICTS.

Author's collection

A huge investigation began during which the identities of some of the gang were revealed. Following a tip-off that two of the anarchists involved in the Houndsditch police killings were hiding in a house at 100 Sidney Street, the building was closely watched. In the early morning of Tuesday 30 January 1911, over 200 armed police surrounded the block, having stealthily evacuated nearby residents to places of safety. Detective Sergeant Ben Leeson was assigned to throw pebbles at a window to try to attract the anarchists' attention and hopefully persuade them to give themselves up. The response was a hail of gunfire and DS Leeson was hit twice. Fortunately, he recovered from his injuries. When it became apparent at the awesome firepower possessed by the cornered men, Scotland Yard Assistant Commissioner Major Wodehouse arranged with Home Secretary Winston Churchill for a Lieutenant and nineteen men of the Scots Guards, stationed in the Tower of London, to be sent to Sidney Street. In the hour-and-a-half from 11.30am to 2.00pm somewhere between 2000-3000 shots were exchanged. Winston Churchill went to view the scene himself. At 1.00pm a plume of smoke was seen coming from an attic window. As it grew thicker fragments of charred paper were scattered throughout the area. It appeared the anarchists were burning thousands of

Postcard view of 100 Sidney Street on fire. Author's collection

incriminating documents. At about 1.15pm a figure, believed to be Joseph Sokoloff, appeared at an upstairs window and began firing a Mauser. He was soon hit in the head by the answering fire. Fifteen minutes later the building was engulfed in flames, as the first floor collapsed. By the time it was deemed safe for firemen to enter 100 Sidney Street, it was little more than a blackened shell. The charred remains of the two anarchists were found inside. Fritz Svaars the other dead anarchist had been overcome by smoke. A rounding up of anarchists began. East End refugees closed ranks and following a trial at the OLD BAILEY lack of evidence resulted in acquittal of those concerned.

SLOWE, CHARLES JEREMIAH

At ten o'clock on the night of Wednesday 23 September 1903, Mary Jane Hardwick, who was assisting her sister Mrs Jane Starkey, landlady of the *Lord Nelson* public house in Whitechapel Road, was violently attacked in the public bar by a customer who then stabbed her with a knife, before fleeing the scene. Miss Hardwick died almost immediately. The man was identified as Charles Slowe of Rowton House, Whitechapel, referred to by many locally simply as Jerry. Slowe, a man without a trade or regular employment had taken a shine to Miss Hardwick but she would have nothing to do with him and did not like having to serve him. Slowe was quickly apprehended nearby and taken into custody. Robert Musgrave, a potman at the *Lord Nelson* said he had heard Slowe say in the bar one night, some seven or eight months before the murder: 'I'll put her light out one of these days.' Slowe's trial began at the Central Criminal Court, OLD BAILEY on Wednesday 21 October 1903. The defence attempted to have the charge reduced to manslaughter by claiming a lack of premeditation but Mr Justice Bingham said: 'In the eye of the law, if a person used a knife with the intent to do an injury, and death ensued, he was guilty of murder.' After fifteen minutes deliberation the jury found Slowe guilty of wilful murder. Before passing sentence the judge said the prisoner had

[Main Picture] *Charles Slowe fleeing the public bar of the* Lord Nelson *after fatally stabbing Mary Hardwick. Miss Hardwick's sister, Mrs Jane Starkey leaps over the bar to go to her younger sister's aid.* [Top left] *Charles Jeremiah Slowe a.k.a. Lyons.* [Top right] *Mary Jane Hardwick.* The Illustrated Police News

been guilty of a cruel and barbarous murder, and he must suffer for the consequences of his act. As he was leaving the dock, Slowe said: 'I shall meet it without fear.' He was executed at PENTONVILLE on Tuesday 10 November 1903 by James BILLINGTON.

SMITH, FRANCIS

For several weeks towards the end of 1803, a white-clad figure had been frightening local residents in Hammersmith. Sufficient numbers had been frightened for an *ad hoc* watch committee to be formed. They were determined to discover if the Hammersmith Ghost, as the spectre had become known, was indeed a malevolent spirit, or simply just a mischievous prankster. Excise officer Francis Smith, aged twenty-nine, was angry that someone was frightening the superstitious locals, particularly women and children. He armed himself and on the night of 3 January 1804 went in search of the ghost. He killed a perfectly innocent bricklayer, John Millwood, who was dressed in white, the usual attire for his occupation. He wore white trousers and a white apron. Smith shot John Millwood in the churchyard in Black Lion Lane, Hammersmith. He died from a bullet wound in the left jaw. Smith gave himself up immediately, and said he thought he was shooting a ghost. Condemned to death at the OLD BAILEY Sessions on 13 January, after the jury recommended mercy, the judge put in a request for the Royal Mercy. He was reprieved on 25 January on condition that he serve one year in prison.

SMITH, GEORGE JOSEPH

George Joseph Smith was one of the most notorious murderers of the twentieth century. On 18 December 1914, a newly married young woman died by drowning in the bath in Bismarck Road, Upper Holloway, a narrow road, which straddles the hillside between Highgate Hill and Archway Road, which was renamed Waterlow Road in the aftermath of the First World War, when German names were unpopular. The tragic death of a bride on her honeymoon excited sufficient attention to warrant its inclusion in the *News of the World,* the nationwide Sunday newspaper, on 27 December 1914. This single article on page eleven of just a few lines one column wide, brought about the downfall of one of the most infamous wife-killers of all time.

George Joseph Smith.
John D Murray collection

George Joseph Smith, the harmonium-playing petty criminal, confidence trickster, antique dealer and serial bigamist known as the Brides in the Bath Murderer was born on 11 January 1872 at 92 Roman Road, Bethnal Green. From an early age Smith was involved in petty crime. By the time he was twenty-four, he had taken to using aliases, the first being George Baker, the name by which he was sentenced to twelve months' hard labour for larceny and receiving stolen goods at North London Sessions in 1896. It was one of his numerous lady friends who had actually done the stealing for him. Smith had an eye for the ladies and judging by his success in the marital stakes, the ladies had an eye for him. He spent years courting ladies of means with varying degrees of success, using a whole series of aliases. If a particular lady took his fancy, having had his wicked way with her, invariably fleecing her of whatever money she had (he also often stole and sold the ladies' belongings), amounting to considerable sums in some cases, he took to his heels. In at least three cases he bigamously married and murdered his brides by drowning them in bathtubs. His first and only legal wife, one Caroline Beatrice Thornhill, he married in Leicester on 17 January 1898, using the alias George Oliver Love. On 9 January 1901

Smith was jailed for two years for receiving stolen goods. In his absence, due to his callous treatment of her, his wife fled to Canada. Smith then went about wooing an assortment of ladies, many of whom succumbed to his charms, some to his bigamous marital bed and three of his six known bigamous wives to a watery death.

Margaret (Peggy) Lofty was a thirty-eight-year-old spinster daughter of a long deceased clergyman. Whilst in Bristol, late in 1914, Smith introduced himself to her as John Lloyd, estate agent. Peggy was a lady's companion, who had worked for various respectable elderly women in the Bristol area. She lived in Bath with her sister and elderly mother and had experienced a deep disappointment earlier that year when she discovered that her fiancé was already married. When Smith, in the guise of John Lloyd appeared on the scene, she must have felt greatly relieved that perhaps she was not going to be 'left on the shelf' after all. He charmed her and told her he would return. He was as good as his word. On 15 December she left her home to go out for tea, but she never returned. She told none of her family about her intentions to marry Mr Lloyd. Perhaps her previous experience made her reluctant to do so, until that knot had actually been tied. Smith married Miss Lofty at Bath Register Office on the morning of 17 December, having visited London a few days previously to arrange accommodation.

They left Bath immediately after the wedding ceremony and took a train for London, arriving in the afternoon, when they went straight to 16 Orchard Road, Highgate, where they intended to lodge. Smith had visited Mrs Heiss, the landlady, a few days previously. However, after he had left, she had second thoughts about allowing the Lloyds to stay. She decided she did not like his manner and thought he might be trouble, so on their arrival she told them that accommodation was not yet available and they would have to lodge elsewhere. Smith being familiar with the area soon found lodgings in which he and his new bride could spend their wedding night. They moved into two furnished rooms at 14 Bismarck Road. The house had a bath. Miss Louisa Blatch was the landlady.

That evening, Mr Lloyd took his wife to see Dr Bates at 30 Archway Road. Mr Lloyd, the dutiful husband expressed his concerns to the doctor about his dear wife's poor state of health

14 Bismarck Road (now Waterlow Road).
Paul T Langley Welch

(This was a ploy he had used at least twice previously with his other 'brides', who shortly afterwards had drowned in their baths). The following morning, Friday 18 December, the last day of Peggy Lofty's life, Smith took her to a solicitor to make her will. Her life was already insured for £700. He also took her on a visit to the Post Office to withdraw her savings. She wrote to her mother informing her of her marriage. She described her husband as 'a thorough Christian man... I have every proof of his love for me...He has been honourable and kept his word in everything. He is such a nice man'. Shortly after 7.30 that evening, Mrs Lloyd took a bath. Miss Blatch, who was ironing in the kitchen, heard splashing coming from the bathroom directly above. She also heard Mr Lloyd playing *Nearer My God to Thee* on the harmonium in the Lloyds' sitting room. Shortly after that the front door slammed.

Margaret (Peggy) Lofty.
John D Murray collection

About ten minutes later the doorbell rang. When she answered it, Mr Lloyd was standing on the doorstep. He mentioned the key which she had given him, but which he had forgotten. He told her that he had been for some tomatoes for Mrs Lloyd's supper and asked if his wife was down from the bathroom yet. He called to her and when she didn't answer he went up the stairs. Then he called out to Mrs Blatch: 'My God! Its my wife! She doesn't answer! I do hope nothing has happened to her!' When Mr Lloyd entered the bathroom he found that his wife was dead. He tried to resuscitate her but to no avail, she had drowned. Peggy was buried on Monday 21 December. The verdict at the inquest was accidental death. Smith left London and went about his usual business. Meanwhile, the article in the *News of the World* had attracted the attention of the families and friends of his two other victims, despite him having used an alias of Henry Williams in one case and his real name in the other, the similarities in the mode of death of the ladies concerned aroused sufficient suspicion to warrant a thorough police investigation.

Mr Lloyd was placed under close observation and the police travelled to various parts of the country making exhaustive enquiries in the four weeks that followed. The police investigation revealed sufficient evidence to enable them eventually to amass an astonishing 264 exhibits to show at the trial and no fewer than 112 witnesses were called. On 4 January 1915, Smith, calling himself John Lloyd, instructed solicitors in Shepherd's Bush to have Peggy's will proved and to realise the proceeds of her life insurance policy. When he went to his solicitor's office again on 1 February, he was arrested outside the building. That same day Peggy Lofty's body was exhumed and examined by Dr Bernard SPILSBURY, who later travelled to Blackpool in Lancashire and to Herne Bay in Kent, to examine the bodies of Alice Burnham and Bessie Mundy, Smith's two other known drowned 'brides'. Following further investigations Smith was charged on 23 March with the wilful murder of Bessie Mundy, Alice Burnham and Margaret Lofty, although he was actually indicted only for the killing of Bessie Mundy.

George Joseph Smith, aged forty-three, stood in the dock at the OLD BAILEY on Tuesday 22 June 1915 at the commencement of his nine day trial, before Mr Justice Scruton. His defence counsel, the formidable Edward MARSHALL HALL came within a hair's breadth of getting an acquittal but Dr Spilsbury's evidence and a convincing demonstration of how he actually drowned his victims sealed Smith's fate. On 1 July the jury took just twenty-two minutes to find him guilty. Smith stood pale faced and was sweating profusely, gripping the dock tightly as the death sentence was passed on him. He was removed from PENTONVILLE to Maidstone Prison where, at 8.00am on Friday 13 August 1915, he was taken across the prison yard to the execution shed and hanged by John ELLIS. On the scaffold, George Joseph Smith was in a state of collapse, maintaining he was innocent of murder to the end.

SPILSBURY, SIR BERNARD HENRY

(pathologist and forensic scientist)
Sir Bernard Spilsbury (1877-1947), became Britain's first internationally famous forensic scientist. Dr Bernard Spilsbury, as he then was, rose to prominence after his involvement in the high profile case of Dr CRIPPEN (1910). Forensics was still in its infancy and Spilsbury was a driving force behind the pioneers of this new form of crime detection. His other early cases included the SEDDONS (1912) and George Joseph SMITH (1915). He rose to such eminence that it was said of him even his presence in a witness box could sway a jury. One of his last high profile cases was the ANTIQUIS CASE (April 1947). Towards the end of his life Sir Bernard became aware that his once razor-sharp intellect was beginning to fail him. Terrified at the thought of the loss of his mental powers, he was found gassed in his laboratory at London's University College on 17 December 1947. Westminster coroner Bentley Purchase, recorded that he had taken his own life.

Parish church of St James's, Clerkenwell. Ellen Lefevre and her children were buried in the churchyard.
Paul T Langley Welch

STEINBERG, JOHAN (JOHN) NICHOLAS

John Steinberg, a German, was a forty-five-year-old whipmaker. He lived with Ellen Lefevre, aged twenty-five, a lady later described as his mistress, and their four children aged between six years and eight months, at 17 Southampton Street, now renamed Calshot Street, a turning off the Pentonville Road. On 8 September 1834, Steinberg murdered Ellen and their children by cutting all their throats from ear to ear. He then fell upon the knife, without leaving any explanation or clues as to his motives. Ellen and the children were buried by public subscription in the churchyard of the parish church of St James, Clerkenwell. Steinberg was buried in the Paupers' Burial Ground in Ray Street. In lieu of the old custom of driving a stake through the body Steinberg's skull was broken with an iron mallet.

STITCHELL, EWEN

On New Year's Day 1926, in a house in Arlington Road, Camden Town, seventeen-year-old Polly Edith Walker was discovered lying beneath her bed in her nightdress, by her widowed mother. She had been strangled with one of her own silk stockings by her twenty-five-year-old, French Canadian, one-legged street musician lover Ewen Stitchell, also known as Eugene de Vere. In addition to being strangled, Polly had also sustained several head injuries. A copper-handled poker was found lying on the blood-soaked eiderdown, as were some broken fire tongs. Stitchell had a charismatic personality but lived life almost like a vagrant. Polly was attracted to him and felt sorry for him and had taken him under her wing. Following his arrest at Hitchin in Hertfordshire on Sunday 3 January, Stitchell admitted killing Polly. He said he had done so out of jealousy having discovered that she had taken another lover. *The Times* reported that, despite his artificial leg, Stitchell is believed to have walked the thirty-two miles to Hitchin, following the murder. Ewen Stitchell was hanged at PENTONVILLE on 24 March 1926.

STOCKWELL, JOHN

In 1934, the Eastern Palace cinema stood in Bow Road, Mile End. On 7 August an employee, nineteen-year-old John Stockwell, attacked the cinema's owner Dudley Horde and his wife, Maisie, with an axe and stole a little under £100. Mr Horde was found lying in a pool of blood unconscious, in the circle of the cinema. He died without regaining consciousness. Mrs Horde had only been knocked out and recovered. Stockwell had formulated an elaborate fake-suicide by drowning plan, which might have worked if only he had got the chronology right. After stealing the money from the safe he fled the scene and went to Aldgate East station, where he deposited the suitcase in a left luggage locker. Establishing that he was still alive and on the run was made easy for the police partly through a slip he made in signing a hotel register, and through the discovery of his clothes on the seashore before the time a postcard sent by himself to the police was postmarked, on which he announced his intention to commit suicide. Discovered under an alias, Stockwell was arrested at the *Metropole Hotel*, Great Yarmouth. He was tried at the OLD BAILEY, convicted of murder and hanged at PENTONVILLE on 14 November 1934.

STOCKWELL STRANGLER, THE – see ERSKINE, KENNET

STRATTON BROTHERS

In the early hours of Monday 27 March 1905, a pair of petty criminals, the Stratton brothers, Alfred, aged twenty-two and Albert, aged twenty, broke into the business premises of Mr Thomas Farrow, at 34 Deptford High Street. Next morning, when his assistant arrived at the paint shop, he found Mr Farrow dead in the parlour, with his head battered in. Mrs Ann Farrow lay unconscious in one of the bedrooms. She died four days later. A cash box had been forced open. On its metal tray was a thumbprint. A milkman had seen two men hurrying from the shop early that morning. The brothers were arrested and their fingerprints taken. This case is a landmark case in British legal history, as Alfred and Albert Stratton were the first criminals to be convicted of murder by fingerprint evidence. The brothers were hanged together at WANDSWORTH on 23 May 1905. Each blamed the other.

STRODTMAN, HERMAN

German-born Herman Strodtman came to London in 1694 along with a school friend Peter Wolter, to be apprenticed to city firm Stein & Dorien. They lodged together and were diligent in their work. In 1701, after Wolter's sister made an advantageous marriage, he assumed an air of superiority over Strodtman which he resented. Such was the rift between the two former friends that they began to fight. Wolter struck Strodtman twice, once in the counting-house, another time in the kitchen before the servant-girls. Dislike turned to hatred and Strodtman resolved to murder Wolter. He first tried to poison him by mixing mercury with some white powder Wolter used as a remedy for the scurvy, but Wolter had ceased to use the powder at that particular time. Matters came to a head over the Easter period. One night while Woter was asleep, Strodtman entered his room and hit him on the head. He then stabbed him several times before finishing him off by suffocating him with a pillow. He stole some money, about £8 in cash, from the counting-house and was apprehended when he tried to cash a bill for £20 from his employers at a bankers in Lombard Street. He was taken to NEWGATE and tried at the OLD BAILEY in the second Sessions following. He died full of contrition, penitence and hope. As he was hanged at TYBURN on 17 June 1701, it was remarked that he kept his hand up for a considerable time after the cart was driven away.

T

THOMAS, DONALD GEORGE

On St Valentine's Day, February 14 1948, during the early evening, PC Nathaniel Edgar was on plain-clothes duty, in Wade's Hill, Southgate following a spate of burglaries in the area. He stopped a man and questioned him. Three shots were heard and passers-by reported the sound of running footsteps along Broadlands Avenue. PC Edgar was found dying outside 112 Wade's Hill. Before he died he managed to whisper the name of his assailant to colleagues. PC Edgar had also written the name of the man in his notebook along with his address and identity number. The name read Donald Thomas, 247 Cambridge Road, Enfield.

Donald George Thomas was a twenty-three-year-old army deserter and had been on the wanted list since the previous October. He was not at the Enfield address but was later traced to a boarding house, run by Mrs Smeed, in Stockwell through the publication of a photograph of a married woman, Mrs Winkless, with whom he was having an affair. He was arrested in his room and the murder weapon, a Luger pistol was found under his pillow, which he had vainly tried to reach as the police burst into the room. He had also a large quantity of ammunition, a rubber cosh and a book, *Shooting to live with the One-Hand Gun*. When arrested Thomas remarked: 'You were lucky. I might as well be hung for a sheep as a lamb.' He was tried, convicted of murder and sentenced to death. However, Thomas was uniquely reprieved because Parliament was testing abolition of the death penalty and the trial took place during the five-year suspension period.

THRIFT, JOHN

John Thrift, described as being illiterate, nervous and hotheaded, was appointed hangman in 1735, when he is believed to have carried out thirteen hangings on 10 March. Following the rebellion of the Young Pretender in 1745, as well as hanging a great many soldiers at TYBURN and elsewhere, he beheaded several noblemen on Tower Hill including the last to be executed there, Lord Lovat, in April 1747.

Thrift lived for many years in Coal Yard (present day Stukeley Street, Covent Garden). On 11 March 1750, in the aftermath of the rebellions, when Jack Ketch (the name by which all London hangmen had been popularly known since about 1678), was an even less popular figure, David Farris, his wife and child, and two companions, Timothy Garvey and Patrick Farrel, passed Thrift's house, and Farris was heard to utter some uncomplimentary remark about Jack Ketch, which Thrift overheard. Thrift armed himself with a hanger (a short broad sword) and rushed out of the door and chased them off. They crossed Drury Lane and entered Short's Gardens, where an altercation took place, all the while Jacobite slogans were being chanted, by the ever increasing mob. At the end of this altercation David Farris, was wounded, stabbed by Thrift's hanger. Farris was carried to the house of Henry FIELDING (magistrate and novelist), before whom he and his wife accused Thrift of inflicting the wounds. Thrift himself went to see Fielding the following day to ask for a warrant to be issued against Farris for a violent assault. Fielding refused, saying he had already issued a warrant regarding the matter and could not issue cross-warrants. Farris died of his injuries on 19 March and Thrift was charged with murder, and incarcerated in NEWGATE, where the thought of Jack Ketch being hanged by his own noose seemed to please the inmates considerably.

Thrift was tried at the OLD BAILEY on 27 April. Although Thrift maintained that the hanger had been taken from him by one Enoch Stock, who had then slain Farris, Stock admitting that having been knocked senseless in the brawl he could neither confirm nor deny this, Thrift was found guilty of murder and sentenced to death. At the intervention of the City fathers, who had no intention of condoning mob rule and certainly not at the expense of endorsing Jacobitism, his sentence was firstly reduced to fourteen years' transportation, then within a matter of days he was granted a free pardon, after which he resumed his post as hangman, which he held until his death on 5 May 1752. He was buried at St Paul's Church, Covent Garden.

TILLETT, LEONARD

On Saturday 17 April 1869, Leonard Tillett, a one-time sailor in the Royal Navy, but lately a ne'er-do-well widower, murdered Harriett Stallion at 33 Fleet Lane, Farringdon Street, by slitting her throat with a razor. He then committed suicide by slitting his own throat. The bodies were discovered by Tillett's ten-year-old son. Harriett Stallion, a widow since March 1864, whose husband, a highly respected mechanic, by whom he had three children, had left her well provided for (she had about £900 settled on her),

Murder and suicide, Fleet Lane, 1864. [Left] *The house in Fleet Lane.* [Right] *Master Tillett at the scene of the crime.* Illustrated Police News

had refused to marry Tillet, despite his repeated requests. As a result of these refusals he had on more than one occasion been heard to utter the words: 'I will do for you and myself too.' According to witnesses, although Mrs Stallion showed some degree of courtesy to Tillett, she sometimes gave him the odd shilling to enjoy a pint or two of beer, by all accounts it appeared that it was more out of fear than out of any kind of affection. Some witnesses said they believed Tillett was not of an entirely sound mind. Mrs Stallion's seventeen-year-old daughter was adamant that there had been no intimacy between her mother and Tillett but a letter found in Tillett's pocket gives his apparent motive, although the couple believed to be those mentioned by him, Mr and Mrs Pickering, were according to witness reports family friends of long standing, and it was a totally innocent relationship. The letter read:

> *I have done a foul deed because she took a married man and used to go with him, and his wife knew it, and that is through how it was done. May the Lord have mercy on my soul. Amen. So good bye to this world.*

At the inquest the jury returned a verdict of wilful murder against Tillett and one of *felo de se* in the case of the self-murder.

TOTTENHAM OUTRAGE, THE

On Saturday 23 January 1908, an extraordinary chase took place through North and North-East London. The murders associated with it became known as the 'Tottenham Outrage' and the chase came about after the a pair of Russian anarchists snatched the wages (£80, the equivalent of over £4,000 today) as they were delivered to Schnurrmann's rubber factory in Chesnut Road. Having grabbed the money, Paul Hefeld and Jacob Lepidus ran down Chesnut Road with a policeman chasing after them. They turned into Scales Road, then left into Dawlish Road and right into Mitchley Road. It was there beside the Mission Hall that Hefeld shot PC Tyler; ten-year-old Ralph Jocelyn was also shot and killed as he ran for cover. Both victims were later buried in Abney Park Cemetery in Stoke Newington.

The chase continued along Park View Road, then over the railway into the marshes and northwards until at Lockwood Reservoir, realising police reinforcements were waiting for them, they went east across Walthamstow Avenue to Chingford Road. There they hijacked a tram travelling south, still firing guns at their pursuers. The anarchists forced the conductor to operate the tram, as the driver had fled, along with most of the passengers. The police requisitioned a milk cart in an attempt to follow the tram, but the anarchists shot the pony. They continued to fire their guns and in all over 400 rounds were discharged. Fortunately, although seventeen civilians and seven policemen were injured, there were no further fatalities.

The two men then made their way through the railway arch that runs across the Ching Brook, where they found themselves confronted by a 6ft fence that formed the boundary of a newly built housing estate. Realising they were cornered, Hefeld panicked and shot himself in the head (he died of his injuries on 18 February), but Lepidus escaped over the fence, crossed the railway lines and made his way from Beech Hall Road towards fields bordering Prestons Avenue, where the *Royal Oak* stood at the top end. He crossed Hale End Road to the rear of the pub and followed a hedge bordering some cottages. He leapt over the hedge and entered Oak Cottage, the home of coal carrier Charles Rolstone and his family. He ran upstairs and locked himself in the front bedroom. Several shots were fired but as police closed in on him, Lepidus shot himself dead.

TRUE, RONALD

In 1922 twenty-five-year-old Gertrude Yates, or to give her her 'professional name', Olive Young, lived in the basement flat at 13 Finborough Road, situated on the border of Fulham with Earls Court. There she earned her living as a high-class prostitute. She had entertained one particular client before and was not keen to do so again as he had stolen £5 from her purse. Unfortunately, on the evening of Sunday 5 March 1922 she allowed this man to stay the night. At 9.00am on Monday 6 March, Emily Steel, Miss Young's maid, let herself in to the flat in order to start making breakfast. A man appeared from Miss Young's bedroom and Emily recognised him as Major True. He told her not to disturb her mistress as they had gone to bed rather late. He then gave her a half-crown tip and left.

Described by some commentators as a 'Walter Mitty character' and others as a 'toff', Ronald True was a thirty-year-old ne'er-do-well, whose undistinguished early career with a variety of employers in New Zealand, Argentina, Canada and Mexico was marred by his dishonesty. At the beginning of the First World War he obtained a commission in the Royal Flying Corps. His time as a 'pilot' ended during training after a serious accident, caused through his ineptitude. He was invalided out in 1917 and thereafter made extravagant claims about his rank and war record. He went to New York, where he married an actress, Frances Roberts. By then True was addicted to morphine. Shortly after returning to England with his new wife, his well-placed family obtained a position for him on the Gold Coast. He flunked it once again. With a history of failed enterprises and false starts behind him, to add to his troubles his increasing dependency on morphine made him unpleasant to his wife. After his return to England, in his all too often deluded state, he built up debts, forged cheques and indulged in bouts of petty thieving.

True became friendly with James Armstrong and in the days before he made that final visit to Olive Young, he hired a car along with a chauffeur, Frank Sims, and he and Armstrong went out in it. On three separate nights they drove to the end of Finborough Road. True told Armstrong that someone was impersonating him and he intended to sort the matter out. On the last night, Sunday 5 March, True, having driven to Finborough Road with Armstrong, got out and sent the car away.

Olive Young was found in the bathroom by her maid, when she failed to get up. Emily discovered all that was in the bed in the blood-spattered bedroom were two pillows placed under the blankets. Her murderer having made her a cup of tea, had attacked her while she was drinking it, hitting her three times over the head with a rolling pin, before stuffing a towel in her mouth and strangling her with a dressing gown cord; then her lifeless body had been dragged into the bathroom. As True had made no effort to cover his tracks he was easily found and arrested on Monday evening at the Hammersmith Palace of Varieties. He denied any knowledge of the murder. True's trial began at the OLD BAILEY on Monday 1 May 1922, before Mr Justice McCardie. His defence counsel, Sir Henry Curtis-Bennett, in applying the McNAGHTEN RULES, failed to establish his client's insanity to the jury's satisfaction. Prosecutor Sir Richard Muir expressed the view, that while the prisoner might be deranged, he certainly knew the difference between right and wrong. True was found guilty and sentenced to death. With the advance in medical knowledge there was considerable unease about the validity of the McNaghten Rules, and having subsequently been examined by three medical experts, True's sentence was commuted to life imprisonment. There were protests that his class background had favoured him. He had killed a prostitute, whereas Henry JACOBY, a hotel servant, who had murdered Lady White and was in PENTONVILLE with True under sentence of death, was not reprieved. Ronald True died in Broadmoor aged sixty in 1951.

TURNER, ANNE – see OVERBURY, SIR THOMAS

TURNER STREET MURDERS – see SEAMAN, WILLIAM

TYBURN

The first execution known to have taken place in the vicinity of Tyburn was that of William Fitzosbert, hanged there in 1196 for sedition. However, in 1236, Alfred Marks refers to many ancient documents in his *Tyburn Tree Its History And Annals* and the earliest record of what thereafter was referred to as Tyburn Tree is mentioned in 1236, when:

...a dreadful machine called a gibbet, was set up in London...

The name is derived from the River Tyburn that runs nearby, a river long since culverted which feeds the River Thames. The dreaded 'triple tree' stood at the junction of Edgeware Road, Bayswater and Oxford Street close to Marble Arch. Until 1783, when the last execution took place, over 1,100 men and somewhere in the region of 100 women were executed there. Many of those executed had committed relatively minor crimes. The vast majority were hanged, some were burned and a few were beheaded or hanged drawn and quartered. After 1783, because of increasing fears of public disorder both at Tyburn itself and along the route from NEWGATE, along Holborn, St Giles and Tyburn Road (today's Oxford Street), executions were moved to Newgate itself to afford greater security.

The Idle Apprentice executed at Tyburn, as depicted by William Hogarth. Author's collection

V

VAN BERGHENS, THE, AND DROMELIUS

All three murderers in the case were born in Holland. In 1700, Michael Van Berghen and his wife, Catherine ran a public house in East Smithfield. Apart from their bar staff, the Van Berghens were attended by a servant, Geraldius Dromelius. One evening a gentleman named Oliver Norris was drinking in the Van Berghens' house from about eight o'clock until after eleven. He became extremely intoxicated and asked a maid servant to procure a coach to take him to his lodgings at an inn in Aldgate. No coach could be found, so Norris set off home on foot. On finding his purse was missing he returned to the Van Berghens and accused them of stealing it. Dromelius joined in as tempers became severely heated and Mr Van Berghen seized a poker and struck Norris on the head, fracturing his skull. Dromelius stabbed Norris in several parts of the body, while Mrs Van Berghen looked on. She then helped the two men to strip Norris of his hat, wig, and waistcoat, after which the body was carried to a nearby ditch which drained into the River Thames. While the Van Berghens cleaned up the blood Dromelius took the clothes in a hamper to dispose of at Rotherhithe, where he took lodgings in anticipation of securing a passage to Holland at the first opportunity. The next morning, the body of Oliver Norris was found at low tide. Someone had seen Van Berghen and Dromelius near the spot the night before. A search was made at the Van Berghan's but apart from a few bloodstains, little else was found. Suspicion was aroused when the Van Berghens could give no satisfactory explanation for Dromelius having left their service. The maid servant provided crucial evidence against them when she said her mistress had told her to tell Mr Norris that she could not find a coach for him. Dromelius was taken into custody at Rotherhithe and all three were taken to NEWGATE and tried at the next OLD BAILEY Sessions. They were executed near the *Hartshorn Brewhouse*, East Smithfield, on 10 July 1700. The bodies of Michael Van Berghen and Geraldius Dromelius were afterwards hanged in chains between Bow and Mile End. Catherine Van Berghen was buried.

VOISIN, LOUIS

On 2 November 1917, a road-sweeper was at work in Regent Square, Bloomsbury. He noticed a large parcel covered in sackcloth, behind the iron railings in the shrubbery of the central gardens. He opened the parcel and discovered, wrapped in a bloodstained sheet, and dressed in delicate lace underwear, the headless torso of a woman. On a paper wrapper was scribbled the miss-spelled message 'Blodie Belgiam'. Nearby, wrapped in brown paper, was a second parcel and this contained the woman's legs. There was one clue that was to prove crucial in the identification of the remains. On the bloodstained sheet in which the torso had been wrapped, was an embroidered laundry mark 'II H'. It was established that the remains had been dismembered by someone who had some knowledge of anatomy, and the time of death was established as being within the previous two days.

Chief Inspector Frederick Wensley was placed in charge of the case. The usual rounds of launderers were instigated and eventually the laundry mark was tracked down to a house in Munster Square, situated off Albany Street, Regents Park. At No. 50 a young Frenchwoman lodged. Thirty-two-year-old Emilienne Gerard, estranged from her husband, Paul, had been missing from her rooms since 31 October. A search revealed an IOU for the sum of £50, signed by Louis Voisin. There was also a framed photograph, which later proved to be of Louis Voisin, who was discovered to be her lover.

Voisin was traced to the basement flat at 101 Charlotte Street, Fitzroy Square. When the police called there, Voisin was in the company of Berthe Roche, who apparently lived with him. They also discovered that his trade was a butcher. As Voisin spoke hardly any English, it was decided to conduct the interview through an interpreter and Chief Inspector Wensley had them brought to Bow Street for questioning. There it was established that Voisin had known Emilienne Gerard for about eighteen months and an intimate relationship had developed between them. On 31 October they had met to say their goodbyes, on the eve of Madame Gerard's departure for France. She was going to see her husband who was a cook in the French army. For the moment all that had been established was the fact that Voisin and Madame Gerard were lovers. It had not at that point been established that the dismembered remains were actually those of Madame Gerard. Nevertheless, Voisin was detained at Bow Street overnight.

The following morning, through an interpreter, Chief Inspector Wensley asked Voisin if he would mind writing out the words 'Bloody Belgium'. Louis Voisin was a hulking brute of a man, who had great strength but little intelligence. He laboriously wrote down the words five times. The last effort was strikingly similar to that written on the parcel. On seeing this, Chief Inspector Wensley was confident that he was on the right track.

After a further visit to Charlotte Street there was no doubts all as to whose remains had been discovered in the parcels found in Regent Square. The kitchen contained the tools of Voisin's trade. As well as saws and knives hanging on the walls, there was also a big knife-sharpening wheel. The walls of the kitchen were spattered with blood. This proved to be human. An earring was found caught in a towel. It was later established this belonged to Madame Gerard. Further searching revealed even more daming evidence. In a little arched recess in the coal cellar the police found a cask of alum which also contained Madame Gerard's head and hands. Voisin owned a pony and trap. The trap was covered with blood. When questioned about the discoveries, Voisin said he had found Madame Gerard's body in its dismembered state on the previous Thursday at her flat, adding:

I did not know what to do. I thought someone had laid a trap for me.

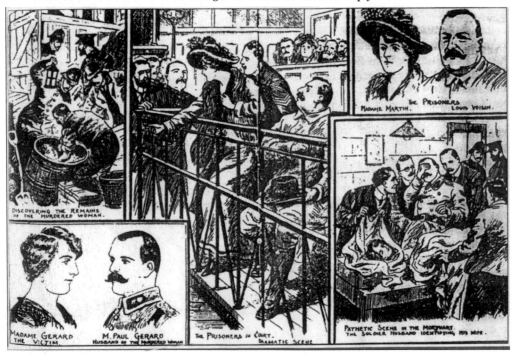

The murder of Madame Emilienne Gerard by Louis Voisin and Berthe Roche.
Illustrated Police News

However, his story did not tally with the evidences and what Voisin had intended to be a false clue, to suggest a xenophobic anti-war motive, served only to trap him. Semi-literate, and not at all bright, he was clearly unaware of the mis-spelling of what he had intended to read 'Bloody Belgium. His inability to spell, in part, proved to be his downfall. The theory put forward by Home office pathologist Bernard SPILSBURY based on the evidence provided by the wounds to the body, was that a large number of wounds had been inflicted by a far weaker hand than the powerful brute of a man Voisin. However, what the police believed may have happened was never admitted by Voisin or Roche. This theory or at least something very like it, seems the most likely explanation, based on the known facts. On the night of 31 October 1917, London suffered one of the worst Zeppelin raids. It is believed that Emilienne Gerard was in the vicinity of Charlotte Street that night, and in fear of her life, she called at her lover's home seeking shelter and comfort from the raids but an argument resulted in her being murdered.

Voisin's trial before Mr Justice Darling, at the OLD BAILEY, was only remarkable for the fact that after being found guilty of murder, the judge pronounced sentence of death in French. Louis Voisin was hanged at PENTONVILLE on 2 March 1918. Berthe Rohe was tried separately before Mr Justice Avory on 1 March 1918. She was acquitted of murder but charged as an accessory. The jury found her guilty and she was given a seven-year prison sentence. However, she didn't serve it, as within a very short time she was certified insane. She died on 22 May 1919.

VRATZ, STERN AND BOROSKY

Captain Christoher Vratz (some accounts spell the name Uratz, others Vrats) was born in Pomerania (a small country adjoining Poland), and although of good birth was a man of little fortune. He became a highwayman and once held up the King of Poland, during the Siege of Vienna, robbing him and his attendants of many diamonds and a considerable quantity of gold. He also committed robberies in Hungary after which time he bought himself a commission in a regiment in the Emperor of Germany's service, where he became acquainted with the Swedish Count Coningsmark, with whom he came over to England. The Count having been thwarted in his advances to a certain Lady Ogle by one Thomas Thynn, Esq, decided nothing would satisfy him but the death of his rival. The Count allegedly requested thirty-eight-year-old Vratz to carry out

The murder of Thomas Thynn Esq, in Pall Mall. Author's collection

the killing. Captain Vratz enlisted the assistance of John Stern, a lieutenant, who was the illegitimate son of a Swedish baron, afterwards made a count and George Borosky, who was Polish. A little after eight o'clock on the night of Sunday 12 February 1681, Thomas Thynn, having visited the Countess of Northumberland and only shortly before been accompanied by the Duke of Monmouth, was riding in his coach up to St James's Street, when Borosky fired a blunderbuss at him. Five bullets tore into his guts, wounded his liver, stomach and gall bladder and broke one of his ribs, of which wounds he died. Vratz, Stern and Borosky were arrested the next day by Sir John Reresby and brought before Justice Bridgman, who committed them to NEWGATE. Count Coningsmark attempted to leave the country but was found at Gravesend disguised and about to board a ship for Sweden. He was brought back to London and taken before the King and Counsel but confessed nothing to either being privy to or concerned in the murder. Vratz, Stern and Borosky were tried at the OLD BAILEY on Tuesday 28 February before Lord Chief Justice Pemberton. All three were found guilty of murder. Count Coningsmark was acquitted as not being an accessory by the same jury. Vratz, Stern and Borosky were hanged in Pall Mall on Friday 10 March 1682. Borosky was afterwards hung in chains near Mile End at the express command of King Charles II. The diarist, John Evelyn wrote:

March 24th 1682.- I went to see the corpse of that obstinate creature Colonel [sic] Vrats [sic], the king permitting that his body should be transported to his own country, he being of a good family, and one of the first embalmed by a particular art, invented by one William Russell, a coffin-maker, which preserved the body without disbowelling [sic] or to appearance using any bitumous matter. The flesh was florid, soft, and full, as if the person were only sleeping. He had now been dead for near fifteen days, and lay exposed in a very rich coffin lined with lead, too magnificent for so daring and horrid a murderer.

W

WAINWRIGHT, HENRY

On the afternoon of Saturday 11 September 1875, a sensational chase began in the Whitechapel Road. A four-wheeled cab was followed on foot by a perspiring and breathless young brushmaker named Alfred Stokes. He called out from time to time for police assistance but none came. Stokes followed the cab to the Commercial Road, where it stopped briefly near the corner of Greenfield Street to pick up a female passenger. The chase continued through the City as the cab made its way to the river, then across London Bridge, before it ended its journey in High Street, Borough, coming to a halt at the junction with Southwark Street, at a group of buildings known as the Hen and Chickens.

A smartly dressed, bearded man got out of the cab and took from the front seat a parcel, which he carried into the Hen and Chickens. While this was happening, Alfred Stokes spotted a policeman and went to talk to him. A little later the man came back to the cab and took out another parcel and Stokes and the policeman approached him, joined by another policeman. They accompanied the man, still carrying the parcel, into the Hen and Chickens and emerged a few minutes later. The bearded man and the woman who remained inside the cab, were taken into custody and driven to Stone's End Police Station. The two parcels were taken to St Saviour's mortuary.

The bearded man was Henry Wainwright, a mat and brushmaker, who had until his recent bankruptcy operated from business premises at 84 and 215 Whitechapel Road. Back in 1871, thirty-three-year-old Henry Wainwright, a keen amateur actor and public speaker, was a successful businessman who was living with his wife and family in Chingford. By chance, he met twenty-year-old Harriet Louisa Lane, apprenticed to a milliner and dressmaker. She became his mistress. They conducted their affair using various aliases and he moved her into lodgings at 14 St Peter Street (now Cephas Street), Mile End. Well placed in business, Wainwright gave his mistress £5 a week. Harriet bore him a daughter on 22 August 1872. After Wainwright moved his family into 40 Tredegar Square, Bow, he moved Harriet to the West End. She later bore him another child, also a girl. Both children were looked after elsewhere, paid for by Wainwright.

As Wainwright's business dealings began to flounder Harriet became an increasingly irritating encumbrance. To economise he had moved her back to Whitechapel, to lodgings in Sidney Street. His business continued on the downturn and he had debts of over £3,000. Harriet's constant demands on his purse and her increasing bouts of drunkenness were beginning to cause him embarrassment, particularly as she had taken to calling in at his place of business. He decided to off-load her and conceived a plan to procure a new lover for her. He persuaded his brother, Thomas, to pose as her admirer, and the name he chose for him was that of one of his acquaintances, Teddy Frieake. His plan was for Thomas, in the guise of Frieake to endear himself to her and to take her to some far-flung place on the continent, and leave her without means, so that her return to England would be impossible. This highly implausible plan was only partially put into operation with several liaisons between Teddy and Harriet. Meanwhile, Wainwright attempted to rescue his failing business, by mortgaging his warehouse at 215 Whitechapel Road in September 1884.

Clearly by this time Wainwright had realised the continuance of his relationship with Harriet Lane posed too great a risk. On 10 September he ordered half a hundredweight of chloride of lime. At four o'clock the following afternoon, Harriet Lane left her lodgings. The living space above Wainwright's warehouse was vacant, she intended staying there. She was never seen alive again.

Henry Wainwright. Author's collection

Three men working next door to Wainwright's warehouse swore that, on an evening about this time in September, between half-past five and six o'clock they heard three pistol shots fired in rapid succession, which appeared to come from the direction of Wainwright's premises. The discoveries made almost exactly a year later would seem to bear that out. Certainly Harriet's body was buried in chloride of lime in an area towards the back of the warehouse, known as the 'paint shop'. Harriet Lane had been shot through the head and her throat had also been cut. Wainwright clearly believed that the chloride of lime would quickly dissolve the soft tissue and soon there would be no remains to link him to the murder. How wrong he was. Harriet's family made enquiries concerning her whereabouts and the real Teddy Frieake, appearing on the scene caused considerable consternation, which later was explained at the Wainwright brothers' trial.

On 27 November 1874, Wainwright's shop at 84 Whitechapel Road burnt down. He claimed £3,000 insurance money from the Sun Fire Office but they disputed the claim. He brought an action against them, which had not yet come to trial at the time of his arrest. On 30 June 1875, Henry Wainwright was declared bankrupt. A fellow Whitechapel businessman, Mr Martin, took over Wainwright's former business in an amicable way, and advanced him £300. He paid Wainwright a salary of £3 a week as manager, and intended to eventually restore his business to him. Wainwright had by this time moved from Tredegar Square to School Lane, Chingford. Mr Martin also took on Alfred Stokes, Wainwright's former long-term outworker.

The mortgagees having foreclosed on his warehouse, made Wainwright realise that Harriet's remains had to be removed. He still retained a key and gained unobtrusive access to the rear of the warehouse via Vine Court. Exactly when Thomas Wainwright became aware of what had happened to his brother's mistress is not known. But once Wainwright realised Harriet's remains were extremely well preserved, he enlisted his assistance. On 10 September 1875 the brothers purchased between them some American cloth, rope, a spade and a chopper, after which Harriet's body was crudely chopped up. About four o'clock that afternoon Henry Wainwright asked Stokes to help him remove some parcels from the warehouse. He did so and carried one heavy package into Whitechapel Road, Wainwright carried the other, all the time puffing on a cigar to disguise the offensive smell. While Wainwright went for a cab, Stokes untied the rope and peered into one of the parcels. He saw a human hand. When Wainwright put the parcels into the cab Stokes followed it and the chase began.

Henry Wainwright's shop was situated next to the Pavilion Theatre. He was very friendly with the artistes who appeared there, and often took them out. In the Commercial Road, when he saw Alice Day, who worked at the theatre as a seamstress, Wainwright stopped the cab and invited her to join him. He continued to puff on his cigar until the cab reached the Hen and Chickens in Borough High Street, where until recently his brother, Thomas, had run an ironmongery business. There were deep cellars there with plenty of places to secrete unwanted encumbrances. But as Wainwright attempted to dispose of Harriet once and for all, he was arrested but not before attempting to bribe the two police officers who apprehended him in the act.

The remains were examined and three bullets were found in Harriet's skull. It was concluded that her throat had been cut either immediately before or immediately after death. Although her facial features were unrecognisable, she was positively identified by her father because of a scar on her right knee.

It soon became clear that Miss Day knew nothing about the contents of the parcels and she was released but Henry Wainwright's brother, Thomas was also arrested. The Wainwright brothers' trial commenced at the OLD BAILEY on Monday 22 November 1875, before the Lord Chief Justice of England (Sir James Alexander Cockburn, Bart). The whole story of Wainwright's connection with Harriet Lane was revealed, as was his brother's involvement. Thomas Wainwright was sentenced to seven years' imprisonment as an accessory. Henry Wainwright was found

The execution of Henry Wainwright, Newgate, 21 December 1875. Illustrated Police News

guilty of murder and sentenced to death. He was executed at NEWGATE by William MARWOOD on Tuesday 21 December 1875. Wainwright strode to the execution shed with a smile on his lips. His smile faded when he beheld the unexpected crowd of spectators, because the execution itself was only nominally private, as some sixty-seven people were present. It was rumoured that some women were there disguised as men. Wainwright said to the assembled company: 'Come to see a man die have you, you curs?' He was afterwards buried in 'Dead Man's Walk', within the precincts of Newgate. Alfred Stokes was awarded £30 by the judge. A public collection raised £1,200 for Henry Wainwright's widow and their children.

WALTERS, ANNIE – see ISLINGTON BABY-FARMING CASE, THE

WANDSWORTH PRISON

Wandsworth Prison was built in 1851, as the House of Correction for the County of Surrey. From 1877 Wandsworth was used to hold short-term prisoners. After HORSEMONGER LANE GAOL closed in 1878, executions for South London crimes were carried out at Wandsworth.

WARD, ROBERT

On Thursday 20 July 1899, twenty-seven-year-old out of work bricklayer Robert Ward, returned to his home in Boundary Road, Camberwell Gate after indulging himself in a heavy drinking session, which had been his wont for the last six months or so since he had been out of work. He was very depressed, having been unable to find any permanent employment. This last drinking session had lasted for a full week. On 20 July, having left the house at about 6.00am to seek work in Peckham, he returned home about noon and asked for some food. His wife, Florence, a somewhat delicate, though hard-working woman, maintained the household by charring and other labour; and always managed to keep her children, two little girls, clean and tidy. She went out immediately to make some purchases. Meanwhile, Ward called his daughters, Mary and Violet, who were playing in the street, into the house and took them to an upstairs bedroom, where he hacked at their throats with an ordinary clasp knife. Great force must have been used, as the knife was not sharp. He then tried to commit suicide by slitting his own throat. Mrs Mills, the landlady heard the commotion and cries of 'Don't Daddy' and went to investigate.

As her horrified gaze fell on three bodies surrounded by blood, she fled the scene and fetched a policeman, who returned with her and sent for the divisional surgeon. Both little girls were dead but their murderer was still alive. Ward said to policeman PC 165L:

I have done it and I want to die as well. I did it with that penknife that lies at my feet.

His throat was bandaged up and he was able to walk to the ambulance, which took him to Guy's Hospital. Robert Ward was charged with the murder of his daughters, Margaret Florence (Mary), aged five and Ada Louisa (Violet), aged two and with attempting to commit suicide (still a criminal offence, remaining so until 1961). Ward was tried at the Central Criminal Court, before Mr Justice Phillimore. The only reason he could give for his appalling act of cruelty was that his wife was too friendly with a

Walworth tragedy. Robert Ward murders his two daughters then attempts to commit suicide.
Illustrated Police News

soldier. After he discovered she had once been his sweetheart he had become very jealous. Evidence of insanity in his family did not sway the jury. He was found guilty of murder and sentenced to death, the judge adding, he could hold out no hope that the law would not take its course. Ward was hanged at 9.00am on Wednesday 9 October 1899 at WANDSWORTH by James BILLINGTON, assisted by his son Thomas.

WEILS, THE, LAZARUS AND PORTER

Mrs Hutchings was the widow of a farmer. She had three children, two boys and a girl. Her late husband had left her well provided for and she lived in the farmhouse in King's Road, Chelsea, attended by servants. John Slow and William Stone who worked as labourers on the farm also lived there.

One Saturday evening just as the Jewish Sabbath had ended, a gang of Jews assembled in Chelsea Fields. At about 10 o'clock they went to the Hutchings' farmhouse and demanded admittance. The household had retired with the exception of Mrs Hutchings and her two female servants. On being asked what was their business the gang rushed in and threatened the women with death if they resisted. Mrs Hutchings' petticoats were tied over her head and the servant girls were tied back to back. While the remainder of the gang stood guard five of the villains proceeded to ransack the house. When they came across the rooms occupied by the sleeping labourers it was decided they must be murdered. Levi Weil aimed a blow at William Stone's chest, which only stunned him. Slow woke up and a pistol was instantly fired at him. He exclaimed:

Lord have mercy on me! I am murdered!

Still alive, Slow was dragged to the head of the stairs, and while the gang proceeded to ransack the rest of the house, Stone, having recovered his senses, made his escape through a window onto the roof. The thieves took all the plate they could find and threatened to kill Mrs Hutchings if she did not reveal where she kept her money. She gave them her watch and a purse containing £65, after which the gang fled. Mrs Hutchings having freed the girls found Slow, who told her he was dying. He died the following afternoon.

This daring raid by a gang of Jews caused a great deal of ill feeling against the whole Jewish people for a considerable time. Fortunately, appeasement came in part after some of the gang were apprehended and brought to justice following one of their number a German Jew named Isaacs, being tempted by the prospect of a reward. It was revealed that the gang consisted of eight Jews headed by Dr Levi Weil, a physician, who had studied at the University of Leyden. On coming to London, Dr Weil did not practice medicine for long. He decided that robbery was a much more profitable occupation to follow and formed a gang of thieves consisting of poor Jews brought over from Amsterdam. Dr Weil sent his men out during the daytime to look for houses that might provide rich pickings; the gang would go back some time later and attack them at night.

Six Jewish men were brought up at the Sessions held at the OLD BAILEY in December 1771, being tried on Friday 6 December. Dr Levi Weil, Asher Weil, Marcus Hartagh, Jacob Lazarus Solomon Porter and Lazarus Harry were indicted for the robbery at Mrs Hutchings' farm and for the murder of John Slow. Dr Weil, Asher Weil, Jacob Lazarus and Solomon Porter were found guilty as charged but

Marcus Hartagh and Lazarus Harry were acquitted, for want of evidence. A rabbi attended the four condemned men in the press-yard at NEWGATE but declined to accompany them to the place of execution. Having prayed together and sung a Hebrew hymn on the scaffold they were hanged at TYBURN on Monday 9 December 1771.

WEST, GRAEME

On Saturday 2 January 1993, fifty-five-year-old millionaire businessman Donald Urquhart had been enjoying a drink in the *Queen's Head*, Marylebone, with his Thai girlfriend, Pat, when they left to get a taxi to take them to their favourite restaurant. As they reached the junction of St Vincent Street with Marylebone High Street a black Yamaha 250cc motorbike drew up a little ahead of them. The rider got off and, leaving the engine running, approached the couple, and before about a dozen witnesses, pulled a gun from inside his leather jacket and shot Mr Urquhart in the head. As he fell to the floor outside Robert Dyas, the ironmongers, the gunman stooped to fire two more shots into his victim's head, before speeding off on his Yamaha. In recent years there had been a spate of such incidents, many of the killings being a result of competition between criminals. The police believed that Mr Urquhart's murder was a contrast killing carried out on the orders of a business rival. Amongst other interests Urquhart owned an exclusive block of flats, was a major shareholder in a construction company and a golf course. Eventually, enquiries led police to south London, where they had heard a group of hitmen were operating. Graeme West, a former nightclub bouncer turned hitman was arrested on 28 September 1993, after unguardedly admitting that he had carried out the Urquhart killing, to a man he believed was a potential client. An accomplice was also arrested. West's trial commenced at the OLD BAILEY in October 1994 and lasted for six weeks. He was found guilty of murder and given a life sentence. His accomplice received five years for conspiracy to murder. The person who put out the contract on Donald Urquhart was never discovered.

WESTON, RICHARD - see OVERBURY, SIR THOMAS

WHEELER, ELEANOR - see PEARCEY, MARY ELEANOR

WIGGINS, JOHN

John Wiggins, a thirty-five-year-old lighterman, was found guilty at the OLD BAILEY of the murder of Agnes Oates at Temperance Cottage, Limehouse, in the early hours of Wednesday 31 August 1867, when her throat had been savagely slit open. Agnes, a young woman in her late teens, hailed from Liverpool. Wiggins met her when she was working as a barmaid at the *Crown Tavern*, in Salmon Lane, Limehouse. She subsequently worked as a servant at the *Cock*, Wapping, leaving her position to live with Wiggins about six months before her death, after he seduced her and promised they would marry. Witnesses reported that the couple quarrelled over money. Wiggins, who had knife wounds to his neck and himself expected to die, later maintained that Agnes had attacked him with a knife and then cut her own throat. The evidence suggested otherwise. He was hanged outside the Debtors' Entrance at NEWGATE on Tuesday 15 October 1867 by William CALCRAFT. It was not without incident. The *Illustrated Police News* reported:

…the prison bell began to toll, and the convict was escorted to the scaffold, which he ascended with a light step, attended by the ordinary and the executioner. There a very unusual and very painful scene occurred. The crowd on seeing the convict, became very excited, and he began to resist the efforts of Calcraft to place him below the beam. First, one of the stalwart prison warders and then another were summoned to assist in restraining him, until four or five of them, with the executioner were upon the scaffold at one time. After the cap had been drawn over his face, the convict shouted to the crowd "I am innocent; on my dying oath. I am innocent. Cut my head off, but don't hang me. I am innocent.

Ward continued to struggle and to protest his innocence to the crowd, until at last he was overcome by sheer force. The rope was adjusted and the drop fell. The *Illustrated Police News* reported that the convict was soon dead.

John Wiggins struggles on the scaffold at Newgate as William Calcraft places the noose around his neck. Illustrated Police News

WILFORD, THOMAS

Thomas Wilford was born in Fulham. Born with only one arm, he was received into the workhouse, where he ran errands for the paupers, as well as errands for members of the public in the vicinity and was noted for his inoffensive behaviour. A girl of disreputable character, Sarah Williams, was sent from the parish of St Giles-in-the-Fields to the same workhouse and persuaded Thomas, then aged seventeen, to marry her. On hearing of the intended marriage, the church wardens gave Sarah forty shillings with which to begin married life. They moved to lodgings in St Giles'. On the Sunday following the marriage Sarah, having been out with an old acquaintance, returned after midnight. Thomas and Sarah began to argue, as she would not give him a satisfactory explanation as to where she had been and he was consumed with jealousy. During the violent quarrel he seized a knife and cut her throat so savagely that it almost severed her head. As he left the room to go downstairs, a woman in an adjacent room asked who was there. Wilford replied: 'It is me. I have murdered my poor wife, whom I loved as dearly as my own life.' He did not make the slightest effort to escape.

Wilford was committed to NEWGATE the next day and tried at the following OLD BAILEY Sessions, where he was convicted of murder. Thomas Wilford was the first be sentenced under the terms of an Act of 1751 for the more effectual prevention of murder, which decreed the convict should be executed on the second day after conviction and that the convicted murderer should either be hanged in chains or anatomised. The sentence was as follows:

> *Thomas Wilford, you stand convicted of the horrid and unnatural crime of murdering Sarah, your wife. This Court doth adjudge that you be taken back to the place from whence you came, and there be fed on bread and water till Wednesday next, when you are to be taken to the common place of execution, and there hanged by the neck until you are dead; after which your body is to be publicly dissected and anatomised, agreeable to an Act of Parliament in that case made and provided; and may God Almighty have mercy on your soul!*

Thomas Wilford was hanged at Tyburn on 22 June 1752. He displayed the most genuine signs of contrition for his crime.

WILLCOX, SIR WILLIAM HENRY (physician and toxicologist)

Sir William Willcox (1870-1941). Physician at St Mary's Hospital, Paddington, where he lectured on chemical pathology and forensic medicine. As honorary medical adviser to the Home Office, he was involved in many high profile murder cases, including Doctor CRIPPEN and the SEDDONS.

WILLIAMS, JOHN – see RATCLIFFE HIGHWAY MURDERS, THE

WILLIAMSON, JOHN

John Williamson, a shoemaker, lived in Moorfields. He was happily married with three children. His wife died. He proposed to a young woman who had inherited some money. The woman was simple-minded. Once he got his hands on her money he began to abuse his new wife. He beat her, handcuffed her and locked her in a closet for several weeks and gave her very little food. She died as a result of this ill treatment and Williamson was charged with murder. Found guilty at the next Sessions at the OLD BAILEY, Williamson was hanged before a large crowd on a specially erected gallows opposite Chiswell Street in Moorfields, on 19 January 1767 and afterward his body was dissected in Surgeons' Hall.

WILSON, CATHERINE

Catherine Wilson has the distinction of being the last woman to be hanged in public in London. She was found guilty of the murder of Mrs Maria Soames in Alfred Street, Bloomsbury, who she was nursing. Mrs Soames died on 17 October 1856, having been poisoned with large doses of colchicum, but it was not until Wilson attempted and failed to kill Mrs Sarah Carnell in February 1862 that an investigation was held into Mrs Soames' death. Following a trial at

John Williamson's ill treatment of his wife. Author's collection

the OLD BAILEY for attempted murder, which resulted in Catherine Wilson's acquittal, she was immediately rearrested and charged with the murder of Maria Soames. Evidence suggested that Wilson had murdered several other patients by poisoning them, all for financial gain but she would not confess to anything. Found guilty of murder, she was hanged at HORSEMONGER LANE GAOL on 20 October 1862.

WITNEY, JOHN EDWARD – see BRAYBROOK STREET MASSACRE, THE

WOOD, ROBERT – see CAMDEN TOWN MURDER, THE

WOOD, THOMAS – see HAYES, CATHERINE

WOOLF, GEORGE

George Woolf has the dubious distinction of being the last man to be hanged at NEWGATE. He became friendly with Charlotte Cheeseman while her own sweetheart was fighting in the Boer War. When the soldier returned from active service an unpleasant confrontation took place after he discovered her connection with Woolf and he and Charlotte broke off their relationship. Twenty-four-year-old Woolf callously ditched Charlotte having promised to marry her, after she became pregnant. He sent her a letter in which he informed her he had met someone else he liked better and not to try to put the blame on him if she found herself in a 'certain condition'. The letter went on:

> *I hope I shall never hear of you or see you again, as I am indeed thankfull I have got rid of you so easily.*

Charlotte sent a reply:

> *Dear George,*
> *Don't be offended because I am writing this letter to you. Will you go out with me again as you know what you have done to me. I think it is a shame how you have treated me, but I will forget that and think of you all the more. You don't know how much I love you...*

Woolf had also written to Charlotte's employer at the cigar factory at Hoxton, where she worked, implying that she was not of good character and should not be trusted. Her employer thought otherwise and showed the letter to the police.

Woolf met Charlotte on the evening of 25 January 1902. They were seen drinking together in the *Rosemary Branch*, in Southgate Road, Hoxton. The following morning some children discovered Charlotte's blood-soaked, battered body in a ditch on Tottenham Marshes. She had been brutally killed with a chisel. Woolf attempted to escape by enlisting in the army but justice caught up with him and he was tried at the OLD BAILEY and hanged on 6 May 1902. Shortly afterwards, work began on Newgate's demolition.

The execution shed, seen here on the right. Author's collection

Acknowledgements

I am particularly grateful to John D Murray who has assisted me over several years; and to Keith Atack, Vera Atack, Iris Ackroyd, Michael Barber, Susan Barber, Sue Barnes, Edward Black, Joan Bostwick, Christine Boyce, Norma Braddick, Tracy Brown, Carole Conlon, Cherrie Conlon, Robert (Bob) A Dale, Kathleen Dale, Iris J Deller, Joanna C Murray Deller, Ricky S Deller, Tracy P Deller, Brian Elliott, Gill Fleming, James Friend, Jeff Gerhardt, John Goldfinch, Leo Gonzales, Doris Hayes (1924–2007), Deborah Hedgecock, Ann Howse, Doreen Howse, Joy Howse, Kathleen Howse, Richard Huggett (1929-2000), Dr Hidayat Hussein, Tammy Jones, Eamon Keane, Sister Julia Keane, Brendan E McNally, Raymond Mellor-Jones, Eleanor Nelder, Stanley Nelder, Dr Declan O'Reilly, Sharon Owen, Kerry Quinn, Sammy Quinn, Anthony Richards, Annie Souter, Brian Gregory Thomas (1943-2004), Jackie Thomas, Karen Thomas, Breda Toh, Helen Vodden, Katie Vollans, Adam R Walker, Anna Walker, Christine Walker, Darren J Walker, David Walker, Ivan P Walker, Paula L Walker Suki B Walker, Kate Ward, Helen Weatherburn, Dave and Terry Webster of D Webster & Son, Paul T Langley Welch, Julia Wiggett, Angela Williamson, Clifford Willoughby, Margaret Willoughby, the staff of the British Library, the staff of the British Library Newspaper Archive, Colindale, the staff of the Guildhall Library, the staff of the National Archive, Kew, the staff of Islington Local History Centre at Finsbury Library, Bruce Castle Museum, Hornsey Historical Society.

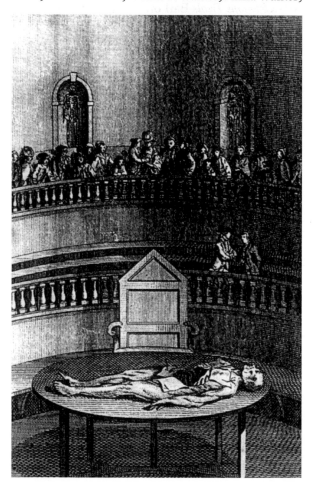

Eighteenth century engraving of Surgeons' Hall, Old Bailey.
Author's collection

Selected Bibliography

The Notable British Trials series. William Hodge & Company, London, Edinburgh and Glasgow

Murder Guide To London Grafton Books, London, 1987

Tyburn Tree Its History And Annals Alfred Marks, Brown, Langham & Co., London

The Complete Newgate Calendar Vols 1-5 Navarre Society, London MCMXXVl

The Chronicles of Newgate Arthur Griffiths, Bracken Books, London, (originally published 1883, this edition published 1987)

The Common Hangman James Bland, Ian Henry Publications, Hornchurch, 1934

Charles Macklin Edward Abbott Parry, Kegan Paul, Trench, Trubner & Co., Ltd, London, 1891.

The Detective-Physician: The Life and Work of Sir William Willcox Philip Henry Almroth , Willcox, Heinemann Medical, London 1970

More Famous Trials Earl of Birkenhead, Hutchinson, London, 1938

Executioner Pierrepoint George G Harrap, London, 1974

Prick Up Your Ears John Lahr, Penguin, London, 1978

The Orton Diaries Ed. John Lahr, Methuen, London, 1986

The Murders of the Black Museum, 1870-1970 Gordon Honeycomb, Bloomsbury, London, 1982

Crimes that Thrilled the World John Garland, Mellifont Press, London, 1937

I Caught Crippen Walter Dew. Blackie & Son, London & Glasgow, 1938

North London Murders Geoffrey Howse, Sutton Publishing, Stroud, 2005

Foul Deeds and Suspicious Deaths in London's East End Geoffrey Howse, Wharncliffe Books, Barnsley, 2005

Foul Deeds and Suspicious Deaths in London's West End Geoffrey Howse, Wharncliffe Books, Barnsley, 2006

The Times

Daily Mail

Daily Telegraph

Daily Mirror

Daily Express

Daily Sketch

Star

London Evening Standard

London Evening News

London Evening Star

St James's Gazette

News of the World

Sunday Pictorial

The Sunday Times

Sunday Mirror

The Observer

Sunday Telegraph

Walthamstow Guardian

Islington Gazette
Hackney Gazette
Hornsey Journal
Penny Illustrated Paper and Illustrated Times
Illustrated Police News
Illustrated London News
Police Gazette
Real Life Crimes and How They were Solved, Vols.1-133 Eaglemoss Publications, London, 2005

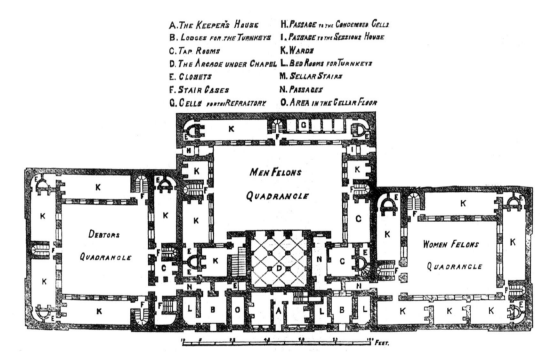

Floor plan of Newgate Gaol, demolished in 1902. Author's collection

TRUE CRIME FROM WHARNCLIFFE

Foul Deeds and Suspicious Deaths Series

Barking, Dagenham & Chadwell Heath
Barnsley
Bath
Bedford
Birmingham
Black Country
Blackburn and Hyndburn
Bolton
Bradford
Brighton
Bristol
Cambridge
Carlisle
Chesterfield
Colchester
Coventry
Croydon
Derby
Durham
Ealing
Folkestone and Dover
Grimsby
Guernsey
Guilford
Halifax
Hampstead, Holborn and St Pancras
Huddersfield
Hull

Leeds
Leicester
Lewisham and Deptford
Liverpool
London's East End
London's West End
Manchester
Mansfield
More Foul Deeds Birmingham
More Foul Deeds Chesterfield
More Foul Deeds Wakefield
Newcastle
Newport
Norfolk
Northampton
Nottingham
Oxfordshire
Pontefract and Castleford
Portsmouth
Rotherham
Scunthorpe
Southend-on-Sea
Staffordshire and The Potteries
Stratford and South Warwickshire
Tees
Warwickshire
Wigan
York

OTHER TRUE CRIME BOOKS FROM WHARNCLIFFE

A-Z Yorkshire Murder
Black Barnsley
Brighton Crime and Vice 1800-2000
Durham Executions
Essex Murders
Executions & Hangings in Newcastle
    and Morpeth
Norfolk Mayhem and Murder

Norwich Murders
Strangeways Hanged
The A-Z of London Murders
Unsolved Murders in Victorian and
    Edwardian London
Unsolved Norfolk Murders
Unsolved Yorkshire Murders
Yorkshire's Murderous Women

Please contact us via any of the methods below for more information or a catalogue.

WHARNCLIFFE BOOKS

47 Church Street – Barnsley – South Yorkshire – S70 2AS
Tel: 01226 734555 – 734222 Fax: 01226 – 734438
E-mail: enquiries@pen-and-sword.co.uk
Website: www.wharncliffebooks.co.uk